"After reading this book, I can recognize G⸺ His hand in my present, and the direction He is pointing to for my future."

—GARY LAU, executive director, New Hope Christian College–Hawaii

"A paradigm buster! *The Making of a Leader* turned my understanding of Christian leadership upside down. I have reread and referred to this book again and again over the years. I especially like how this new edition contains updated research and new resources to explore in deeper and more transformational ways. A classic just got better!"

—DR. PAUL G. LEAVENWORTH, executive director,
The Convergence Group

THE MAKING OF A
LEADER
SECOND EDITION
RECOGNIZING THE LESSONS AND
STAGES OF **LEADERSHIP DEVELOPMENT**

Dr. J. Robert Clinton

A NavPress resource published in alliance
with Tyndale House Publishers

NavPress is the publishing ministry of The Navigators, an international Christian organization and leader in personal spiritual development. NavPress is committed to helping people grow spiritually and enjoy lives of meaning and hope through personal and group resources that are biblically rooted, culturally relevant, and highly practical.

For more information, visit NavPress.com.

For information about special discounts for bulk purchases, please contact Tyndale House Publishers at csresponse@tyndale.com, or call 1-855-277-9400.

Clinton, J. Robert.
  The making of a leader : recognizing the lessons and stages of leadership development / J. Robert Clinton. — [Rev. ed.].
     p. cm.
  Includes bibliographical references (p.   ) and indexes.
  ISBN 978-1-61291-075-8
  1. Christian leadership. I. Title.
  BV652.1.C56 2012
  253'.2 — dc23

                              2012016756

Printed in the United States of America

26 25 24 23 22
13 12 11 10 9   8

CONTENTS

ILLUSTRATIONS

Figures

Tables

FOREWORD

"Leadership" is a topic high on many agendas today, whether in politics, business, or the church.

In part, this is because of a perceived leadership vacuum. In his leadership essays, John Gardner pointed out that at the time the United States was formed, the population stood at around 3 million. That 3 million produced at least six leaders of world class: Washington, Adams, Jefferson, Franklin, Madison, and Hamilton. Today's American population of 240 million might be expected to produce eighty times as many world-class leaders. But, asks Gardner, "Where are they?"

At a convention of the National Association of Evangelicals, college president George Brushaber spoke of "a missing generation" of younger leaders ready to take the places of the senior post–World War II group of evangelical pioneers.

My own travels and observations have led me to believe this is a worldwide phenomenon. Yet I am encouraged to believe there is a new group of younger men and women, roughly forty and under, emerging into leadership around the world.

In response to both the lack of and the new wave of leaders, there is an urgent need for the cultivation of godly and spiritual leadership.

There are a number of responses to this challenge. The Lausanne Committee for World Evangelization has called several conferences for emerging younger leaders. My own ministry, Leighton Ford Ministries, is focused upon identifying, developing, and networking these younger people. A number of graduate schools are focusing some specific programs on leadership development. One is the School of Intercultural Studies at Fuller Theological Seminary, where Dr. Bobby Clinton taught. It is out of his experience in teaching that his important book *The Making of a Leader* developed.

I believe we can make either of two opposite mistakes in viewing leadership emergence. One is to attach a mystique to leadership that says in effect, "God calls leaders. Leaders are born. There is nothing we can do about it." The opposite is to say, "Leaders are made. With the right techniques, we can produce them."

It is always true that God gives leadership to His church and His kingdom: "Promotion cometh neither from the east, nor from the west, nor from the south. But God . . . putteth down one, and setteth up another," said the psalmist (Psalm 75:6-7, KJV).

But it is also true that there are processes that God uses to produce His leaders. A study of Scripture shows the stages of development in a Moses, a David, or a Paul.

It is the strength of Dr. Clinton's work that he takes seriously both parts of this process. He sets forth clearly that leadership is a God-given call and gift. Out of his own study of Scripture, life, and leadership, he has identified some of those common experiences that God uses to grow leaders.

I know of no other book that so carefully and thoroughly outlines the stages of leadership development from the early inner growth of the leader through the crises and challenges that mature a person's ministry and life.

The principles set forth will be of help both to younger people who sense that God is calling them to leadership and to senior people who have increasing responsibility to encourage the development of new leadership in their churches and organizations.

I warmly commend this book and pray that it will help to produce a new generation of pioneers for the gospel.

LEIGHTON FORD, president
Leighton Ford Ministries

PREFACE

What does it mean to be a leader? What does it take to become the leader God wants you to be? What are the processes, the cost, and the result?

For six years I have been researching and teaching the answers to these questions at Fuller Theological Seminary's School of World Mission in Pasadena, California.[1] My students and I have shared the excitement of applying new concepts to our lives and seeing ourselves as emerging leaders whom God is developing. In this book I hope to capture the dynamics of these ideas and provide biblical insights into the patterns and processes God uses to develop a leader.

This is a book about spiritual dynamics. Effective spiritual ministry flows out of being, and God is concerned with our being. He is forming it. The patterns and processes He uses to shape us are worthwhile subjects for leadership study. Those who study patterns and processes, and use insights from them in life and ministry, will be better prepared leaders.

My students and I have studied hundreds of lives from three categories of leaders: historic, biblical, and contemporary. As we've compared findings from these studies, we've gained insights that are transferable to other leaders' lives, including our own.[2]

My classes have helped me identify, label, define, and suggest ways to use these insights in the process of selection and training of leaders. These insights can help leaders in all kinds of situations to identify and become more sensitive to God's working in their own lives as He forms them into the leaders He wants them to be.

Leadership is a dynamic process in which a man or woman with God-given capacity influences a specific group of God's people toward His purposes for the group.[3] This is contrary to the popular notion that a leader must have a formal position, a formal title, or formal training. Many who are called to lead in church or parachurch organizations may not have formal titles such as pastor or director. They may be Sunday school teachers, small group leaders, or lay people functioning in any number of other leadership capacities. To be considered a leader, one does not require a professional position nor need to be a "full-time Christian worker." This book is written for all who influence a specific group of people for God's purposes, whether or not they are professional, paid leaders.

I directed my original research toward professional Christian leaders, that is, leaders who are paid to lead—full-time pastors, evangelists, missionaries, and nationals who direct mission organizations, lead denominations, establish Bible schools, and teach in seminaries. Most of these have had some formal training for their profession.[4]

Most, if not all, of the patterns and processes in these leaders' development are applicable to nonprofessional leaders.[5] These nonprofessional leaders work as volunteers in local churches or small organizations. They usually have not received any formal training in Christian leadership. In this book I am applying what I've discovered to both professional and nonprofessional Christian leaders.

Development includes all of life's processes, not just formal training. Leaders are shaped by deliberate training and by experience. "Leadership emergence," as one of my colleagues so often emphasizes, "is a much broader term than leadership training." Leadership training refers to a narrow part of the overall process, focusing primarily on learning skills. Leadership emergence includes this but much more.[6]

In general, readers with little or no ministry experience will not identify with as many of the processes and patterns mentioned in this book as those who are further along in their development. If you have more experience as a leader, you will grasp the underlying concept of

God's processing for leadership and be sensitized to the general idea of a development pattern. You will be able to see your own pattern as it develops and respond with a more teachable attitude.

If you are even further along in your leadership emergence, you will probably identify readily with all of the processes described. You will have either gone through them or seen others experience them. You can benefit from the discussion of how these processes are used by God to develop leaders by applying this wisdom to yourself and others.

Four things will happen as you read this book:

1. You will learn about the *providence* of God.
2. You will begin to sense a *continuity* of God's working in your past to develop you as a leader.
3. You will have a high degree of *anticipation* because God is going to use you in the future.
4. Finally, you will perceive yourself and others in terms of insights gained from this book. You will become more *deliberate in using these insights* for the development and training of others.

When you look on leadership emergence in terms of life's processes, you quickly realize who the academic dean really is. It is God. Each of us has leadership courses that are individually tailored for us by the Academic Dean. Each learner, a potential leader, can graduate with honors—the right knowledge, skills, and character needed for the specific job God has in mind for him.

PREFACE TO THE REVISED EDITION

It is gratifying to know that the original edition of *The Making of a Leader* was helpful to many. I was delighted when Don Simpson informed me that NavPress wanted to issue a revised edition of the book. At the time of the writing of *The Making of a Leader*, I had researched about five hundred case studies of leaders' lives. Over the next fifteen years, I researched another three thousand case studies. My comparative findings from the study of these leaders' lives continues to confirm much of what was included in the original material of *The Making of a Leader*.

As I have read back through the material, I feel that very little needs to be changed. Two helpful additions include:

- I have written a bit more about testing patterns (that is, how God uses integrity checks, word checks, obedience checks, and ministry tasks as He works with the response of the leader to them). See endnotes 5 and 10 in chapter 3. In the entire book, these are probably two of the most important endnotes for young emerging leaders. All leaders will go through at least one of these testing patterns — probably both positive and negative testing patterns. But young leaders will see the testing patterns more frequently as God seeks to instill character in them.

- I have included in chapter 8 on ministry philosophy a basic concept that is important to the foundation of a ministry philosophy. There I define the concept of leadership value. Even though a given leader may not be able to derive a full-blown ministry philosophy, he can certainly identify a core of leadership values that ought to be passed on. I talk about the use of three modal auxiliary verbs for writing a good leadership value. I also give some good examples of leadership values. I have found that very few folks will actually try to work on a ministry philosophy, but many can identify convictions they hold in the form of leadership values. So I minimally modified that chapter by adding the concept of a leadership value. All leaders should be able to identify some of their core leadership values. If they do, they have a good start toward their ministry philosophy.

I have not altered much of the original text, except for the changes noted here. But what I have done is put a lot more information in the endnotes concerning things that I've seen in the last fifteen years of my research on leaders' lives. You may want to scan those endnotes carefully; they contain a lot of good information. And I have added many references in the endnotes to writings I have done since I originally wrote *The Making of a Leader*. These writings will give the reader my further findings on leadership emergence theory.

I am hopeful that leaders who are more aware of God's lifetime of shaping activities will finish well, and *at a higher percentage* than we now see.

Dr. J. Robert (Bobby) Clinton
Summer 2011

WHO NEEDS THESE LESSONS ANYWAY?

The Challenge: "Well begun is half done. Forewarned is forearmed."
(Miss Warren)

The pithy lessons given by Miss Warren, my English and American literature teacher at the Columbia Graduate School of Columbia Bible College, have become part of my ministry philosophy. A good start on anything in life—a term paper, a reading assignment, a ministry task, personal leadership emergence—almost ensures continuance and closure. And to know about something ahead of time is to allow much better planning to take advantage of it.

WILLIAM JAMISON – LAY OR CLERGY, WHICH WAY?

From the time he was a little boy, Bill Jamison had a quick mind and was always two or three grades ahead of his class in both math and reading. He came from a Christian home and made an early decision for Christ. He loved to share with others. Before he was born, his mother had covenanted with God to accomplish great things through Bill.

In his teens, at a camp retreat, he made a commitment to the lordship of Christ. At the counseling that occurred after the campfire challenge, Bill's counselor made a prophetic statement: "You remain true to God in your heart and He will use the great mind He has given you for His purposes." Bill never forgot those words.

In his last two years in high school, Bill developed some skills in talking to people about Christ. At the same time, his reading skills and mathematical abilities continued to grow. He was a computer whiz and published several public domain computer programs.

In college, he decided on a double major involving physics and computer science, made the honor roll every semester and was tapped for several honorary societies, was active in a campus ministry, headed up several organizations, and displayed excellent administrative skills. He founded a new organization that helped students learn how to apply computers to research projects.

In his junior year, his research resulted in a patent in his name and a large grant for graduate studies. Toward the middle of his senior year, he was challenged by a campus ministry worker: "If you really want to count for Christ, then you need to give up your secular ambitions and go into ministerial training." This was a crucial decision for Bill.

If Bill had come to me at this crucial decision point, I would have used several concepts to evaluate his situation: destiny processing, giftedness, influence-mix, and double confirmation.[1] (See the Glossary for explanations of technical terms used in this book.)

The special times when God spoke to Bill's mother and when He gave a word about the future at the campfire commitment were events in which God began to communicate to a potential leader His intentions to use that person (destiny process items). This form of guidance deals with the accomplishments of a lifetime.[2] The experience of Bill's mother seemed to indicate that God's hand was on Bill's life. The word given by the camp counselor seemed to indicate that Bill's special intellectual capacities would be central in what God planned to accomplish.

These are enough to opt for a lay career dedicated to God. However, other indications are there also.

Bill's giftedness set[3] includes natural abilities (a sharp mind, a disposition to share generously with others), spiritual gifts (evangelism, leadership, maybe apostolic gifts), and acquired skills (computers, research, and so on). Frequently there is a focal element[4] in the giftedness set that the other elements enhance. In Bill's case, the natural abilities are the focal element, and the spiritual gifts and acquired skills will work to support that element.

Leaders influence followers in different ways. Direct, indirect, and organizational influence are three main ways a leader influences. Bill has the potential to influence directly (personal evangelism), indirectly (by giving), and organizationally (administrative skills, board membership). I can point to men and women who have become successful in secular roles and who influence the course of Christianity through giving and membership on boards of Christian organizations.

Bill is going to be highly successful, perhaps with computers in business. If his heart is set on pleasing God, then that success can be greatly used by Him.

But as a caution, Bill should seek double confirmation, through which God leads first by giving guidance to a person and then by confirming it through another person who is not familiar with the situation. He then brings the two together to unmistakably affirm the guidance. This is described in chapter 6.

JIMMY THOMPSON — YOUNG MINISTERIAL CANDIDATE

After graduating from college with a degree in literature, Jimmy Thompson decided to go on to seminary. His Christian experience during nineteen years of schooling was minimal, though regular and consistent. After seminary he joined the staff of a large church as a youth worker. During the two years that followed, Jimmy became discouraged and confused, and even doubted his gifts and abilities.

Chapters 4 and 5, on ministry maturing, point out that God works through tasks in the life of a Christian entering ministry: entry task, training task, relational task, and discerning task. God first works on the entry and training tasks, where Jimmy is right now. He probably already has faced some relational processing also.

Further, God moves a worker into ministry through ministry tasks, ministry assignments, and various ministry challenges. Also, the foundational ministry pattern focuses on faithfulness. Jimmy needs to see that God works first on character through the testing patterns described in chapter 3. Integrity and faithfulness are preludes to success and giftedness.

The timeline of chapter 2 gives a long-term perspective on what is happening to Jimmy at this point. Also, the dropout pattern (a possibility for him) frequently occurs among pre-service ministerial trainees.[5]

A mentor is helpful in bringing along a young leader to maturity. Mentoring is a special process described in chapter 6. I would suggest that Jimmy trust God to give him a mentor. If he perseveres through the next two or three years, learns from a mentor, and becomes increasingly aware of God's processing toward the four ministry tasks, then he will make it past the dropout stage and will be used fruitfully by God.

MARY THAMES – ORGANIZATIONAL LEADER

Mary Thames joined Kids Outreach International when it was about twenty years old and she was in her mid-thirties. She was assigned a city to begin children's work. At first she worked bi-vocationally, with a part-time job to support herself. As her ministry flourished, she was able to relinquish her part-time job and concentrate fully on ministry.

Right from the start she displayed evangelistic and teaching gifts. She started small, went deep, and then expanded. She developed one neighborhood, trained workers to take over the work, and took along one or two most promising helpers to begin Kids Outreach in another neighborhood. This pattern was repeated several times in that first city. Then Mary was led by God to move on to another city. This was approved by the organizational leaders. The pattern was repeated. Mary now split her time between the two cities.

Increasingly, her time was spent in training the lay workers and solving problems, and not in direct evangelism. To make a long story short, Mary opened up the work in six different cities over a period of about twelve years. She developed a basic strategy to penetrate a neighborhood and a city, designed materials for training lay workers, and demonstrated outstanding qualities of leadership. In each of these assignments the organization concurred. Each, however, was essentially the same kind of task.

Ministry took a toll on Mary. In her mid-forties she wondered if she had enough energy to repeat the successful pattern again. Was there not some role in the organization that might use her experience and gifts at a higher level of responsibility? She felt that she could be used by the organization to do what she had been doing so well. She had some things to say to the organization. But the top leadership didn't want to listen. This was due partly to their view of what a leader was and who could be a leader. And it was due partly to their shortsightedness in developing middle-level leadership.[6]

Probably Mary's superiors need this book more than she does. They need to learn two major lessons of leadership emergence:

- Effective leaders recognize leadership selection and development as a priority function.
- Effective leaders increasingly perceive their ministries in terms of a lifetime perspective.

Mary has seen these two principles. She has used the first repeatedly in her ministry. Now she is at a crossroads and is beginning to sense the need for the second in her own life. But the organizational leaders have not perceived these two lessons yet. Kids Outreach has obligations to Mary as well as she to it. Organizations need to keep two tensions in mind — the needs of the individual and the needs of the ministry.

An understanding of Mary's timeline and the related concepts of patterns, processes, and principles as discussed in chapter 2 gives one a breadth of understanding needed to make responsible decisions. Mary's development and maturity in giftedness, as well as her age, should have cued the top leaders of the organization to design a role and provide opportunities that would bring convergence for Mary.[7] Unless such a role develops, she will probably leave the organization.

Leaders who make decisions for others need to understand the various factors that allow convergence: role-match, giftedness, experience, spiritual maturity, destiny, geographic location, and so on. They should consider the needs of the individual as well as the needs of the organization.[8] This book gives perspectives that help leaders make responsible decisions concerning people like Mary who have grown since joining the organization.

PASTOR JEFFREY MCDONALD — MATURE MODEL

Pastor Jeff has had a long and fruitful ministry. Hundreds of people have been released into ministry as a result of his mentoring. He has served in numerous successful pastorates and taught at seminary. Wherever he has gone, he has increased missions awareness. Today he holds an honorary position at a seminary, where he is still influencing people toward godliness.

Admittedly, Pastor Jeff does not need much help. In fact, he could probably contribute much to this book. But, he has a heritage that should be passed on. This book gives definitions and labels that would help him to identify God's working in his life and to articulate it to others. Pastor Jeff can illustrate the ideas in this book with firsthand experiences that can inspire and challenge many. Chapter 8 could challenge Pastor Jeff to identify and write up his ministry philosophy[9] that has evolved over the years. This statement of a ministry philosophy backed with spiritual authority that goes with a lifetime of fruitful ministry can affect younger leaders who are not clear on what ministry is all about. Very few experienced leaders know how or have taken the time to articulate a ministry philosophy. Younger leaders need such models.

WHO NEEDS THIS BOOK?

God has His ways of developing a leader. If you are aware of them, you are well on your way to responding to God's means of developing you. If you know that God will be developing you over a lifetime, you'll most likely stay for the whole ride. If you are a potential leader or a practicing leader, then this book will give insights that allow you to persevere.

This book was written for leaders or potential leaders who:

- Are wondering what God is doing
- Are beginning to seek their place of ministry
- Need a fresh challenge from God
- Need to understand how to select and develop younger leaders
- Are at a crossroads, facing a major decision
- Want to know how God develops leaders

Leaders, or those emerging as leaders, need a road map to point out where God will take them as He develops their gifts. Each journey is unique, but a map helps a person organize what is happening as God works, anticipate the future, understand the past, and respond to God's leading. Leadership emergence theory does what a good map is supposed to do. It is a set of well-integrated ideas to help us:

- Organize what we see happening in leaders' lives
- Anticipate what might happen in future development
- Understand past events so as to see new things in them
- Better order our lives

We need overall perspective, the big picture that can keep us from hastily forming conclusions and making decisions that are not compatible with long-range development. When I wrote to Dan (chapter 1), I knew roughly where he was on his timeline, moving into important first steps in ministry. I suspected that some of the events in his life would be testing events, like the integrity check and the ministry tasks.

It helps to have labels to describe things that are happening to us. Comparative studies of these same kinds of things that have happened to others give us some predictability. If God uses certain kinds of process items in others' lives to accomplish certain tasks, then He most likely will use them in your life and my life to accomplish the same kinds of tasks.

My leadership emergence theory can be stated in relatively simple terms:

> God develops a leader over a lifetime. That development is a function of the use of events and people to impress leadership lessons upon a leader (processing), time, and leader response. Processing is central to the theory. All leaders can point to critical incidents in their lives where God taught them something very important.

As with any theory, there is a feeling of being bombarded with so much new material. New terminology is always difficult at first. I will label between fifty and one hundred concepts in this book. I realize that you won't remember all these at first. I count on three factors to reduce the tension associated with learning new labels:

- The labels describe concepts that are real to life. Many of you will have experienced the reality described by the label. That will help.
- The labels are descriptive of the reality. For example, an integrity check is a check or test of one's integrity. The isolation process item does describe separation.
- I provide a glossary for quick reference to labels and definitions used in the text. Use it frequently!

I've structured the book to introduce you systematically to the ideas involved in leadership emergence; my theory is rooted in biblical principles. The first two chapters give the big picture, first through a letter I once wrote to a friend and next by considering the process of development along a timeline. Leadership emergence is a lifetime process. You need an overall perspective in order to understand what is happening at any given time. The timeline introduced in chapter 2 is then explained piece by piece in the remaining chapters.

Chapter 3 talks about the early lessons God uses to formulate foundational leadership traits. These processes for developing character are readily recognized by both lay leaders and full-time leaders. All have experienced them as God's prerequisites for leadership.

Then come the most complex chapters in the book. Chapters 4 and 5 are complicated because they describe the many things God does to develop a leader in ministry. The four stages of ministry development—entry, training, relational, and discernment—entail numerous leadership emergence ideas. Chapter 4 covers the entry and training stages. Chapter 5 touches on the relational and discernment stages.

Chapter 6 talks about guidance processing and other multi-phase processing. God first teaches a leader lessons in personal guidance. Then He uses those lessons as a springboard for developing a leader to perceive guidance for groups he's leading. This chapter highlights the central task of Christian leadership: influencing a group of people toward God's purposes for them.

Chapter 7 emphasizes the importance of maturity in a leader. Mature ministry flows from a mature person. God deepens, sometimes painfully, the character of a leader in order to produce riper fruit.

Chapter 8 points out the need for integrating the lessons being learned into a ministry philosophy. Such a framework becomes the bedrock for a leader. It will provide support in the decisions of future leadership.

Chapter 9 throws out three challenges of leadership. I hope you will respond to all three. I emphasize in this chapter the concept of continuing well and especially finishing well. Most leaders who drop out of ministry do so in the middle-game; they do not continue well.

I have designed this book both for initial and referential learning. I hope you will use and reuse this book. But I know you won't always remember the many definitions I introduce to you. The glossary is a quick reference aid.

I have been selective. There is more to leadership emergence theory than I have included here.[10] This is repeatedly noted in the explanatory notes, which are placed at the end of the book rather than on each page. Though this is not convenient for the thorough reader, it keeps from cluttering up the pages for the average reader who usually skips over them in a first reading. These notes give explanations and challenges that should stimulate you to further learning and provide you with sources for additional information about leadership emergence theory. I have added extensively to these endnotes in this revised edition.

Leadership is a lifetime of God's lessons. Yours will be unique. God will take you through several "leadership stages" on your way to a lifetime of service. I anticipate that this book will give you insights for your journey.

CHAPTER 1

A LETTER TO DAN, THE INTERN

Dan was a seminary student, in his late twenties, who felt God had called him to be a missionary to the Chinese. During his second year in seminary, he became restless with all the study involved and wanted to get out there where the action was. With this in mind, he dropped out of seminary and went to Hong Kong for a nine-month internship.[1] Things did not turn out as he had hoped. He was asked to do academic research into Chinese history and culture, but the job description was fuzzy. His supervisor was rarely available.[2]

Dan wanted to be involved in ministry among the Chinese, but he knew very little of the Chinese language. He started an English class with several Chinese. Mainland China was also beckoning. Perhaps he should quit his internship and pursue these efforts. He felt perplexed, even frustrated. It was at this point, about halfway through his internship, when I wrote to him.

Dear Dan,

Your prayer letter was a welcome treat. Marilyn and I always enjoy hearing from you. I was delighted to hear of your situation. I see great potential for inner-life growth. It's great when we realize we are in God's training program. He always adapts the curriculum to fit us. Talk about long-range development! God has that in mind as He tailors every person's curriculum individually to suit His work in their lives. You are going through a required course just now. You probably thought you were signing up for an elective course—but not so.

One of my areas of study, research, and teaching is that of leadership emergence theory. Leadership emergence theory forces you to look at a lifetime with long-range perspectives. When you step back and view a person's life history telescopically, you see things that you may otherwise miss. Let me suggest four things I see happening in your situation. I do not say these things dogmatically, but offer them as insights that may help you see more clearly God's present working in you.

First, some necessary background so you'll understand my language. Leadership emergence theory begins with the concept of formulating a timeline. A timeline study for each individual is unique. However, when you see enough timelines, you notice some overall general patterns. The following is an idealized general pattern synthesized from a study of many individual patterns. Though it is not true specifically for anyone, it does give a functional framework. Notice that there are five development phases.

Phase I. Sovereign Foundations	Phase II. Inner-Life Growth	Phase III. Ministry Maturing	Phase IV. Life Maturing	Phase V. Convergence

Figure 1-1 Five-Phase Generalized Timeline

Sometimes, though rarely, there is a sixth phase called "Afterglow" or "Celebration." In real life, the development of Phases III and IV often overlap, though I show them here in a sequential pattern.

In Phase I, God providentially works foundational items into the life of the leader-to-be. Personality characteristics, both good and bad experiences, and the time context will be used by God. The building blocks are there, though the structure being built may not be clearly in focus. Character traits are embedded. These same traits in mature form will be adapted and used by God. Many times the personality traits later will be seen to correlate with the spiritual gift-mix that God gives.[3]

A retrospective view during the convergence stage makes it easier to clarify just how the foundational issues correlate with mature leadership. Usually the boundary condition between Phase I and Phase II is the conversion experience (or an all-out, surrender commitment) in which the would-be leader aspires to spend a lifetime that counts for God.

In Phase II an emerging leader usually receives some kind of training. Often it is informal[4] in connection with ministry. The leader-to-be learns by doing in the context of a local church or Christian organization. The basic models by which he learns are imitation modeling[5] and informal apprenticeships,[6] as well as mentoring.[7] Sometimes it is formal training (especially if the person intends to go into full-time leadership) in a Bible school or seminary.[8] Sometimes, during the academic program, the person gets ministry experience. Superficially it may appear that ministry training is the focus of this development phase. But closer analysis shows that the major thrust of God's development is inward. The real training program is in the heart of the person, where God is doing some growth testing. This testing is what I think is happening to you in Hong Kong.

In Phase III the emerging leader gets into ministry as a prime focus of life. He will get further training, informally through self-study growth projects[9] or nonformally through functionally oriented workshops and so on.[10] The major activities of Phase III are ministry. The training that goes on is rather incidental and often not intentional. It is the ministry that seems so all important! Most people are anxious to bypass Phase II and get on with the real thing—Phase III, ministry. That appears to be your case. You are anxious to get to ministry with the Chinese.

The amazing thing is that during Phases I, II, and III God is primarily working in the leader. Though there may be fruitfulness in ministry, the major work is that which God is doing to and in the leader, not through him. Most emerging leaders don't recognize this. They evaluate productivity, activities, fruitfulness, and so on. But God is quietly, often in unusual ways, trying to get the leader to see that one ministers out of what one is. God is concerned with what we are. We want to learn a thousand things because there is so much to learn and do. But He will teach us one thing, perhaps in a thousand ways: "I am forming Christ in you." It is this that will give power to your ministry. Phase IV will have this "you-minister-from-what-you-are" emphasis.

During Phase IV the leader identifies and uses his gift-mix with power. There is mature fruitfulness. God is working through the leader using imitation modeling (see Hebrews 13:7-8). That is, God uses one's life as well as gifts to influence others. This is a period in which gifted-ness emerges along with priorities. One recognizes that part of God's guidance for ministry comes through establishing ministry priorities by discerning gifts.

During Phase V convergence occurs. That is, the leader is moved by God into a role that matches gift-mix, experience, temperament, and so on. Geographical location is an important part of convergence. The role not only frees the leader from ministry for which there is no gift, but it also enhances and uses the best that the leader has to offer. Not many leaders experience convergence. Often they are promoted to roles that hinder their gift-mix. Further, few leaders minister out of what they are. Their authority usually springs from a role. In convergence, being and spiritual authority form the true power base for mature ministry.

In the long haul, God is preparing you for convergence. He is conforming you to the image of Christ (see Romans 8:28-29), and He is giving you training and experience so that your gifts may be discovered. His goal is a Spirit-filled leader through whom the living Christ minis-ters, utilizing the leader's spiritual gifts. The fruit of the Spirit is the mark of the mature Christian.[11] The gifts of the Spirit are a mark of a leader being used of God. God wants that balance. His approach is to work in you, and then through you.

During all the development phases, God processes a person by bring-ing activities, people, problems—you name it—into his life. We call these *process items*. God's ultimate purposes for these process items I have explained earlier. In studying people's lives, we have been able to identify and label some of the process items. One is an integrity check.[12] Usually this occurs in the Inner-Life Growth phase and in the early part of the Ministry Maturing phase. I sense that your Hong Kong internship is an integrity check. A successful integrity check results in a stronger leader able to serve God in a wider sphere of influence.

An integrity check tests inner character for consistency. Will you follow through on a commitment? Perhaps God is using your time in Hong Kong to let you see if you will persist in your desire to minister to the Chinese. It is one thing to make a decision in the heat of the moment (or quietness as the case may be). It is quite another to serve for a lifetime. Perhaps what God is saying to you through this experience is the message of Jeremiah 12:5: "If you have raced with men on foot and they have worn you out, how can you compete with horses? If you stumble in safe country, how will you manage in the thickets by the Jordan?"

Isolation is another process item. Several times in a leader's life the leader may be set aside. Usually this process item is seen in the Ministry Maturing phase and Life Maturing phase. These times can occur because of crises, illness, persecution or discipline, self-choice, or providential circumstances.

Why? (I know you're asking that!) Isolation process items are used by God to teach important inner leadership lessons that could not be learned in the pressures and activities of normal ministry. God has to get your attention first. Then He teaches.

I see God processing you with a form of isolation. Yours is a cross between self-choice and providential circumstances. In those forms of isolation, God desires to teach one or more of the following lessons:

- A new perspective on ministry
- Rekindling of a sense of destiny
- Flexibility in openness to new ideas and change
- Broadening through exposure to others
- Inner convictions from the Word
- Guidance

Your part is to respond to this isolation processing and identify the lessons that God has for you in it.

A ministry task, which usually occurs in Phase II, is an assignment from God in which the leader is tested on some basic lessons. Upon successful completion of the ministry task, the leader is usually given a bigger task. You can see this process item in the life of the biblical leader Titus. I also saw it in the life of Watchman Nee, a Chinese leader. I point out these and other examples in my self-study manual on leadership emergence theory.

Ministry tasks can be formal or informal. They may look as if they are assignments from somebody or due to your own self-choice. But sooner or later, if a person is open and sensitive to God's processing, there is recognition that God really gave the assignment. Hence, ultimate accountability is to Him. Ministry tasks involve getting experience, gaining knowledge, or doing things that will bring out character and giftedness. Often the "little-much" principle stated in Luke 16:10 is operating. Can you be faithful in little things? You may not see the importance of small tasks now, but can you do faithfully what is given you? If you can, then you'll be given greater things. If not, God will have to teach the same lesson again.

Your English class in that Chinese home may well be a ministry task from God. He will teach you lessons about yourself and your love (or lack of same) for the Chinese. It will be experiential learning dealing with your sphere of influence.[13] Can you learn to influence a small group because of who you are (your modeling of your life with Christ) and what you teach? Your research project involving study of Chinese culture and history also may be a ministry task. Be faithful in accomplishing it. God may be giving you information that He intends to use with you later.

Ministry tasks are not always clear-cut and easy to see. But they are stepping stones to other ministry. Your job is to do them as unto the Lord. When you are in a church or Christian organization and have influence in it, you will see this all the time with younger emerging leaders. As a matter of fact, you will probably deliberately use it in the testing and training of leaders-to-be.

Perhaps the key issue in all of this is submission. Are you willing to submit to God's purposes right now for you? Anyone can submit to something he wants. Submission is tested only when the thing is not desired. Learning submission could be the most important reason God has taken you to Hong Kong. It is one thing to know what God's will is; it is another thing altogether to know the timing (both what and when). From what I see, you are not ready yet for a full ministry. God is not in as big of a hurry as you and I are. He is more interested in shaping you and me first. Submission is an essential leadership lesson.

Some suggestions:

Work on submission. I just returned from a seminar in New Zealand. As I was talking about my growth projects, one of the participants gave me these words from Andrew Murray, a great South African Christian.

1. He brought me here. It's by His will I am in this straight place. In that fact I will rest.
2. He will keep me here in His love and give me grace to behave as His child.
3. Then He will make the trial a blessing, teaching me the lessons He intends for me to learn.
4. In His good time, He will bring me out again—how and when only He knows. So let me say: I am (1) here by God's appointment, (2) in His keeping, (3) under His training, and (4) for His time.[14]

At the time I didn't see exactly why he gave them to me. But after reading your letter, it became clear that they weren't for me as much as they were for you. As I was thinking this morning, I was prompted (by the Holy Spirit I believe) to send them along.

Read the chapter on "Time" in *Principles of Spiritual Growth* by Miles Stanford.[15] It has something to say to you right now, where you are. You are in a hurry to get on with ministry. Particularly note the quote concerning the difference between a squash and an oak tree.[16]

Wait on the Lord. He will lead in a plain path in His time.

Talk to my friend Steve Torgerson. He is an "evangelical free missionary" in Hong Kong. He is going through isolation because of Chinese language study. He has been superbly trained by God. His multi-apprenticeship is a form of informal training that has been used by God to equip him for ministry. But he can't do it yet because of the language barrier. He knows what you are going through. Spend some time with him. Cultivate his friendship and seek his advice. He'll be a good sounding board for you.

Read the story of J. O. Fraser who served in China (*Behind the Ranges* by Geraldine Taylor). He was prepared by isolation.[17] I think you are ready for it now. God will meet you as you read.

Well, I was just going to write a little letter and it has turned out to be quite an epistle. If you were here, I wouldn't hesitate to talk and share these things — so why not by letter? The apostle Paul did such things.

A colaborer with you,
Bobby Clinton

CHAPTER 2

THE BASIS FOR LESSONS: THE BIG PICTURE

The Challenge/The Problem: Remember your leaders, who spoke the word of God to you. Consider the outcome of their way of life and imitate their faith. Jesus Christ is the same yesterday and today and forever. *(Hebrews 13:7-8)*

Today there are more churches, more Christian organizations, and more mission organizations than ever before, all of which present a crying need for leadership. We need men and women whose lives imitate those people in the Bible who were worthy of the name "leader." The church worldwide is in need of a committed group of disciples, like those past leaders, who can lead the way by demonstrating through their lives a faith worth imitating.

In order to imitate the faith of former leaders, we study their lives. We need to think back and remember. Are the lessons learned by biblical and spiritual leaders who lived years ago applicable to us today? The answer to that question is a resounding yes. Why? Because Jesus Christ is the same yesterday, today, and forever. It is no accident that those words follow the admonition to "think back" and "imitate." The same lessons He taught in the past apply to me today. The same Jesus Christ who enabled those leaders to live lives of faith will enable me to live a life of faith today. He is both the source and the reason for our study of leadership.

Leadership is a lifetime of lessons. It is not a set of do-it-yourself correspondence courses that can be worked through in a few months or years. In our attempt to "think back on how they lived and died," we will learn to analyze these lessons. Through this, we will accumulate data and process it by using a tool, the timeline. As we reflect on this data, we will see various patterns emerge that will indicate the many ways God developed and strengthened leaders in the past for their particular leadership roles. We can profit from both *how* God developed them and *what* God taught them. As we apply these lessons to our lives, we will be imitating their faith.

Let's look at several mini case studies of leaders worthy of being imitated. All of them imitated God-directed leaders before them. Examine the differences and similarities in their lives and be sure to notice the timeline displays for each of them. I will continually refer to them in my explanation of the patterns, processes, and principles of leadership.

Aiden Wilson Tozer combined the touch of the mystic with the passion of the prophet.[1] He came from humble rural beginnings. He was primarily self-trained and never received formal training. His early ministry involved a series of new beginnings as he moved from one pastorate to another. Tozer was a person of solitude and, because he believed in developing his inner life, he used times of solitude to learn. What he learned during these quiet times he disclosed in his writings, demonstrating the indirect influence of the written word. Tozer's timeline follows.

I. Inner-Discipline Foundations	II. On-the-Job-Training — New Beginnings	III. City Leadership — Expanding National Sphere of Influence	IV. Wrap-Up — Reflection	
1897	1919	1928	1959	1963

Figure 2-1 Timeline of A. W. Tozer

Those who knew Dawson Trotman well called him Daws.[2] He was a dynamic person who did everything with all his might. He called the church back to authentic Christianity by focusing on committed discipleship.[3] His pragmatic approach to learning and his drive to see others reproduce what he had learned characterized his life. The worldwide spread of The Navigators can be traced directly back to his prayer life. His is the story of what God accomplishes with a life that is willing to trust and do. Here is his timeline:

I. Restless Foundations	II. Developing the Model	III. Broadening the Vision	
1906	1933	1948	1956

Figure 2-2 Timeline of Dawson Trotman

Watchman Nee was born as an answer to prayer.[4] His name, Watchman, was divinely given and prophetic. He lived during a transition time in China, when the winds of dynastic change were blowing. During that foment he came to know Christ. He founded indigenous churches that were greatly persecuted. His work was founded on principles and God-given convictions. His emphasis on union life[5] and his insights on spiritual authority,[6] the major power base of a spiritual leader,[7] can give important direction to leaders today. Consistency characterized Watchman Nee's life and ministry.

		III. Direct to		
I. Sovereign Foundations	II. Foundational Lessons	Indirect Ministry	IV. Maturity Years	
1903	1921	1927	1941	1972

Figure 2-3 Timeline of Watchman Nee

BIRD'S-EYE VIEW – PATTERNS, PROCESSES, AND PRINCIPLES

The terms *patterns*, *processes*, and *principles* are foundational to understanding the analysis of a person's life. Patterns deal with the overall framework, or the big picture, of a life. Processes deal with the ways and means used by God to move a leader along in the overall pattern. Principles deal with the identification of foundational truths within processes and patterns that have a wider application to leaders.

When studying patterns, the timeline is useful for making long-term observations. When studying processes, we analyze process items—those providential events, people, circumstances, special interventions, and inner-life lessons that can be God's way of indicating leadership potential. Process items also develop potential, confirm the leadership role, and move the emerging leader along to God's appointed ministry level.[8]

Principles are different from both patterns and processes in that they identify foundational truths. A long time ago in my Navigator training, I was taught the importance of identifying principles and applying them to my life. This has been reinforced over the years as I have met others who have that same bent. One such influence was Warren Wiersbe. He once wrote an excellent article that stressed this whole idea of principles. In it he said,

> About the only thing I remember from one of my courses at seminary is a bit of doggerel that the weary professor dropped into a boring lecture:
>
> > Methods are many,
> > Principles are few.
> > Methods always change,
> > *Principles never do.*
>
> That conviction led me into a lifelong search for principles, the foundational truths that never change and yet always have a fresh principle behind them. I learned to evaluate men and ministries on the basis of the principles that motivated them as well as on the basis of the fruit they produced.[9]

Now that I have introduced you to these three terms, we will concentrate on patterns. We will discuss process items and principles as they apply to patterns in greater detail in later chapters.

THE GENERALIZED TIMELINE

A timeline is an important tool for analyzing the life of a leader, for it reveals the overall pattern of God's work in a life. If you look back at the case studies, you will see that I included a timeline for each of them. Below you will see a generalized timeline that is a synthesis of the many I have studied. While it rarely fits anyone exactly, it does give perspective. A timeline is a linear display along a horizontal axis that is broken up into development phases.[10]

Phase I. Sovereign Foundations	Phase II. Inner-Life Growth	Phase III. Ministry Maturing	Phase IV. Life Maturing	Phase V. Convergence	Phase VI. Afterglow

Figure 2-4 The Generalized Timeline

A development phase is a unit of time in a person's life. We identify different units by the nature of the development or the means for development in a leader's life. These significant units of time are labeled "sovereign foundations," "inner-life growth," "ministry maturing," "life maturing," "convergence," and "afterglow." Development phases are not absolutes.[11] They are helpful, however, because they force one to analyze what God was doing during a given time in a person's life.

In Phase I, Sovereign Foundations, God providentially works through family, environment, and historical events. This begins at birth. You might find it hard to believe that God was working through your family or your environment, especially if these were not godly influences, but He was. It is exciting to see how the providence of God was—and is—working through all our experiences. Keep in mind that it is often difficult to see the importance of all these items until later phases.[12] Ask God to put together some of the pieces of your sovereign foundations. As He does, you will come to a deeper appreciation of His power.

In Phase I, God is developing the leader by laying foundations in his life. This operation is sovereign. The potential leader has little control over what happens in this phase. His primary lesson is to learn to respond positively and take advantage of what God has laid in these foundations. There was little significant spiritual input in the lives of our three case studies (Tozer, Trotman, and Nee) during their foundational phases, yet we can see that God was sovereignly directing each life.

The next phase an emerging leader enters is one in which he seeks to know God in a more personal, intimate way. This period is defined as Phase II, the Inner-Life Growth phase. The leader learns the importance of praying and hearing God. As he grows in discernment, understanding, and obedience, he is put to the test. These early tests are crucial experiences that God uses to prepare the leader for the next steps in leadership. The growing leader invariably gets involved in some form of ministry. In this context of learning by doing, he gains new inner-life lessons.

In this phase, leadership potential is identified and God uses testing experiences to develop character. A proper, godly response allows a leader to learn the fundamental lessons God wants to teach. If the person doesn't learn, he will usually be tested again in the same areas. A proper response will result in an expanding ministry and greater responsibility.

In Phase III, Ministry Maturing, the emerging leader reaches out to others. He is beginning to experiment with spiritual gifts even though he may not know what this doctrine is. He may get training in order to be more effective. Ministry is the focus of the rising leader at this stage. Many of his lessons will zero in on relationships with other people or on the inadequacies in his personal life.

God is developing the leader in two ways during this time. Through ministry, the leader can identify his gifts and skills and use them with increasing effectiveness. He will also gain a better understanding of the body of Christ as he experiences the many kinds of relationships it offers. These relationship experiences teach both negative and positive lessons.

Ministry activity or fruitfulness is not the focus of Phases I, II, and III. God is working primarily *in* the leader, not *through* him.[13] Many emerging leaders don't recognize this and become frustrated. They are constantly evaluating productivity and activities, while God is quietly evaluating their leadership potential. He wants to teach us that we minister out of what we are.

By Phase IV, Life Maturing, the leader has identified and is using his spiritual gifts in a ministry that is satisfying. He gains a sense of priorities concerning the best use of his gifts and understands that learning what not to do is as important as learning what to do. A mature fruitfulness is the result. Isolation, crisis, and conflict take on new meaning. The principle that "ministry flows out of being" has new significance as the leader's character mellows and matures.

In this phase the leader's experiential understanding of God is being developed. Communion with God becomes foundational; it is more important than success in ministry. Through this change, the ministry itself takes on an increased relevance and fruitfulness. The key to development during this phase is a positive response to the experiences God ordains. This response will deepen communion with God that will become the base for lasting and effective ministry.

In Convergence, Phase V, God moves the leader into a role that matches his gift-mix and experience so that ministry is maximized.[14] The leader uses the best he has to offer and is freed from ministry for which he is not gifted or suited. Life Maturing and Ministry Maturing peak together during this period.

Many leaders do not experience convergence, and there are various reasons for this. Sometimes they are hindered by their own lack of personal development. At other times, an organization may hinder a leader by keeping him in a limiting position.[15] Some reasons are providential, as in the case of Dawson Trotman, and may be hard to understand because we do not have the full picture.[16] In general, however, when and if convergence occurs, the leader's potential is maximized.

The major developmental task for Phase V is the guidance of the leader into a role and place where he can have maximum effectiveness. His response to God's guidance must be to trust, rest, and watch as God moves him toward a ministry that embodies all the development of preceding phases. Convergence manifests itself as he responds consistently to God's work in his life.

For a very few, there is Phase VI, Afterglow (or Celebration).[17] The fruit of a lifetime of ministry and growth culminates in an era of recognition and indirect influence at broad levels. Leaders in Afterglow have built up a lifetime of contacts and continue to exert influence in these relationships. Others will seek them out because of their consistent track record in following God. Their storehouse of wisdom gathered over a lifetime of leadership will continue to bless and benefit many.

There is no recognizable developmental task in Phase VI other than to allow a lifetime of ministry to reflect the glory of God and to honor His faithfulness over a lifetime of emergence.[18]

IDENTIFYING DEVELOPMENT PHASES

Development phases are consistently characterized in at least three different ways.[19] First, different kinds of process items occur in different phases. Second, each phase is terminated by specific boundary events. Third, there is a different sphere of influence.

God uses providential events, people, and circumstances (process items) to develop a leader. While all of life is used to shape us, some items in life can be tied more directly to leadership emergence. I have grouped the various process items into six general categories: foundational factors, inner-life growth factors, ministry factors, maturity factors, convergence factors, and guidance factors. Different types of items occur at different times in the leader's life. These process items can occur, though infrequently, in other than their characteristic phases. Guidance process items occur throughout all the phases. They are often crucial during transitions between phases.

Early development phases are characterized by process items known as inner-life growth items. Dawson Trotman's life reflected these just after his conversion.[20] He prayed that God would allow him to witness at work. God tested his sincerity with a series of three checks. First of all, was his conversion secret or would he reveal it by taking his New

Testament to work? Dawson took his Bible to work. Word quickly spread that Trotman had religion. God tested him again. Would he identify himself with other Christians, specifically a preacher who came to the lumberyard and preached once a week? Trotman did, and this led to another check. The preacher asked Trotman to give his personal testimony. Dawson agreed to this, and word spread quickly among his co-workers. Trotman's first public testimony turned out to be a preaching service to all two hundred of his fellow employees. Through these three specific checks, God began to shape and prepare Trotman for an expanded ministry of evangelism. Great usefulness in the future hinges on little issues like these.

The middle phases of development often display ministry process items. These concern lessons about ministry and take different forms. Some, called power items, involve recognition and appropriation of God's power in a ministry.

Watchman Nee experienced power process items several times in his life. Nee and a team of Chinese were evangelizing a small island village. In January 1925, the fisherfolk and farmers, who were taking part in the new year celebration, were not very open to the gospel teams. The fisherfolk believed in a god named Ta-Wang, whom they claimed had demonstrated his power by bringing perfect weather on his special festival day for 286 years. In a re-creation of the encounter between Elijah and the Baal priest, Nee's team and the villagers saw a confrontation between God and Ta-Wang. Nee's God broke through and a deluge of rain came in response to the faith of his team. Those who had said, "If your God is stronger than Ta-Wang, then we will follow Him," did just that. This event was a breakthrough in the ministry, not only on that island but on all the others in the chain.

The second identifying factor in development phases is the boundary event. Process items that happen during a boundary time and are instrumental in bringing about the shift from one phase to the next are called boundary events. Boundary events include such factors as crises, promotions, a new ministry, learning a major new concept, unusual experiences, life-changing encounters with a person, a divine guidance experience, or a geographic move. As you can see, there are no set guidelines. Boundary events vary from individual to individual, but in general boundary events are change signals. They mark the end and then the beginning of a significant time in a leader's life.

A. W. Tozer's Phase I ended with his conversion experience. His second phase terminated with a move from small pastorates in Virginia, Ohio, and Indiana, to a pastorate in Chicago. Not only was this a geographic move, but it was a shift from a small rural conservative constituency to a much larger metropolitan congregation.

There are three significant boundary events in Dawson Trotman's passage from Phase I to Phase II. God moved him to a lifetime conviction that was to shape the ministry he began. The actual boundary was not sharp, but spread over several months. The three boundary events built on and enforced one another.

The first was a word process item, something God often uses from His Word to significantly alter a leader's thinking. During a nine-month period Trotman had formed only three boys clubs. At that rate it would take a long time to reach the nation, much less the world. Could he speed up the rate? Was there a better way to get the job done?

During this time of questioning God renewed and expanded upon a promise He'd given to Dawson earlier: "Since you are precious and honored in my sight, and because I love you, I will give men in exchange for you, and people in exchange for your life" (Isaiah 43:4). He had prayed for laborers for God's harvest. He began to see the vast difference between a mere believer and a laborer, and to see the need to concentrate on building laborers on whom God could depend. He began to preach, "God can do more through one man who is 100 percent dedicated to Him than through 100 men who are only 90 percent."

About that time Dawson wrote in the margin of his Bible, near the Isaiah promise, this request: "That God will soon bring us into touch with a mighty band of young men, strong rugged soldiers of the cross, with an eye singled to His glory."[21] Something had happened over the last six months. Dawson's goal had been changing from winning souls to building strong disciples and recruiting laborers for God. This boundary item, a challenging promise from God's Word, began to shift his emphasis from evangelism alone to evangelism with follow-up, the trademark of The Navigators for the past seventy years.

Not all boundary events are positive, as we see in the next item:

> Dawson picked up a hitch-hiker whose speech indicated he was not a believer. Within moments he discovered this man was one of his "converts" of the previous year whose decision had not been followed up and who had virtually died on the vine. Shaken, Dawson reasoned that there must be countless such persons who had sincerely, perhaps with tears, called on the name of the Lord, but whose lives had not been changed. What was wrong?
>
> From that time on Dawson resolved to follow up anyone he led to Christ – a work more difficult than soul-winning – and to encourage others to give their converts their rightful opportunity to grow in Christ. The truth had come into focus, and he made an axiom of it: "You can lead a man to Christ in twenty minutes to a couple of hours, but it takes twenty weeks to a couple of years to adequately follow him up." The hitch-hiker convert startled him into realigning his ministry – less emphasis on getting the decision and more on growing up into Christ.[22]

The third boundary event involved a guidance item, which preceded the final shift into the next phase. It was a divine contact, to be defined more fully in chapter 6. Trotman was given the name of a sailor on the USS *West Virginia*. After praying about Spencer's growth in Christ, Trotman decided to meet with him. During Bible study, Trotman and Spencer were approached by another man who asked what they were doing. Trotman skillfully used Scripture to witness to the man, and Spencer was impressed with his use of the Bible.

> On the way back to the landing he said, "Boy, I'd give my right arm to know how to use the Word like that." "No you wouldn't," Daws baited him. After a brief exchange the sailor insisted, "I would. I mean it."

It was the response Dawson wanted. "All right, you can. And it won't cost your arm, but you'll have to be willing to dig in and study and apply yourself. I'll give you all the time you'll take."[23]

Trotman worked one-on-one with Spencer to train him in the basics of Christian discipleship. Out of this contact and training experience grew the concept of reproduction by multiplication rather than by addition, another trademark of The Navigators today.[24]

God used the word item, the negative preparation item, and the guidance item (divine contact) during this boundary time in Trotman's life. If he had not responded in the way he did, he may not have moved on to his next phase of leadership emergence.

Because the very nature of leadership is influence, God endows leaders with the capacity to influence. A leader will exercise his gifts most effectively at a given level of influence.[25] God uses various means to develop a potential leader into the full exercise of leadership at that level. Sphere of influence describes a level or type of influence, and the people being influenced and for whom that leader will give an account to God.[26] A change in sphere of influence, either an increase or decrease in numbers, or a change in the kind of sphere of influence, usually signals a change in development phases.

Tozer's transition from Phase II to Phase III illustrates how sphere of influence can differ greatly in different development phases. In Phase II Tozer's influence was only direct—a face-to-face ministry to the people he saw on a daily or weekly basis in a small church. In this phase he grew from a new believer influencing individuals into an ordained pastor. In Phase III Tozer's sphere of influence increased both in size and kind. His direct ministry was a large city church. But his influence went beyond this as he began writing books, speaking on the radio and at conferences, and teaching in training institutions, such as Moody Bible Institute and Wheaton College. This sphere of influence in Phase III did not develop overnight, but even at the start it was different from that of Phase II.

SUB-PHASES

Because a development phase can cover an extensive time period, it is helpful to use sub-phases, which can show the step-by-step development of a leader within a long phase. Sub-phases are characterized by boundary events and by small changes in sphere of influence.

Phase IV. Watchman Nee's Maturity Years

A. Isolation years	B. Urgency years	C. Glory years — prison isolation	
1941	1945	1952	1972

Figure 2-5 Sub-Phases in Development Phase IV for Watchman Nee

During the first eleven years of this phase, Nee had a tremendous sense of urgency. He anticipated the drastic effect that the revolutionary movement would have on the lives of Chinese Christians. During his isolation years, in sub-phase A, he began to prepare his strategy. Because he was preparing for the future, his emphasis during sub-phase B was on intensive leadership training. In sub-phase C, his direct sphere of influence decreased because he was in prison, but his indirect sphere of influence increased greatly because of the publication of his writings. All of this occurred during Phase IV of Nee's life.

Development phases are identified by three factors: process items, boundary events, and changes in sphere of influence. There is usually an interplay between these three factors that also helps to determine development phases.

As a leader, you should recognize that God is continually developing you over a lifetime. His top priority is to conform you to the image of Christ for ministry with spiritual authority. Enduring fruitfulness flows out of being. In addition to transforming your character, God will increase your capacity to influence through developing your spiritual gifts.

While the details of the generalized pattern will differ greatly from individual to individual, and not all leaders will go through all the stages, the overall concept holds and is useful in evaluation and decision making.

SUMMARY

Where have we been? We defined three foundational terms: patterns, processes, and principles. We looked at a tool for analysis called the timeline. We defined development phases on the timeline. We studied what a development phase is and how it is identified. We found that process items, boundary events, and sphere of influence help us determine individual development phases. We took an overall look at leadership as a lifetime of lessons.

Has this chapter caused you to reflect on your own pattern of development? I hope it has given you a fresh understanding of the touch of God in your life by giving you new perspectives to identify God's development in your own leadership pattern. With an expectant learning attitude you will find yourself responding to His direction and sensing new lessons that previously you might have missed. This kind of reflection on divine activity in a leader's life develops the confidence that leaders in Christian work must have.

HOW ABOUT YOU?

Now, for some practical "how tos." I've listed some questions for you to answer. Don't skip this. As with all types of study, you need to apply what you learn. So, go for it. Accept the challenge of these suggestions. Do them and share them with a friend.

1. Rough out your own timeline. Start by identifying the major boundary events in your life. Then think back to what God was doing in each of those major time periods. Name each development phase with a label that captures what God was doing during the phase.

2. In what ways has your development followed along the generalized pattern? In what ways has it differed?

3. Even though I have not yet told you how to arrive at principles, most leaders can intuitively derive them. As you think about

the timeline and the major boundary events you identified in
question 1, can you identify a major leadership principle that
God has shown you?

4. Twice during this chapter I have mentioned a major
   observation: *Ministry flows out of being.* Do you agree with this?
   Why or why not?

CHAPTER 3

FOUNDATIONAL LESSONS: INNER-LIFE GROWTH PROCESSES

The Challenge/The Problem: Keep thy heart with all diligence; for out of it are the issues of life. *(Proverbs 4:23, KJV)*

Our greatest challenge as leaders is to develop a godly character. Warren Wiersbe addresses this issue:

> Apart from character, ministry is only religious activity or even worse, religious business.
>
> "Let me be taught," wrote Henry Martyn, "that the first great business on earth is the sanctification of my own soul. . . ."
>
> Someone asked financier J. P. Morgan what the best collateral was a customer could give him. Morgan replied, "Character."
>
> G. Campbell Morgan was riding with D. L. Moody . . . when suddenly Moody asked, "What is character anyway?" Morgan knew that the evangelist wanted to answer his own question, so he waited. "Character," said Moody, "is what a man is in the dark. . . ."
>
> Perhaps the key word is integrity. . . . No amount of reputation can substitute for character.[1]

Wiersbe has captured the essence of a godly character in one word:

integrity. There are many lessons in the development of a leader. None are more crucial in timing or in impact than the early ones, which focus on character building.

DEVELOPING A LEADER — EARLY PROCESSES

Let's put this chapter in proper perspective. The previous chapter introduced the concept of patterns, processes, and principles. We used a generalized timeline (see page 37) to see the overall pattern in the development of a leader. This chapter looks at Phase II.

In this phase, God uses four important process items to test an emerging leader's character. Three of the items are called checks because of the testing nature of this phase.[2] These are integrity checks, obedience checks, and word checks. A fourth item, the ministry task, occurs frequently in the inner-life phase. It is a testing item, but its focus is on the emergence of the leader in ministry, so we will deal with it in the next chapter where our focus is ministry processing.

THE INTEGRITY CHECK

At the heart of any assessment of biblical qualifications for leadership lies the concept of integrity — that uncompromising adherence to a code of moral, artistic, or other values that reveals itself in sincerity, honesty, and candor and avoids deception or artificiality.[3] The God-given capacity to lead has two parts: giftedness and character. Integrity is the heart of character.[4]

An emerging leader becomes aware of the importance of integrity through integrity checks. An *integrity check* is a test that God uses to evaluate intentions in order to shape character. This check is a springboard to an expanded sphere of influence. There are three parts to an integrity check: the challenge to consistency with inner convictions, the response to the challenge, and the resulting expansion of ministry.

In Daniel 1:8-21, Daniel faced an integrity check that could have cost him his life.

Daniel made up his mind not to let himself become ritually unclean by eating the food and drinking the wine of the royal court, so he asked Ashpenaz to help him, and God made Ashpenaz sympathetic to Daniel. Ashpenaz, however, was afraid of the king, so he said to Daniel, "The king has decided what you are to eat and drink, and if you don't look as fit as the other young men, he may kill me."

So Daniel went to the guard whom Ashpenaz had placed in charge of him and his three friends. "Test us for ten days," he said. "Give us vegetables to eat and water to drink. Then compare us with the young men who are eating the food of the royal court, and base your decision on how we look."

He agreed to let them try it for ten days. When the time was up, they looked healthier and stronger than all those who had been eating the royal food. So from then on the guard let them continue to eat vegetables instead of what the king provided.

God gave the four young men knowledge and skill in literature and philosophy. In addition, he gave Daniel skill in interpreting visions and dreams.

At the end of the three years set by the king, Ashpenaz took all the young men to Nebuchadnezzar. The king talked with them all, and Daniel, Hananiah, Mishael, and Azariah impressed him more than any of the others. So they became members of the king's court. No matter what question the king asked or what problem he raised, these four knew ten times more than any fortuneteller or magician in his whole kingdom. Daniel remained at the royal court until Cyrus, the emperor of Persia, conquered Babylonia. (GNT)

Daniel, a teenager away from home and parental influence, was forced to decide if the convictions he grew up with were his own. In this case the *inner conviction* was a religious one involving food. He was under pressure to violate this conviction, but he stuck to his conviction (*response*). God gave him relationships that allowed him to work out a plan that did not compromise his convictions. God honored his unyielding character. Daniel and his friends were respected for their knowledge and skills and were given top-level government jobs. This promotion to a strategic position is an example of *expansion*—the third element of an integrity check.[5] Daniel stood firm and saw God provide a solution. This enabled him to stand on even tougher issues later in life. All three elements of the integrity check are found in this passage.

Because character development has many facets, there are a variety of integrity checks. This is a sampling of the many that I have identified: values (which determine convictions), temptation (which tests conviction), conflict against ministry vision (which tests faith), an alternative in guidance situations (which tests calling), persecution (which tests steadfastness), loyalty (which tests allegiance), and restitution (which tests honesty).[6]

Checks are also used in a variety of ways. Some are used to test follow-through on a promise or vow, ensure commitment to a ministry or vision, allow confirmation of inner-character strength, and build faith. Others are used to establish inner values, teach submission, and warn others of the serious responsibility to God.

The following examples are taken from the early lives of leaders, before they were even considered leaders. Like you and me, they were learning about character and integrity through everyday, commonplace experiences and situations.

Patricia Reid and Norma Van Dalen describe an integrity check early in the life of Amy Carmichael, who later became the founder of the Dohnavur Fellowship (the famous mission organization that worked with temple children in India).

The lessons Amy had learned concerning life values and priorities were challenged often during these years of preparation. On one particular occasion while shopping for new clothes with her mother, Amy was especially tested regarding these convictions. When the dressmaker brought out his finest and gayest materials, Amy sensed the Holy Spirit's convictions about such an "extravagant and unpractical" dress. Surprising her mother and the dressmaker, Amy obeyed the still small voice and resisted the temptation to enjoy a beautiful dress she didn't really need. This lesson became the foundation of Amy Carmichael's simplistic lifestyle with regard to her personal needs.[7]

This was an integrity check. It was used to establish an inner value concerning a simplistic lifestyle. God knew Amy would need this in her fifty-five years on the mission field in India.

In his autobiography *On the Mountaintop*, Carlton Booth relates a test of his integrity that occurred just after his conversion:

> I had been converted to Christ shortly before going to work for Sears; but up on that second floor, all alone, I found myself subjected to strong temptation. Some of the orders that came down to me from floors above included unwrapped boxes of chocolates, and I convinced myself that one chocolate lifted from the second layer of a box now and then would never be missed. Candy was a rare treat which we could not afford in those days, and this made the temptation so irresistible that I yielded to it several times.[8]

Booth's conscience began to bother him. The Lord convicted him of the need to tell his supervisor about what he had done. He saved up a dollar to cover the cost of the items he had taken. He then confronted his supervisor. The rest of the account follows:

> He neither chided nor congratulated me when I said my conscience had been troubling me. Those gimlet eyes looked straight through me and he said, "Well, son, what shall I do with this money?"
> I told him I didn't care what he did with it, all I wanted was to have relief from this thing that had been troubling me for many days. So he took the money and said quite calmly, and I think a bit sympathetically, "I shall turn this in to the office marked 'conscience money!'"[9]

This incident tested Booth in the area of restitution. It established the inner value of honesty. Booth was later used by God in an evangelistic music ministry and in a training ministry.

Some do not pass integrity checks. Saul, the first king of Israel, lacked integrity. First Samuel 15 tells the sad story. God told Saul to destroy the Amalekites utterly along with all their possessions. Saul defeated them, but he didn't destroy them or their possessions. He failed an obedience check, but the real issue goes beyond obedience to the lack of integrity in Saul's intentions.

Saul's first words upon seeing Samuel were, "The LORD bless you, Samuel! I have obeyed the LORD's command." Samuel asked, "Why, then, do I hear cattle mooing and sheep bleating?" (1 Samuel 15:13-14, GNT). Samuel confronted Saul and told him that God had rejected him.[10] God won't use a leader who lacks integrity.

Inner-life issues need emphasis. Integrity testing is essential to a leader, especially in these early stages of ministry. Because of the value and use of these tests, it is obvious that a major leadership principle is involved: *Integrity is foundational for effective leadership; it must be instilled early in a leader's character.* An emerging leader who disregards this principle takes a great risk. Those who respond properly to integrity checks will move on in their leadership emergence.

THE OBEDIENCE CHECK

A leader must learn obedience in order to influence others toward obedience. An *obedience check* is a process item through which a leader learns to recognize, understand, and obey God's voice. The leader encounters this early in his development and repeatedly throughout life. Through it God tests a leader's personal response to revealed truth.

One of the classic obedience checks in Scripture is chronicled in Genesis 22:

> Some time later God tested Abraham; he called to him, "Abraham!" And Abraham answered, "Yes, here I am!"
>
> "Take your son," God said, "your only son, Isaac, whom you love so much, and go to the land of Moriah. There on a mountain that I will show you, offer him as a sacrifice to me." (verses 1-2, GNT)

This obedience check was especially difficult because of God's promises concerning Isaac. Abraham knew his future line depended on

Isaac, but he was still willing to obey God.

I once heard a leader say that many are called to lay something on the altar; and they do, but they take along a rubber knife. Our obedience often is not complete but has some strings attached.[11] Abraham took a real knife—and God honored his obedience by sparing Isaac.

It is one thing to obey when it seems logical and necessary, but it is quite another when the obedience calls for something that doesn't make sense. Obedience doesn't always hinge on understanding. It did not make sense ethically or practically to kill Isaac, yet Abraham obeyed. Although this was an obedience check, it was also an integrity check. Would he remain loyal to God and believe in Him when the pressure was on? These tests revealed that faith and loyalty to God were a part of Abraham's character. Hebrews 11:17-19 attests to this.

Abraham's complex experience shows the pattern for a successful obedience check. God requires unconditional obedience. We are to obey, and He is responsible for the results.

Obedience checks occur throughout the Bible and are frequently mentioned in historical and contemporary leadership emergence studies. Some examples include learning about possessions and giving, learning to put God first in the choice of a mate, and learning to be willing to be used by God in ministry. Others include readiness to trust a God-given truth, to forgive, to confess error, or to right a wrong.[12]

Watchman Nee provides us with an excellent illustration involving inner-life growth. He sensed a need to begin printing gospel tracts and then prayed for the money to distribute them. God revealed that there were hindrances to his prayer. Many in his church were criticizing another believer and Watchman silently agreed with them. When he prayed further about the money, God spoke to him about this sin. God required that he go and confess his guilt to his sister.[13]

> Afterwards, I considered doing so, but, when coming face to face with her, I hesitated five times even though I wished to confess to her. It was because I was concerned that she, who had all along been admiring me so much, would then

despise me. I said to God, "It would be all right if You ordered me to do anything else, but I am unwilling to confess to her." I still kept asking God for the printing money, but He would not listen to my reasoning and insisted on my confessing.

The sixth time, through the grace of the Lord, I confessed to her. With tears, we both confessed our faults and then forgave each other. We were filled with joy and from then on loved each other all the more in the Lord.[14]

Not long after this event, a postman delivered a letter that contained fifteen U.S. dollars. The letter read, "I am fond of distributing gospel tracts. Please condescend to accept." God's expansion was clearly identified. The lessons lasted a lifetime. They were on the thought life, a forgiving spirit, hindrance to prayer, and trusting God for ministry provision. Obeying God was the first lesson, and the others hinged on it.

Acts 5:1-11 tells us about two separate obedience checks. Ananias and Sapphira sold their property, but they lacked integrity when they lied about the amount of the sale. Peter was being checked when he confronted each of them about their sin. Peter's obedience in this unpleasant task is carefully recorded by Luke so that all who read it are warned of the seriousness of obedience with integrity. God's discipline was swift and severe. After this event Peter's ministry expanded.

Leaders will be responsible for influencing specific groups of people to obey God. They will not achieve this unless they themselves know how to obey. This brings me to my second major principle in the testing pattern of the inner-life phase: *Obedience is first learned, then taught.*

THE WORD CHECK

A leader must have the ability to receive truth from God. This gift, receiving truth from God, is essential because it builds spiritual authority, which is the basis for a spiritual leader's influence.[15] The right to influence comes from the ability to clarify God's truth to others. Clarifying truth from God is the essence of the cluster of spiritual gifts that I call the word gifts. Leaders always have at least one word gift along with others that make up their gift-mix.[16] The primary word gifts are teaching, prophecy, and exhortation. The secondary word gifts are apostleship, evangelism, and pastoring. Leaders will also use word gifts to discern guidance for the ministry.

Godly leaders display love for truth. They study the written Word to feed their own souls as well as to help others. God teaches a leader to appreciate truth, cultivate habits for the intake of truth, and respond in obedience to truth so that he may be quick to discern God's truth in everyday life and through other people's ministry. The process used to describe this development is the word check.

A *word check* is the process item that tests a leader's ability to understand or receive a word from God personally and then allow God to work it out in his life. When successfully passed, a word check will lead to more truth. Truth will confirm the emerging leader's capacity to lead, which will yield increased spiritual authority as perceived by followers.

Word checks are frequently combined with integrity checks and obedience checks, because the revealed truth will test integrity or obedience. It is important to perceive the overall effect of the test, not which process item is used. I'll talk about this overlap of process items later in the chapter.

Samuel's first encounter with God was a word check. It set the stage for Samuel's guidance ministry to Israel during a time of leadership transition. First Samuel 3:1-10 sets the stage for Samuel's entrance into this transition:

> In those days, when the boy Samuel was serving the LORD under the direction of Eli, there were very few messages from the LORD, and visions from him were quite rare. One night Eli, who was now almost blind, was sleeping in his own room; Samuel was sleeping in the sanctuary, where the sacred Covenant Box was. Before dawn, while the lamp was still burning, the LORD called Samuel. He answered, "Yes, sir!" and ran to Eli and said, "You called me, and here I am."
>
> But Eli answered, "I didn't call you; go back to bed." So Samuel went back to bed.
>
> The LORD called Samuel again. The boy did not know that it was the LORD,

because the Lord had never spoken to him before. So he got up, went to Eli, and said, "You called me, and here I am."

But Eli answered, "My son, I didn't call you; go back to bed."

The Lord called Samuel a third time; he got up, went to Eli, and said, "You called me, and here I am."

Then Eli realized that it was the Lord who was calling the boy, so he said to him, "Go back to bed; and if he calls you again, say, 'Speak, Lord, your servant is listening.'" So Samuel went back to bed.

The Lord came and stood there, and called as he had before, "Samuel! Samuel!"

Samuel answered, "Speak; your servant is listening." (GNT)

After the Lord called Samuel that fourth time, He revealed that terrible discipline would be administered in Eli's family because of his and his sons' sin. This would serve as a warning to Israel. Samuel told the whole truth to Eli the next morning, and Eli submitted to this obvious word from the Lord. The Bible goes on to comment in summary fashion,

As Samuel grew up, the Lord was with him and made come true everything that Samuel said. So all the people of Israel, from one end of the country to the other, knew that Samuel was indeed a prophet of the Lord. The Lord continued to reveal himself at Shiloh, where he had appeared to Samuel and had spoken to him. And when Samuel spoke, all Israel listened. (verses 19-21, GNT)

God speaks to leaders and His message is confirmed. An emerging leader may not always recognize God's voice. A leader who repeatedly demonstrates that God speaks to him gains spiritual authority. One who listens and follows will see God's confirmation and expansion of his ministry. Samuel demonstrates the proper response for all emerging leaders when he says, "Speak; your servant is listening."

Watchman Nee's life illustrates these points. Personal appropriation of truth will change one's personal values and lifestyle. After Nee's conversion he had a new desire to study the Bible.

Soon Watchman came upon Paul's words: "Present yourselves to God as men who have been brought from death to life, and your members to God as instruments of righteousness."

"God required of me therefore," he said afterwards, "that I now regard all my faculties as belonging to Another. I dared not squander a few cents of my money or an hour of my time or any of my mental or physical powers, for they were not mine but his. It was a great thing when I made that discovery. Real Christian life began for me that day."[17]

Nee saw the power of the Word of God to change his own direction, so he decided to take time off from his formal schooling to enroll in a Bible school instead. He read through the New Testament on a monthly basis. As he did, his desire for more truth increased.

Watchman's intake of Scripture was not just for knowledge. He learned to recognize God speaking through the Word. This is shown in the lives of emerging leaders.

It was now that he realized how much Charity Chang had occupied his thoughts. There had of course been no hint of a match, yet at some stage the idea had certainly found lodging in his mind. Their next encounter, however, brought him up short. What he already feared was all too evident from their brief conversation. Her worldly tastes and passion for stylish clothes seemed to him the mark of something deeper. She in no way shared his love for the Lord, with its new scale of priorities but had goals of her own, ambitions for success in the world's eyes that he could no longer entertain. Clearly they were headed in different directions.

For a while he shelved the problem, until one day he was reading Psalm 73:25, "There is none on earth that I desire beside thee," and the Spirit of God arrested him. "You have a consuming desire upon earth. You should give up your attachment for Miss Chang. What possible qualifications has she to be a preacher's wife?" His reply was an attempt to bargain. "Lord, I will do anything for you. If you want me to carry your good news to the unreached tribes, I am willing to go; but this thing only I cannot do." How could he, just coming up to twenty-one, finally detach his mind from one who had so pleasurably engaged it?[18]

Nee did detach his mind, however, and threw himself into the ministry. Later, God graciously worked a radical change in Charity's life and she became an ardent follower of Christ. He then brought these two back together geographically, emotionally, and finally as man and wife. God teaches an emerging leader to hear His Word for personal guidance. This is a natural stepping stone for hearing God's Word for corporate guidance.

Dawson Trotman was saved through a word check. He was memorizing Scripture for a contest.

Dawson was walking to work, lunch pail in hand, along the familiar path beside a slough when suddenly the words of one of the twenty verses he had memorized blazed in his consciousness. *Verily, verily, I say unto you, He that heareth my word, and believeth on him that sent me, hath everlasting life.*

Why, that's wonderful, he thought. *Hath everlasting life.* For the first time in years he prayed when he wasn't in trouble. "O God, whatever this means, I want to have it." As if in telegraphic answer, the verse John 1:12 flashed on his mental screen: *But as many as received him, to them gave he the power to become the sons of God, even to them that believe on his name.* His response was immediate. "O God," he said simply, and meant it, "whatever it means to receive Jesus, I want to do it right now."[19]

Trotman kept walking down the street, but now he was a different man. This experience with the memorized Word became the cornerstone for the discipling model he eventually developed.

Amy Carmichael's early development repeatedly contained word checks, integrity checks, and obedience checks. These checks resulted in foundational principles that guided her all through her ministry.

Amy's life prior to her experience in Belfast had been rather "ordinary" for a person of her age and social status. However, one Sunday morning in 1885 that was all to change. While walking home from church with her brothers, they saw a pathetic looking woman hobbling down the street carrying a heavy load. Moved to help her,

Amy and her brothers took the load and walked with her to her destination. Amy felt uncomfortable doing this as all the respectable people, also on their way home from church, stared at the "group" with disgust. As they were passing an old fountain, Amy heard a voice speaking to her – 1 Corinthians 3:12b-14a, "gold, silver, precious stones. . . . If any man's work abide . . ." (KJV). She was immediately convicted and challenged concerning her life's priorities and ambitions. This verse and experience remained in her memory and became a "measure" for any and all ministries or activities she devoted her time to.[20]

This was primarily a word check, but it became the basis for integrity checks throughout Amy's ministry because it gave her an inner value, a conviction concerning ministry for God. She would from then on measure a ministry in terms of eternal worth and results.[21]

God uses His Word in a variety of ways: to give inner conviction, to assign ministry, to solve problems, to motivate toward vision, to encourage faith, to give divine assurance, and to clarify guidance, to name a few. All are important to an emerging leader. Personal lessons learned through word checks are stepping stones to group lessons.

Word checks also lead to the identification of word gifts in an emerging leader. This usually follows a pattern. An emerging leader is sensitive to God's voice and personally responds to truth through word checks. This opens the door to sharing the truths he's learned with others. The communication of truth allows for the development of various word gifts in the leader.

This pattern leads me to a third principle: *Leadership gifts primarily involve word gifts, which initially emerge through word checks.*

Failure to pass a word check often results in repeated lessons and lengthened development time. It can result, as in the case of Ananias and Sapphira, in discipline and removal from ministry.

I have described three major kinds of tests: the integrity check, the obedience check, and the word check. Sometimes it is not so easy to differentiate them. Life is complex and a given piece of reality does not always fit into neat analytical categories. Often a test involves a combination of one or more process items. See the diagram, which shows possibilities of combinations.

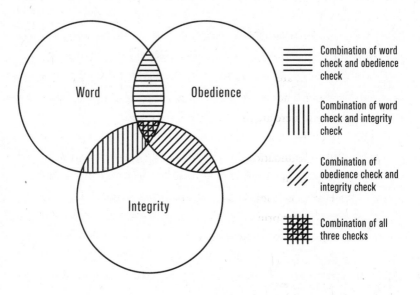

Figure 3-1 Diagram Showing Overlap of Testing Items

Although it is good to identify a given process item it is much more important to see the testing's significance.

SUMMARY

This chapter has examined the major overall pattern of Phase II, the Inner-Life Growth phase. That pattern is characterized by testing followed by expansion of ministry. Integrity checks, obedience checks, and word checks are means by which God tests an emerging leader's intentions. These three items are called checks because of their testing nature. Successful response on the part of the leader results in personal growth and ministry expansion.

I have stated that a godly leader is a person with God-given capacity and God-given responsibility to influence specific groups of

God's people toward His purposes for the group. Inner-life growth testing focuses on developing capacity and responsibility in a leader. Character is foundational if a leader is to influence people for God's purposes.

Let me emphasize again that these tests are primarily for the emerging leader. The results of character, obedience, and the ability to perceive and use God's truth are bridges over which God proceeds in His development of a leader. They are first lessons in a lifetime of lessons. They are crucial ones. Again here are the three principles:

- Integrity is foundational for effective leadership; it must be instilled early in a leader's character.
- Obedience is first learned, then taught.
- Leadership gifts primarily involve word gifts, which initially emerge through word checks.

HOW ABOUT YOU?

Perhaps as I have been describing these process items you have immediately identified with one or more that you have personally experienced or have seen in the life of another. To get a better understanding of the principles, answer the following questions.

1. What is the integrity check that Paul faces in Acts 20:22-23? What kind of integrity check is it? What is its purpose or use? Which of the three elements of an integrity check does it contain?
2. Can you think of another biblical example of an integrity check that I have not shared? Jot it down.
3. Can you identify in your own experience, or that of someone you have observed, an instance of an integrity check? Analyze it in terms of the elements of personal growth and expansion.

4. Can you identify an obedience check in your experience? Perhaps the following checklist will help you identify it:

- Learning about possessions and giving
- Learning about choice of mate and putting God first
- Willingness to be used by God in ministry
- Willingness to trust a truth God has shown
- Willingness to forgive
- Willingness to confess
- Willingness to right a wrong

5. See if you can identify the word checks in Acts 11:27-30. How are they the same as the ones I have been describing in this chapter? How are they different?

6. Can you identify a word check in your own experience or that of someone you have observed? Jot it down and analyze how God used it.

7. Interviewing a mature leader who has been involved in ministry for ten or more years is a helpful exercise. Explain to such a leader the terms *integrity check*, *obedience check*, and *word check*. Then ask him to identify an important word check in his past. My guess is that you will discover some important leadership lessons, and you will know the leader in a deeper way than before.

CHAPTER 4

SECOND LESSONS: MINISTRY MATURING PROCESSES — PART I

The Challenge/The Problem: He who is faithful in a very little and therefore can be *relied upon*, is also faithful in much and *can be relied upon there*. And he who violates law and justice in a very little thing does the same also in regard to much. *(Luke 16:10, Wuest, emphasis added)*

Faithfulness is the yardstick by which God measures ministry maturity. How do you perform those ministries that are assigned to you? Do you see them as coming from God and respond with a joyful rendering of service to Him? Do you view them as chores to be endured or feats to be accomplished for the sake of personal recognition?

With faithful service comes greater responsibility. How do you measure up?

HOW DOES A PERSON BEGIN MINISTRY?

Michele Helin attends The Cornerstone, a singles class at Lake Avenue Congregational Church. There are ten of us on the leadership team of this class. My ministry is teaching and training, while Michele's is organization and service. She is single and in her mid-thirties. She teaches disabled children in the public school system in Los Angeles

County. She embodies faithfulness both in her vocation and in her
ministry of service to The Cornerstone.

Michele's faithfulness goes beyond performing assigned tasks; she
sees things that need to be done and she finds a way to do them. She
spearheads our monthly prayer meeting and frequently hosts it. She coor-
dinates the Bible teaching in the small group she attends. Her influence
in these activities is low key. A casual observer in the class might not
sense this behind-the-scenes leadership, but God does because He
measures in faithfulness.

I asked Michele one Sunday how she got started in ministry. She
replied, "I was challenged by a pastor when I was a young Christian.
There was a need, and I felt I should help out even though I felt inadequate." A small beginning, but sensitivity to need, willingness to serve,
and faithfulness highlight Michele's entrance into ministry.

Michele has responded to many other ministry opportunities over
the past several years. She illustrates several important ideas described in
this chapter. Why do people get involved in ministry? How does God
recruit leaders? How does He develop them? How does He evaluate them?

FROM RECEIVING TO GIVING – MINISTRY PROCESSING

Before jumping into the answers let's review what we've learned so far.
Chapter 3 dealt with the Inner-Life Growth phase of the generalized
timeline. It pointed out that God's first priority in developing a leader is
to refine his character. Integrity is the true measure of the inner life.
Character development comes before ministry. We saw the testing
patterns of integrity checks, obedience checks, and word checks. These
checks identify leadership potential.

At this point, the potential leader moves into ministry.

He has tasted of God's goodness and must pass it on to others. God
takes time and a variety of experiences to move a potential leader through
the transition from receiving to giving.

In this chapter we will see the ways God develops leaders using the
different process items, and we'll identify various patterns. Two of these

are the *foundational ministry pattern* and the *giftedness discovery pattern*. We will then discuss a major leadership principle. Due to the length and complexity of the Ministry Maturing phase—one that may involve many years—we will break our discussion of it into two chapters.

MATURING IN MINISTRY

As a potential leader moves into ministry, God develops his leadership abilities by taking him through four stages. (1) God challenges the leader into ministry. This is called *entry*. (2) He develops skills and spiritual gifts to enhance the leader's effectiveness. This is called *training*. (3) He enables the leader to relate to people in ways that will motivate and influence them. He also teaches him how to set up the means to accomplish these goals. This is called *relational learning*. (4) He helps the leader see spiritual principles that govern ministry that pleases Him. This is called *discernment*.

This development takes place over a long period of time, often many years. It is therefore necessary to divide this phase into sub-phases called early ministry, middle ministry, and later ministry. As with phases, the sub-phases are grouped according to the processes that occur within them. The development stages are not always clearly delineated because there is some overlap in the learning process. For instance, a person in the training stage may learn some lessons about relationships or discernment.

Each sub-phase is characterized by a different set of process items. In the early ministry sub-phase, the process items are ministry task and ministry challenge. In the middle ministry sub-phase, the process items are ministry skills, training experience, and giftedness discovery. In the later ministry sub-phase, the process items are ministry structure insights and power items. Several process items occur throughout the Ministry Maturing phase: faith challenges, authority insights, ministry conflict, and ministry affirmation.

All of this may sound complicated, but it will come to light as we analyze it. The following diagram will help clarify the phase. You may want to refer to it as you read the next two chapters.

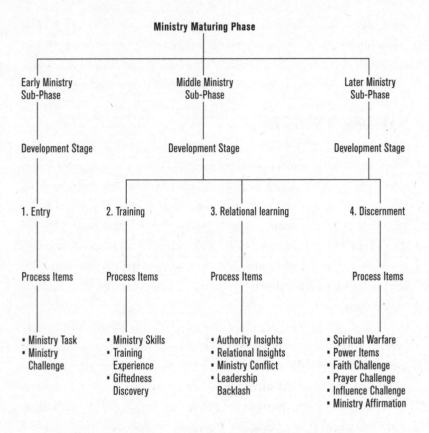

Figure 4-1 Early, Middle, and Later Ministry Sub-Phases and Process Items

In the early ministry sub-phase, entry occurs as God selects those who are faithful and challenges them with ministry tasks and assignments. A developing leader responds and learns to perform faithfully. He develops some ministry skills in the process. God then gives him new assignments with greater responsibility. A leader's good responses lead to new experience and additional skills.

The need to do a responsible job in ministry leads to awareness of the need to expand ministry skills. In the middle ministry sub-phase, ministry skills are learned through many forms of training. The potential leader now recognizes a gift or two and has some skills for exercising his gifts. He gravitates toward new ministry challenges and assignments that allow him to use his gifts more effectively.

In the later ministry sub-phase, the leader learns lessons about relationships in both the relational learning stage and the discernment stage of development. Often these lessons are learned the hard way. A developing leader will usually struggle with someone who is in authority over him. Learning submission is critical to learning what authority is, so emerging leaders must first learn to submit.

Conflict in ministry requires discernment skills. What is from God and what is not? Conflict can arise from different approaches to ministry as well as from personality clashes. Learning to relate in a godly manner in the midst of conflict is closely intertwined with learning to discern the spiritual principles governing ministry. This area of spiritual discernment is difficult for many leaders to learn, but it is crucial because healthy relationships are essential to effective ministry.

Throughout the entire Ministry Maturing phase the leader learns spiritual principles that touch all four of the development stages. He will learn the most in the discernment stage, because maturity will give him added perspective on God's work in his life. He will learn about the use of power that will challenge any overconfidence he may have in his skills and gifts and force him to discern the ultimate purposes of ministry. Increasing responsibilities and the need to minister effectively force him to learn dependence on God and greater faith. God's "well done" in the form of ministry affirmation is sprinkled throughout the phase. It encourages the leader to faithful effort for God.

ENTRY

Two ministry process items are involved in the entry development stage. One is the ministry task, which moves the leader from the Inner-Life Growth phase to the Ministry Maturing phase. The second is the ministry challenge.

The Ministry Task

The first item, the ministry task, was referred to in chapter 3. There I mentioned that a fourth testing item could be included with integrity checks, obedience checks, and word checks, because it tests character and teaches about ministry. It is a boundary process item because it signals a transition time between the Inner-Life Growth phase and the Ministry Maturing phase. A *ministry task* is an assignment from God that tests a person's faithfulness and obedience to use his gifts in a task that has a beginning and ending, accountability, and evaluation.

In early ministry phases, emerging leaders are attracted to others who serve as mentors or masters or supervisors and who challenge emerging leaders to undertake tasks, which can be of any size or nature.[1] These tasks will test loyalty and submission and indicate the emerging leader's gifts, initiative, and potential. An important thing to keep in mind is that the ultimate assignment is from God, even if the ministry task is self-initiated or assigned by another. The leader's accountability is to God. A desire to please the Lord in a ministry task is a sign of maturity.

A ministry task should be differentiated from ministry experience in general because a ministry task is a test. It is a special assignment that can be completed and evaluated. It will test the potential leader's availability, faithfulness, and skills. God's pattern seems to be to start with small ministry tasks. As the leader responds to them properly, God gives him tasks of greater and greater responsibility.

Michele, Barnabas, and Paul — Some Examples

A pastor challenged Michele to teach a Sunday school class. This assignment tested Michele's faithfulness and obedience and also allowed her to use her budding teaching gift. The task had a beginning and ending and some limited accountability. Michele responded positively. She was the major benefactor from this ministry experience.

Barnabas's trip to Antioch in Acts 11 was an apostolic ministry task, which was definable and had closure as well as accountability to the elders in Jerusalem.[2] It tested his apostolic gifts as well as his willingness to obey.

Paul's year or so at Antioch with Barnabas as his mentor was a ministry task that was a springboard to the missionary task of Acts 13 with Barnabas. Barnabas challenged Paul to this task. God evaluated Paul's performance positively when He expanded the ministry of the two men, thus confirming them as apostles to the Gentiles. Small ministry tasks can be early indicators of leadership potential. The primary objective of the ministry task in the early ministry sub-phase is to develop the potential leader. Those given in later ministry sub-phases concentrate on accomplishing the task for those who will benefit. The continuum shown in figure 4-2 indicates these differences.

Little   Much

Task primarily for   Task primarily for
potential leader   ministry to others

Figure 4-2 The Ministry Task Continuum — Luke 16:10 in Action

Let me reemphasize: God uses tasks along toward the left of the continuum to help shape the leader for future ministry—probably even more than ministering to those who are recipients of the ministry. But those tasks toward the right are more for accomplishing the ministry than shaping the leader.

Figure 4-3 expands on the continuum shown in figure 4-2 and gives six categories: A, B, C, D, E, and F. These categories will be used in table 4-1, which follows, giving biblical examples of these types of ministry tasks.

Task primarily for   Task primarily for
potential leader   ministry to others

Figure 4-3 Biblical Ministry Tasks Continuum

Table 4-1 Explanation of Ministry Tasks Continuum

MINISTRY TASK TYPE: A, B, C, D, E, F AND BIBLICAL LOCATION	PERSON(S) ASSIGNED THE TASK	BASIC FUNCTIONS DONE
A. Luke 9:1-6 (Task primarily for leaders)	Twelve disciples	Demonstrate the kingdom through healing and exorcism, test faith, test obedience, experience spiritual authority
B. Luke 10:1-12 (Task more for leaders than followers)	The seventy-two	Test receptivity, test faith, demonstrate the kingdom, experience spiritual warfare and spiritual authority
C. Acts 11:22-23 (Task almost equally for Barnabas and Antioch Christians)	Barnabas	A word check for Barnabas, judge Gentile forms of Christianity, experience and develop spiritual authority, model lifestyle and teaching
D. Acts 13:1-3 (Task more for new Gentile Christians than for Paul and Barnabas)	Barnabas, Paul	Experience contextualization in evangelism and Gentile Christian lifestyle, evangelize Gentiles, plant churches
E. Philippians 2:19-23 (Task predominately for Ephesian elders and church members)	Timothy	Shepherd the people, unify, share Paul's teaching
F. Philippians 2:25-30 (Task primarily for Philippian church)	Epaphroditus	Encourage, unify, affirm giving mission

It is important to recognize the ultimate source of ministry assignments. From a human perspective the task may appear routine or insignificant, but ultimate accountability is to God even though the assignment came through human authority. Knowing this can bring great fervor and give a sense of accomplishing God's purposes. Leaders who give out ministry tasks need to rely upon the Lord's direction in assigning them. They should use ministry tasks as deliberate means for character building and ministry training, but they must have God's leading in making those assignments.

The Ministry Challenge

The *ministry challenge* is closely related to the ministry task. A ministry task is a simple assignment that focuses on the job to be done and its effect on the emerging leader and those he leads. A ministry challenge focuses on the leader's acceptance of his ministry. Specifically it is the means through which a leader or potential leader is prompted by God to sense the need for and accept a new assignment.

My first ministry challenge was to teach a junior high boys' Sunday school class. The invitation came through the person who recruited teachers for the junior high department. I sensed the need and responded, but I was an inadequate teacher. Most of the boys were not interested in spiritual things. I could have seen the experience as a failure, but I did learn several things. I had never tried to discipline boys their age, but by the end of our time I had earned their respect and learned how to prepare lessons. Although at the time I did not sense the hand of God leading me into ministry, I later saw how God used the teaching experience to develop me during the entry stage of my life. It paved the way for other assignments to come.

We don't know what Barnabas said to Paul or how he convinced him. Perhaps Barnabas reminded him of his effort on Paul's behalf in Jerusalem when Paul was trying to gain acceptance with the elders (see Acts 9:27). In any case, we know Barnabas was serious about recruiting Paul. He walked a long way to find Paul, with no guarantee of locating him. We don't have the details of their conversation, but we do have the results. Paul came back with Barnabas and was launched into a continually increasing ministry.

Sources for ministry challenge can be external or internal. A challenge can come from someone else or from a leader's own recognition of a need or an opportunity. Internal challenges are relatively rare among early emerging leaders. The heart of the ministry challenge is twofold: sensing God's direction and the joy of discovering what it means to be a channel through whom God works. There are some typical external challenges that occur in a local church during the early ministry sub-phase. They include calls for people to teach Sunday school classes, be committee members, help someone else perform a service, lead a small group Bible study, do evangelistic visitation, do organizational support work, organize social functions, and plan retreats.

Typical ministry challenges occurring in parachurch groups might include campus witnessing, discipling others, leading Bible study groups, and working with youth groups, summer camps, and inner-city service ministries.

Ministry challenge describes the means whereby a leader is prompted to sense God's guidance and to accept a new assignment. The most common means of entry into a ministry assignment in all three sub-phases is an external challenge by a person to work in an established ministry. The rarest entry pattern in all three sub-phases involves self-initiated challenges to create new ministry roles and structures. This leads to some important implications:

- The majority of leaders will emerge via common entry patterns.
- It is self-initiation in the entry patterns that indicates strong potential for upper-level leadership.
- Plateauing in a leader's development is indicated by a declining frequency of initiative and response to ministry challenges and ministry assignments.

A major responsibility of leadership is the selection and development of potential leaders. Mature leaders should openly and deliberately challenge potential leaders about specific needs and ministry opportunities. A danger sign indicating a plateaued leader is a lack of enthusiasm for challenging and recruiting potential leaders. A growing leader, on the other hand, stimulates the emergence of potential leaders.

Self-initiated ministry challenges or assignments carry with them the seeds of higher-level leadership. Those who self-initiate often disrupt the status quo and threaten those in authority over them. In the resulting conflict, the promising quality of self-initiative can be overlooked. Leaders need to recognize the value of this quality and be on the alert for those emerging leaders who demonstrate it.

Are you still regularly recognizing ministry challenges and ministry assignments? Are you still willing to accept new challenges and assignments, and are you recruiting others for them? If not, you may have reached a plateau. In order to move on, you need to ask God for fresh enthusiasm for ministry.

TRAINING

So far I've talked about two entry process items, the ministry task and ministry challenge. The ministry task provides a transition from the Inner-Life Growth phase to the Ministry Maturing phase. The ministry challenge dominates the processing in the early ministry sub-phase and decreases in the middle ministry sub-phase. It is rare in later ministry processing. It should be noted that training occurs informally with the ministry task, primarily via on-the-job ministry experience.

In the transition between the early and middle ministry sub-phases, the ministry skills process item provides the momentum. A leader's sensitivity to this item indicates whether he is growing or plateauing. Some leaders who sense the need for ministry skills may opt for some kind of formal training. I will say more about this later as I talk about my own transitioning into ministry.

Ministry Skills

My transition started with a simple challenge from one of my Navigator buddies, Dave Stout. Dave was further along than I in the discipleship process, and I admired his personal integrity and sincere walk with God. Dave said, "Bobby, I believe God can use you to teach me some important things about praying. Would you be willing to meet with me on Saturday mornings from 6:00 to 8:00? We could study Ros Rinker's book *Prayer: Conversing with God*." This simple challenge combined ministry challenge, ministry task, and ministry skills process items. The experience lasted three months. The insights and prayer skills that I gained during that time still affect my prayer life today.

An important aspect of development during the Ministry Maturing phase is the acquisition of skills that aid a leader in accomplishing ministry. Most people gain these skills in the early phases of ministry, particularly in the training stage of the middle ministry sub-phase.[3] They include relational, group, organizational, and word skills. These may help the leader gain helpful knowledge or teach him to exercise leadership.

The *ministry skills* process item is the acquisition of one or more identifiable skills that help a leader accomplish a ministry assignment. The skills necessary to lead effectively are varied. An example of a group skill would be learning how to lead various kinds of small groups—such as prayer groups, Bible study groups, or committees. This skill focuses on influencing people. A knowledge-focused group skill would be learning how to prepare Bible study materials for small groups. Skills that mix knowledge and influence include learning how to organize committees, write proposals, or persuade people of the importance of new ideas.

A leader who wishes to have long-term influence will need to learn how to implement change. A very important skill involves learning how to relate to superiors, colleagues, and subordinates in organizational structures. Conflict management skills are especially needed in middle and later ministry development.

Other skills on which God concentrates in the training stage include word skills, Bible study methods, and Bible communication skills. As mentioned earlier, leadership gifts always include a word gift. Skills to enhance this gift are essential.

Leaders who plateau early reveal a common pattern. They learn new skills until they can operate comfortably with them, but then they fail to seek new skills deliberately and habitually. They coast on prior experience.[4]

Ministry skills development offers a twofold challenge: (1) to see the leading of God in each skill learned and to recognize that each is part of a long-term process of training by God, and (2) to maintain the attitude of a seeker in order to benefit from learning opportunities.

Training Experience

In the early part of the middle ministry sub-phase most skills are picked up through experience, observation, and self-study. The *training experience* process item refers to an experience that gives some form of affirmation, assuring the leader that God will continue to use him in the future. The item is characterized by identifiable progress in terms of sphere of influence, leadership responsibility, or self-confidence.

All leaders are constantly being trained by God, but not all of them learn from the training. This is particularly true in informal training, which takes place in the context of everyday life, and in nonformal training, which comes through workshops, seminars, or conferences. In order to learn, a leader needs to analyze specific instances in which formal or informal training has taken place.

Informal apprenticeship. I met Mark Williams when he was a high school student in Reynoldsburg, Ohio. Recognizing his leadership potential at that time, I have followed his progress. Today he is a Conservative Baptist pastor, but before going on to formal ministry training, he served a year-long informal apprenticeship with Josh McDowell. This experience taught Mark evangelistic methods and ways to communicate his faith. It also gave him added confidence in approaching ministry problems. This was a significant time of training, because Mark learned skills and attitudes that will last a lifetime.

Nonformal workshops. These can teach basic skills in Bible study, prayer, or small group leadership. Workshops and conferences are becoming more available as many people and organizations recognize the importance of leadership training at the grass-roots level.

The workshops don't have to be spiritual in focus. In the mid-seventies I attended a week-long workshop for writers in New York City to develop information-mapping writing skills. At the end of that week I began a project that eventually became my book *Spiritual Gifts.*

This nonformal training has significantly affected my teaching ministry.

Formal training. Often during the early or middle sub-phase of the Ministry Maturing phase, a leader will opt for intensive rapid acquisition of knowledge and skills. This training will usually be formal and will require him to leave his current ministry. Formal training means relocation to a training institution, which was my own experience. After two years of Bible teaching in home Bible studies, I decided to resign my position as an electrical engineer with Bell Telephone Laboratories and go to Bible school for a year. Formal intensive training can be helpful, but is not requisite to leadership.

Discovering Spiritual Gifts

I've talked about the ministry skills and training experience process items. Both of these are helpful in understanding God's work in the training stage of a leader's development. Apart from the acquisition of general leadership skills, the most important development during the middle sub-phase of the Ministry Maturity phase involves discovering spiritual gifts and using them confidently. A spiritual gift is a unique capacity for channeling the Holy Spirit's power into a ministry. I identified about nineteen in the book I have written on spiritual gifts.

The *giftedness discovery* process item is any significant advance in the discovery of spiritual gifts and their use along with the event, person, or reflection that brought about the discovery. Figure 4-4 lists the basic giftedness development pattern.

1. ministry experience ▶ 2. discovery of gift ▶ 3. increased use of that gift ▶ 4. effectiveness in using that gift ▶ 5. discovery of other gifts ▶ 6. identification of gift-mix ▶ 7. development of gift-cluster ▶ 8. convergence

(Read "▶" as "usually leads to or which leads to")

Figure 4-4 Basic Giftedness Development Pattern

Full-time leaders of churches or Christian organizations usually manifest more than one spiritual gift. *Gift-mix* describes the set of spiritual gifts a leader repeatedly demonstrates in ministry. *Gift-cluster* refers to a gift-mix in which there is a dominant gift supported by other gifts. In the gift-cluster[5] the supportive gifts harmonize with the dominant gift to maximize effectiveness.

Gifts normally emerge in the context of small groups or when a leader has a ministry assignment. Most lay leaders will discover gifts by using them, without recognizing that they are spiritual gifts. Most of these leaders will reach step 3 and a few will reach step 4. In either case, the gift may not be identified explicitly, but it is usually understood implicitly by an intuitive drift toward a ministry that uses the gift. Full-time leaders will usually reach step 5, where they discover other gifts. Leaders who move on to a ministry beyond a single local church — that is to regional, national, or international spheres of influence — will reach step 6, identification of gift-mix. Often they will reach step 7, developing a gift-cluster, and will rearrange roles and priorities so that their gifts will have the greatest effect. This can lead to convergence, a time of very productive and satisfying ministry.

I will give two examples of giftedness discovery — Barnabas and myself — but will first mention two patterns that supplement the basic giftedness development pattern. Table 4-2 identifies these supplemental patterns that help leaders in the early identification of their spiritual gifts.

Table 4-2 Two Supplementary Giftedness Patterns

PATTERN	EXPLANATION
Like Attracts Like	Potential leaders are intuitively attracted to leaders who have the same spiritual gifts.
Giftedness Drift	Potential leaders respond intuitively to ministry challenges and assignments that call for their spiritual gifts, even if these are not explicitly known.

A leadership emergence study of Barnabas reveals an early discovery of his gift of exhortation.[6] Acts 4:32-37 indicates that Barnabas reached steps 1 and 2 of the basic giftedness development pattern. There were later significant discoveries in Acts 9 (indicating step 3) and Acts 11 (indicating step 5) that brought out manifestations of his gift of apostleship. In Galatians 2:6-10 the affirmation was another step forward in the pattern. When the apostles encouraged Joseph by giving him a new name, Barnabas (meaning "Son of Encouragement"; see Acts 4:36), he received a special ministry affirmation.[7] Barnabas developed this gift of encouragement and it characterized his life.

I first discovered that I have a teaching gift through tasks assigned by my pastor. I was teaching home Bible studies and accepted other openings to teach. This pattern has continued. I taught classes for children, teenage boys and girls, college students, couples, singles, and seniors. Some of these were external challenges, but many were internal challenges that required that I form structures to do the teaching. Step 3 in the basic giftedness discovery pattern is easy for me to see as I look back on my experiences.

My effectiveness as a teacher grew, through experience and through my own growth and understanding of Christianity, as I developed my teaching gift. Step 4 of the pattern involved my efforts to develop complementary skills to aid the effectiveness of my gift. I studied various books on communication and hermeneutics to aid my teaching skills.

Step 5 crept up on me by surprise. At that time, I did not have an explicit doctrine of spiritual gifts, but I began my own biblical studies about them. As I studied, I recognized that I had the gift of exhortation, primarily admonition. As I continued to use my teaching gift I saw that exhortation dominated all that I did in teaching. My study of the biblical teaching on gifts was key in reaching step 5.

Three years later, I began to notice, especially in small group settings, that I was often able to say something wise (a word of wisdom; see 1 Corinthians 12:8) for a situation. My introduction to this gift came by simply observing the way our executive team functioned in decision making. In time I reached step 6 of the pattern. I recognized my gift-mix as exhortation, teaching, and word of wisdom. Though some ministry situations have demanded that I exercise other gifts, my ministry has consistently used my gift-mix.

I am currently at step 7 in the pattern. My gift-cluster has begun to take shape. I've recognized that the dominant gift is exhortation and the teaching gift provides the setting in which to use it. Ideas arise in teaching that stir people and open them to change, and exhortation moves people toward use of ideas. Follow-up counseling often gives me the opportunity to use the word of wisdom gift.

I've experienced the two supplementary patterns in table 4-2, "like attracts like" and "giftedness drift," in my own life and have observed them in others. I was attracted to my pastor's ministry of Bible teaching some time before I discovered my teaching gift: like attracts like. I attended Columbia Graduate School of Bible and Missions in order to observe two professors, Frank Sells and Buck Hatch, in their teaching ministry. One had a dominant exhortation gift, strong in admonition. The other had an ability to organize and conceptualize. I was drawn to them and learned much from what they taught and how they taught. The like attracts like pattern was there. Later on, I was involved with a small group of executive leaders in which I often heard a word of wisdom from one of the members. Again, like attracts like.

"Giftedness drift" was a pattern in my own discovery of the teaching gift. Before I had heard of a spiritual gift of teaching I was constantly challenged to accept assignments that required a teaching gift.

THE LITTLE-BIG PRINCIPLE

This chapter began with the challenge in Luke 16:10, "Whoever can be trusted with very little can also be trusted with much." As we have worked through the various process items that God uses to move us through the stages of development, you may have seen a pattern concerning faithfulness. This pattern is at the foundation of all ministry maturing. It occurs in each of the sub-phases. The pattern indicates that faithfulness in ministry tasks and challenges, along with proper response to testing, leads to an expanded sphere of influence. Faithfulness will continue to be tested at each new ministry level.

This faithfulness pattern is built on repeated instances of the little-big principle: *Faithfulness in a small responsibility is an indicator of probable faithfulness in a larger responsibility.*

SUMMARY

When God directs a potential leader into ministry, He moves him through four stages of development. (1) He challenges a potential leader into ministry—entry. (2) He develops skills and spiritual gifts to enhance the leader's effectiveness—training. (3) He enables the leader to relate to people in ways that will motivate and influence them, and He teaches him how to set up the means to accomplish these goals—relational learning. (4) He helps the leader see spiritual principles that govern ministry that are pleasing to Him—discernment.

In this chapter I have concentrated on the first two stages of development: entry and training. I explained how God uses process items to develop a leader. In the entry stage the process items are the ministry task and the ministry challenge. In the training stage they are ministry skills, training experience, and giftedness discovery.

We looked at two major patterns: the foundational ministry pattern and the giftedness development pattern. Two minor patterns, "like attracts like" and "giftedness drift," were mentioned in connection with giftedness. I also identified the little-big principle, which is the underlying principle in this phase.

This chapter has discussed the first two development stages that occur primarily in the early and middle ministry sub-phases. Chapter 5 will discuss the stages involved in the later ministry sub-phase and some of the more complex issues of a leader's development.

HOW ABOUT YOU?

Perhaps as I described some of these ministry concepts you could identify some incidents in your own pilgrimage. Some of the concepts may be foreign to you, but the following questions may help you grasp and apply them.

1. What was the most recent ministry challenge that you accepted? Describe the details of this process item.
2. What ministry challenges have you personally used to attract other potential leaders into ministry?
3. What is the most important practical ministry skill you have? How did God build that skill into your life?
4. How far along in the giftedness development pattern are you? Pinpoint where you think you may be.

   - Step 1 — ministry experience
   - Step 2 — discovery of gift
   - Step 3 — increased use of that gift
   - Step 4 — effectiveness in using that gift
   - Step 5 — discovery of other gifts
   - Step 6 — identification of gift-mix
   - Step 7 — development of gift-cluster
   - Step 8 — convergence

5. If you are as far as step 5, then describe what you know about your own gift-mix. Use the lists found in Romans 12:3-8, 1 Corinthians 12-14, Ephesians 4:7-16, and 1 Peter 4:10-11. Or you may refer to *Your Spiritual Gifts Can Help Your Church Grow* by C. Peter Wagner, or *Unlocking Your Giftedness* by J. Robert Clinton and Richard Clinton.

6. If this whole concept of giftedness discovery is new to you, perhaps you could interview someone further along in the giftedness development pattern. After explaining some of the concepts, use questions 4 and 5 with that person and determine where he is.

CHAPTER 5

SECOND LESSONS: MINISTRY MATURING PROCESSES — PART II

The Challenge/The Problem: God in his mercy has given us this work to do, and so we do not become discouraged. . . . For it is not ourselves that we preach; we preach Jesus Christ as Lord, and ourselves as your servants for Jesus' sake. . . .

Yet we who have this spiritual treasure are like common clay pots, in order to show that the supreme power belongs to God, not to us. *(2 Corinthians 4:1,5,7, GNT)*

Bob and Alice headed off to their first ministry assignment after graduating from seminary. They were excited about the prospect of doing kingdom work. They had interviewed with a group of people who had a vision to plant a church in their area. Excited about their similarity of vision, the group called the couple to come and pastor.

The job honeymoon was brief. After a few weeks, the first conflicts began. There were differences of opinion and vision concerning the format of services, children's ministries, small group structure and leadership, and the pastor's working hours. Added to these pressures were the stresses of a cross-country move away from family, new schools for the children, and a growing feeling of loneliness and isolation from all that had been familiar.

These conflicts did not occur all at once but were spread over many months. At the end of the first year, after a particularly painful conflict concerning the role of the pastor's wife in the church, they were ready to pack it in. Had God really called them? If so, how could there be so many conflicts within the body of Christ?

However, Bob and Alice stuck it out, and they're still learning about how God develops leaders throughout the Ministry Maturing phase. Their story is not an isolated one. Burnout among pastors and others in ministry is increasing. Many drop out after three to four years.

The ones who stay in ministry over the long haul are the exceptions. Ministry has problems that can easily discourage anyone—lay leader or full-time worker—and discouragement comes from a number of sources. Those who stay have learned how God develops a leader to maturity. Problems are God's stepping stones to maturity.

In chapter 4 we began a study of the Ministry Maturing phase. We saw that this phase was divided into three sub-phases in which God takes a leader through four developmental stages (figure 4-1, page 68). We discussed the first two stages called *entry* and *training*.

This chapter deals with some of the more complex issues in the Ministry Maturing phase. These occur in the last two development stages: *relational learning* and *discernment*. As we study the process items that occur in these stages, we will identify four common problems. The first, the authority problem, occurs in the relational learning stage, and the next three—the spiritual warfare problem, the plateau barrier problem, and the ministry philosophy problem—occur in the discernment stage. Finally, I'll discuss three ways the Ministry Maturing phase ends; two are unsatisfactory and one is progressive.

RELATIONAL LEARNING

A leader is one who influences a specific group of people to move in a God-given direction. In order to influence and motivate people, a leader must learn how to relate to people effectively. He must also learn how to work within existing organizational structures and create new structures to enhance ministry. These fundamental concepts are learned in the relational learning development stage, which occurs during both the middle and later sub-phases. Four process items—authority insights, relational insights, ministry conflict, and leadership backlash—form a cluster of related lessons, which I call the submission cluster. God uses these lessons to teach a leader how to bridge the very important ministry problem of authority. God also uses the submission cluster to teach other relationship lessons.

The Authority Problem

All four of the problems discussed in this chapter can be barriers or bridges to leadership emergence. This is particularly true for the authority problem, because leaders need to use spiritual authority as a power base for their ministry.[1] Spiritual authority is delegated by God and differs from authority that is based on position or force. Leaders who have trouble submitting to authority will usually have trouble exercising spiritual authority. This challenge occurs throughout their ministry, becoming more subtle as leaders mature.

When I faced the authority problem in my own life, God brought Watchman Nee's book *Spiritual Authority* to my attention. It helped me bridge the authority problem. Anyone can submit when decisions appear right; it is when the decisions seem wrong or are wrong that submission is difficult. Submission is tested most when there are differences of opinion over crucial issues.

I call the principles I drew from Nee's book the "ten commandments of spiritual authority" (see table 5-1 on page 88).

Table 5-1 The Ten Commandments of Spiritual Authority

COMMANDMENT #	STATEMENT OF THE COMMANDMENT
1	A leader who learns spiritual authority as the power base for ministry must recognize the essential Source of all authority: God.
2	A leader with spiritual authority ought to know it is God's delegated authority and does not belong to the leader exercising it – that leader is just a channel.
3	The channel of delegated authority must be responsible to God for how that authority is exercised.
4	A leader is one who should recognize God's authority manifested in real-life situations.
5	A leader must know that objection to authority means that a person is subject to God Himself and not to the channel through which the authority comes.
6	A leader should know that rebellion against authority means that the rebelling person is rejecting some impure manifestation of God's authority through a human channel.
7	A leader should know that people who are under God's authority look for and recognize spiritual authority and willingly place themselves under it.
8	A leader must know that spiritual authority is never exercised for one's own benefit, but for those under it.
9	A leader in spiritual authority must know that he does not have to insist on obedience – that is the moral responsibility of the follower.
10	A leader must know that God is responsible to defend spiritual authority.

How does a leader learn these lessons? The submission cluster is part of God's method for teaching these ten principles. Let's look at the four process items in the submission cluster one by one, beginning with a crucial one—the authority insights process item.

Authority Insights

There are many biblical examples of leaders discovering authority insights: the centurion in Luke 7:1-10; the request for James and John in Matthew 20:20-28; the disciples in Luke 8:22-25, when Jesus calms the sea; the Pharisees, lawyers, and disciples in Luke 5:17-26, at the healing of the paralyzed man; and Miriam and Aaron in Numbers 12:1-16, in the incident involving jealousy over Moses' authority.

Jesus' authority is a recurrent theme throughout the Gospels and is a major source of contention with the Jews. Jesus demonstrated authority in His teaching ministry through His wisdom, knowledge, and prophecy. He also demonstrated spiritual authority in His healing ministry, in the various miracles concerning physical creation, and through His power in spiritual warfare. His claim to God's authority was validated throughout His ministry.

The ultimate goal in authority development is to help a leader understand that spiritual authority is the primary authority base in leadership influence. This is not to negate other kinds of authority as legitimate, but to put them in proper perspective. Transition from the Ministry Maturing phase to the Life Maturing phase is characterized by significant progress toward this ultimate goal.[2]

The *authority insights* process item refers to those positive and negative ministry lessons that teach about the use of spiritual authority. These are lessons on submission to authority, on authority structures, on authenticity of power bases, on authority conflict, and on how to exercise authority.

As a leader learns these lessons through the authority insights process item, his development will follow a typical pattern, where each step leads to the next: (1) negative lessons of authority, (2) a search for and understanding of legitimate authority, (3) a desire to model legitimate authority, (4) insights about spiritual authority, and (5) increasing use of spiritual authority as a source of power. This is not comprehensive, but it is suggestive and helpful.

Relational Insights

On the first missionary journey with Paul, Barnabas is an example of one who learned an authority insights process item and a relational insights process item (see Acts 13). Barnabas had been Paul's mentor since Paul's first trip to Jerusalem as a Christian. He brought Paul into the Jerusalem church's leadership (see Acts 9:27-29) and introduced Paul into the Antioch church (see Acts 11:25-26).

During the time of ministry in Cyprus it appeared to Barnabas that Paul was exercising spiritual authority and had, in fact, become the leader. Paul was at the point where he needed to move beyond the mentoring relationship with Barnabas. From Acts 13:13 onward, with only three exceptions, the biblical record always refers to Paul and Barnabas. Prior to this it was Barnabas and Paul. Paul led from this time on.

It takes grace and maturity for a man like Barnabas not only to allow such a leadership switch but to work to make it successful. Barnabas's relational insight was that Paul didn't need a mentoring, subordinate, or co-equal relationship; he needed to lead. It took a big man to be willing to step down and become the follower. Barnabas recognized spiritual authority, recognized a leader with capacity beyond his own, and took the necessary steps to encourage that leader in his calling. Barnabas bridged the authority problem, learned to relate to Paul in a different way, and thus entered the Christian record book as one who significantly influenced missionary history.

A negative example of a relational insight is Paul's conflict with Barnabas over Mark (see Acts 15:36-39). Mark left the team during the first missionary journey (when the leadership switched from Barnabas to Paul). Later when Paul suggested to Barnabas that they return to Turkey for follow-up, Barnabas wanted to take Mark along. Paul disagreed, not yet having learned the importance of patience and forgiveness in a mentoring relationship (this time toward Mark). The two parted ways. Later Paul recognized that Barnabas's patient ministry with Mark had paid high dividends. In Colossians 4:10, Paul's change in attitude is shown by his encouragement to the Christians at Colosse to welcome Mark.

The authority problem concerns how a leader gets along with people: his leaders, his peers, his subordinates. Influence depends on relationships with people, so many of the lessons learned during this phase will focus on relationships. Many lessons will be learned through negative experiences. The ability to establish relationships and see God use them to accomplish His purposes is an art and a skill. The relational insights process item focuses on expansion of leadership capacity in terms of relationships. The development of a leader via this process item is broader than just helping him bridge the authority problem. It is also useful in working through authority issues.

Relational insights process items are those instances in ministry in which a leader learns either positive or negative lessons about relating to other Christians or non-Christians in the course of ministry decisions. Lessons learned through relational insights can significantly affect future leadership.

The centurion in Matthew 8:5-13 knew about legitimate authority: "I myself am a man under authority, with soldiers under me. I tell this one, 'Go,' and he goes; and that one, 'Come,' and he comes. I say to my servant, 'Do this,' and he does it" (verse 9). He transferred his understanding of legitimate earthly authority to the spiritual realm when he saw Jesus as one who had spiritual authority. Furthermore, he saw his relationship to Jesus through that insight, and he acted in faith. "Just say the word," he said, "and my servant will be healed" (verse 8). Jesus did, and the servant was healed. Jesus went on to pay him one of the highest compliments recorded in the New Testament, "I tell you the truth, I have not found anyone in Israel with such great faith" (verse 10).

What would you say if I were to ask you, "What is the most important relational insight you have learned? How did you learn it?" Often a relational insight comes as a result of an authority clash, a submission lesson, or a ministry crisis. These lessons in relationships, whether learned negatively or positively, are turning points in the development of a leader.

The most important relational insight I have learned is that subordinates must be very careful in their correction of those in authority over them. One needs to be more than just right on issues to correct such a leader. Rightness or wrongness is not the whole matter. Sometimes being right on certain issues is less important than maintaining a positive relationship. I learned this lesson the hard way, but it has stayed with me.

There were two results of this lesson: I learned that I was not very flexible and needed to allow God to begin changing my rigidity, and I learned to give up the right to be right.

The authority insights process item and relational insights process item often work together to awaken an emerging leader to the authority problem. Sometimes the authority problem cannot be perceived apart from conflict, which is the third process item in the submission cluster.

Ministry Conflict

In Acts 6 the apostles faced conflict from within the church between the believers who spoke Greek and those who spoke Hebrew. The conflict concerned the distribution of food to widows, but it was rooted in authority and relational problems. The apostles solved this conflict with everyone's approval.

When people influence other people, conflict inevitably arises. This is particularly true during the Ministry Maturing phase, because many of the decisions a leader makes affect others. These decisions are usually made without the hindsight of valuable experience.

The *general conflict* process item describes any conflict that is used to develop a leader in his spiritual life or ministry. Conflict is a powerful tool in the hand of God and can be used to teach a leader lessons that he would not learn in any other way.

The *ministry conflict* process item refers to those conflicts in ministry through which a leader learns either positive or negative lessons about the nature of conflict, possible ways to resolve or avoid conflict, creative ways to use conflict, and about conflict as one of God's means to develop the leader's inner life. A leader's grasp of these lessons can significantly affect his future leadership.

Conflict may come from without—that is, from those who are not believers—and from within—from those who are believers. Sometimes the conflict from within is the most difficult to face because a leader has higher expectations for believers.

Ministry conflict, like general conflict, tests a leader's personal maturity. What we truly are is revealed in a crisis. Conflict processing is important not so much for learning problem solving, but for its value in revealing character. What we *are* in the conflict is much more critical than what we *do*. Ministry conflict processing is to the Ministry Maturing phase what integrity processing is to the Inner-Life Growth phase.

One of the most important things to learn from the ministry conflict process item, as it relates to the submission cluster, is that it is often necessary.[3] That is, authority insights and relational insights—rooted in the authority problem—may never be learned apart from conflict.

In conflict processing, closure is often weak. Closure completes an experience in order to put it behind and gain lessons from it for the future. A leader could leave a ministry conflict either successfully resolved, partially resolved, or unresolved, but it is important to have closure in conflicts. Otherwise, it will be hard to see and learn the necessary lessons.

Another important lesson in the Ministry Maturing phase is that God uses conflict for His purposes in a leader's ministry, as well as in his personal life. It is bad enough to go through conflict; it is worse to go through conflict and not profit from it.

The authority principle is derived from these lessons: *Leaders in the Ministry Maturing phase must learn to submit to authority in order to learn how to use authority properly.* This learning process involves insight in submission, recognition of God's authority, and willingness to submit.

Leadership Backlash

Moses faced backlash situations throughout his ministry. The Israelites needed to submit to God. They followed His will in leaving Egypt; however, in the wilderness God's purposes were no longer so clear. Hot, tired, thirsty, and discouraged, the people murmured against God. He showed that He was still in charge by meeting their needs through supplies of food and water, delivering them from persecution, and giving them guidance throughout the entire ordeal. Moses learned to submit to

God through these tests, and God vindicated Moses in his leadership by proving Himself faithful.

The fourth process item in the submission cluster, leadership backlash, is a special case of ministry conflict. A leader experiencing leadership backlash learns through conflict with others to submit to God in a deeper way. This fourth process item usually involves discerning guidance from God and implementing it in ministry.

The *leadership backlash* process item refers to the negative reactions of followers, other leaders within the group, and Christians outside the group to a course of action taken by a leader once ramifications develop from his decision.[4] It is helpful to recognize the normal pattern:

Table 5-2 Eight-Stage Leadership Backlash Cycle

STAGE	STATEMENT OF THE COMMANDMENT
1	The leader gets a vision (direction) from God.
2	The followers are convinced of the direction.
3	The group moves in the direction given.
4	The group experiences persecution, hard times, or attacks from Satan — spiritual warfare is common.
5	There is backlash from the group.
6	The leader is driven to God to seek affirmation in spite of the action's ramifications.
7	God reveals Himself further: who He is, what He intends to do. He makes it clear that He will deliver.
8	God vindicates Himself and the leader.

Leadership backlash tests a leader's perseverance, clarity of vision, and faith. This process item is a complicated one and usually combines aspects of all three of the other items in the submission cluster. The primary lesson, learning submission to God, is often lost because of the other problems of authority, relationships, and conflict.

Sometimes in the backlash, people actually forget what the situation was like before the action was taken. They may have a distorted view of it.

Usually the action's unforeseen consequences involve persecution or hard times of some kind. Although followers may have originally agreed on the course of action, they now blame the leader for having taken it. A leader's ultimate success brings with it problems. All leaders need to be aware of this and persevere through the trials associated with effective ministry.

God may have several purposes for trials. A leader may be easily taken up with a plan of action and may need to be reminded of *who* is ultimately responsible for the plan and its success. God uses complications in general to develop inner-life maturity. Leadership backlash is a form of integrity testing in which the leader's actual motivation can be revealed.

Followers need to realize that submitting to spiritual authority involves obeying God by being loyal to the leader who is following God's direction. Loyalty is not tested until difficult times come. God can use difficult times to set the stage for deliverance that can come only from Him. He can then deliver, receive glory, and lay foundations for future work.

DISCERNMENT

To develop a leader to maturity, God enlarges the leader's perspectives of the spiritual dynamics of ministry. The leader must learn to sense the spiritual reality (spiritual warfare) behind physical reality, as well as to depend upon God's power in ministry. Also, the leader must learn to know God's voice in the challenge process items—faith, prayer, and influence—and the affirmation process items—divine and ministry. He will need this discernment ability throughout his lifetime.

The heart of the discernment stage is the enlargement of the leader's outlook. God develops discernment throughout the whole Ministry Maturing phase, but it peaks in the later ministry sub-phase. Spiritual warfare and power process items are the focus of discernment processing in spiritual reality. Personal expansion processing involves the challenge cluster of process items—prayer challenge, faith challenge, and influence challenge—and the special destiny item, ministry affirmation.

Spiritual Warfare Process Item

In Daniel 10, we read that Daniel was comforted by an angel. He had been fasting and praying for the nation of Israel for three weeks. The angel explained that God heard Daniel's prayer when he first began to pray, but the answer was delayed because the angel had to fight with the spiritual powers that ruled Persia. The angel's explanation reveals the reality of the unseen spiritual warfare behind the physical scene. Daniel's prayer ministry was part of the spiritual warfare.

The *spiritual warfare* process item refers to those instances in ministry where the leader discerns that ministry conflict is primarily supernatural in its source and essence. He depends on God's power to solve the problem in such a way that his leadership capacity, particularly his spiritual authority, is demonstrated and expanded.

This process item occurs whether or not a leader possesses the spiritual gift of discerning spirits. Those with that gift will naturally see spiritual reality more quickly and recognize spiritual warfare. All leaders, however, need the ability to discern spiritual reality in general and spiritual warfare in particular. Some leaders have a tendency to go overboard, blaming all conflict and problems on spiritual warfare. They see spiritual forces behind all human realities. Other leaders are blind to spiritual reality and see no spiritual forces behind human actions. Scripture strikes a balance between these two extremes.

The sequence of events in Matthew 16:13-23 shows the subtlety of the spiritual reality behind apparently normal human reactions. Jesus asked His disciples, "Who do you say I am?" and Peter answered, "You are the Christ" (verses 15-16). Jesus told Peter he was blessed by God with the ability to discern the truth. Jesus then foretold His suffering in Jerusalem. Peter reacted by suggesting that such a thing should never happen. Jesus rebuked Peter, exposing the subtle relationship of spiritual reality and spiritual warfare, by saying, "Get behind me, Satan! You are a stumbling block to me; you do not have in mind the things of God, but the things of men" (verse 23).

Ephesians 6:10-20 warns us that we must be alert to discern spiritual reality behind human facades. Verse 12 says, "Our struggle is not against flesh and [human beings], but against the rulers, against the authorities, against the powers of this dark world and against the spiritual forces of evil in the heavenly realms." Verses 18-20 identify one of the most effective weapons to use in spiritual warfare: intercessory prayer.

Studying these passages leads to an important principle regarding spiritual warfare: *Physical situations may well be caused, controlled, or instigated by spiritual beings.*

You can see that discernment is necessary in spiritual warfare, and that one must avoid the twofold spiritual warfare problem. Maintaining dynamic balance between the two extremes takes discernment. A leader must heed two cautions concerning the spiritual warfare process item. Don't *underestimate* and don't *overestimate* the spiritual warfare behind every situation. God will give the necessary discernment as the leader is open to learn.

Discernment alone is not enough to deal with spiritual warfare. A leader also needs power. The power items broaden discernment and focus on solutions to spiritual warfare.

Power Process Items

Four process items form the cluster called power items. Power items are characterized by gifted power, prayer power, power encounters, and networking power. The ultimate purpose of the power cluster is to train a leader to habitually appropriate God's power through faith.[5]

Acts 11:27-28 records gifted power. Agabus, a prophet from Jerusalem, is empowered by the Holy Spirit to prophesy to the Christians at Antioch concerning a famine in Israel. The Antioch church responds to the prophecy by sending money to the church in Jerusalem. It is clear that God used Agabus to challenge the Antioch church.[6] God expanded the ministry of these Christians as their church became the center of missionary activity for Paul's cross-cultural ministry journeys.

In the *gifted power* process item a leader uses a specific spiritual gift that clearly demonstrates the Holy Spirit's power.

The story of Samuel's last public leadership act, in 1 Samuel 12, describes prayer power. The issue was spiritual authority. An unusual answer to prayer—a rainstorm in the midst of the dry season—gave Samuel the spiritual authority he needed to give his closing words of admonition.

The *prayer power* process item involves a situation or need that is resolved or met through specific prayer. The prayer is answered in such a way that God's power and the authenticity of the leader's spiritual authority are clearly demonstrated.

I described in chapter 2 the incident of Watchman Nee and his evangelistic team who saw God's power vindicated in a tense situation with the islanders' god, Ta-Wang. It was evident to all that evil powers had been confronted. That was a classic example of the power encounter process item. Most leaders will at some time face this type of special power process item.

The *power encounter* process item involves a crisis situation in which there is confrontation between people representing God and people representing other supernatural forces. The issue is power, and God's credibility is at stake. He vindicates it in an unusual demonstration of His power.

We have already discussed the relationship between Barnabas and Paul to some extent, so we will just look at what part Barnabas played in a networking power process item in Paul's life. Barnabas was sent to give wisdom and direction at a crucial time in Paul's life and ministry. His authority and influence drew Paul into his God-given ministry, thus demonstrating the power of networking—God's having the right person in the right place at the right time to facilitate another's ministry.

The *networking power* process item involves God's use of mentors or other mature leaders to accomplish goals for the leader so that he senses the importance of relationships with other leaders and understands how God works through networks of people.

Breaking the Plateau Barrier

The second major area where a leader needs discernment concerns the expansion of his own ministry. In this area God concentrates on expanding a leader's discernment regarding his own capacity to lead. Recognizing and responding to God's direction in the process items of prayer challenge, faith challenge, and influence challenge indicate significant development in the discernment function. Plateaued leaders rarely discern or respond to this challenge cluster of items.

All leaders have the capacity to influence. God wants to develop that capacity over a lifetime. Leaders often reach a point in the later stages of the Ministry Maturing phase in which their development seems to be arrested. This is the plateau barrier. Leaders have a tendency to cease developing once they have some skills and ministry experience. They may be content to continue their ministry as is, without discerning the need to develop further.

When a leader has potential for leadership, which is not yet developed or used, God will challenge that leader to take steps to develop and use that capacity for His purposes. Often a leader is unaware of his capacity until God brings guidance through people or events to encourage him toward development. Let's look at God's challenges.

Prayer Challenge Process Item

A classic prayer challenge process item is recorded in Genesis 18 where Abraham prayed for Sodom. After God revealed His plan for Sarah to conceive a son, He informed Abraham of His intended judgment upon Sodom. Abraham pleaded with God to spare the city. Similarly, down through the ages, God reveals His plans to a leader, challenges him to pray concerning that revelation, and thus involves him in the outcome.

At the heart of leadership is communication between God and the leader. A leader must know God's purposes for a group before he can communicate them.

In the hectic pace of ministry, vital communication with God via prayer is often neglected. Prayer is one of the major "being" items that is constantly reemphasized by God in this "doing" phase.

The prayer challenge may be stimulated by pressing personal needs or ministry needs, but its essence is more than the answer to those needs. It is a reminder that prayer is a necessary leadership habit that enhances communication with God and secures vision for ministry.

The *prayer challenge* process item refers to those instances when God reminds the leader that he must pray in order to have effective ministry. A leader's proper response to this challenge will produce positive growth that will affect later ministry.

Samuel was reminded of this essential fact and thus serves as the prototype for leaders. He had anointed a new king and was also stepping out of active ministry. However, his commitment to praying for that ministry remained. We should imitate his response to a prayer challenge when he said, "As for me, far be it from me that I should sin against the Lord by failing to pray for you. And I will teach you the way that is good and right" (1 Samuel 12:23).

A major principle can be drawn from this passage: *If God calls you to a ministry, then He calls you to pray for that ministry.*

Leadership emergence studies of numerous giants in missions history (Hudson Taylor, Jonathan Goforth, and others) testify to the importance of this principle.[7] The New Testament record does not always tell how God gave prayer challenges, but we can assume He did because these leaders frequently took time to pray for their ministries. We see in Scripture that Christ responds to the prayer challenge before major decisions or crises in His ministry. His prayer time away from crowds and alone with the Father strengthened Him and gave Him vision for His future ministry.

The ultimate goal of this process item is to help the leader see prayer not as a burden but as a release, a privilege to be entered joyfully. An intermediate goal is gaining discernment to see God's challenge and guidance for ministry.

Faith Challenge Process Item

While I was working as an electrical engineer, I began to sense the need for further training in Bible study. I didn't know what would come after the training, but I felt compelled to pursue it. My wife, Marilyn, and I knew we didn't have the money to cover the cost of schooling. I remember the night we discussed this problem. How could we manage? We had four children and there was a great difference between an engineer's salary and a student's.

God had challenged us with the promise from Matthew 6:33: "Seek first his kingdom and his righteousness, and all these things will be given to you as well." As we considered this promise, we became convinced that God would provide for our family. As we were actually talking, we received a phone call from my brother-in-law who promised to support us during my time in Bible college. God honored our step of faith. During the three years in Bible school, God met all our financial needs.

God's call to a leader to increase his faith in ministry is one of the strongest challenges a leader will face. Faith challenges almost always stretch one beyond his present understanding. They are not restricted to those who have the spiritual gift of faith.

Faith challenges are directly linked to effective ministry. Leaders are people with God-given vision, and one of their essential functions is to inspire followers with that vision and hope. They can't fulfill this function without faith.

The *faith challenge* process item refers to those instances in ministry when a leader is challenged by God to take steps of faith in ministry and sees God reward those steps with divine affirmation and ministry achievement. God's faithfulness increases the leader's capacity to trust Him in future ministry.

A faith challenge involves three elements: (1) a revelation from God concerning some future plan, (2) a realization by the leader that God is challenging him to act on the basis of this revelation, and (3) a mindset that determines to make leadership decisions based on this firm conviction. A faith challenge may come all at once or it may be given over time.

Influence Challenge Process Item

The challenge to send Barnabas and Paul on their first missionary trip was more than just a corporate challenge to the church at Antioch. It was also an influence challenge process item for both Barnabas and Paul. Their influence was expanded to include target groups in other cultures. The basic kind of influence was still direct — person to person.

The *influence challenge* process item refers to those instances in which a leader is prompted by God to expand his sphere of influence.[8] A sphere of influence refers to the number of people for whom a leader will give an account to God. The influence challenge can come through an increase in extensiveness, intensiveness, or scope of influence.

The challenge to encourage the Thessalonian church through writing an epistle was an indirect influence challenge for Paul. He constantly expanded this indirect influence throughout his lifetime as he wrote. His influence spread throughout the Christian world to people he did not directly know, and we are affected by it today as we read the epistles.

Understanding the sphere of influence and influence challenge is a step forward in discernment, but please note this caution: A leader is not to consciously seek to expand his sphere of influence as if bigger were better. A leader is to respond to God's challenge to accept varying spheres of influence in order to find God's proper sphere for him.

Ministry Affirmation

First Kings 19:1-16 illustrates a ministry affirmation process item. The prophet Elijah was in the midst of a severe depression. His ministry was successful, but it left him lonely and frightened. God sent an angel to minister to him, and then God Himself gave Elijah an affirmation. In a gentle whisper, God spoke to Elijah and gave him a ministry assignment as well as a junior prophet to teach, Elisha. Clearly, strong leaders as well as weak leaders need ministry affirmation.

Potential leaders trained for full-time ministry often become discouraged and drop out of ministry. This is also true of leaders who aren't in full-time ministry. Discernment about how God develops a leader is a major factor in overcoming this barrier. A second antidote to the discouragement-dropout syndrome is the ministry affirmation process item. It encourages a leader and gives him a renewed sense of ultimate purpose in leadership. It is God's pat on the back.

The *ministry affirmation* process item is a special kind of ministry assignment or experience through which God gives approval to a leader, resulting in a renewed sense of purpose for the leader.

Ministry affirmation includes such things as vision, sign, successful ministry incident, human expressions of appreciation, inner satisfaction, word of knowledge, word of wisdom, prophecy, promotion, and expansion of sphere of influence. Vision, signs, and promotions are easy to see, but real growth in discernment comes when a leader can sense God's approval through the less spectacular affirmations like human expressions of appreciation and inner satisfaction.

Ministry affirmation serves as encouragement, but it can also serve as confirmation of God's guidance. Quite often divine affirmation comes when a leader seeks God in a time of isolation. Deliberate times of fasting and days of prayer spent alone with God produce the needed affirmation. The need for ministry affirmation is not a sign of weakness but a harbinger of renewal and refreshment that will motivate the leader to further service.

There are many recorded instances of ministry affirmations in Jesus' life, beginning with the Father's words at His baptism, "This is my Son, whom I love; with him I am well pleased" (Matthew 3:17). John's gospel records another ministry affirmation in the life of Christ:

> "Father, I thank you that you have heard me. I knew that you always hear me, but I said this for the benefit of the people standing here, that they may believe that you sent me."
>
> When he had said this, Jesus called in a loud voice, "Lazarus, come out!" The

dead man came out, his hands and feet wrapped with strips of linen, and a cloth around his face.

Jesus said to them, "Take off the grave clothes and let him go." (11:41-44)

God often uses ministry affirmation not only to establish the leader but also to vindicate that leader before followers.

MINISTRY PHILOSOPHY

Leaders frequently pursue ministry without a clear ministry philosophy. Either they do not learn lessons or they fail to identify these lessons and integrate them into a system that can undergird future ministry decision making. Whether or not a leader stops at a plateau or moves on to the Life Maturing phase and Convergence phase depends on how he handles this problem.

Ministry philosophy refers to ideas, values, and principles that a leader uses as guidelines for decision making, for exercising influence, or for evaluating his ministry. An effective ministry philosophy should develop during the Ministry Maturing phase. This is such an important stage and can cause such a significant problem that I will return to it and devote chapter 8 to it.

REACHING THE END OF THE MINISTRY MATURING PHASE

There are three patterns for terminating the Ministry Maturity phase. Two leave the leader in the ministry phase, and the third leads him on to the next phase: Life Maturing.

The leaders who terminate their development in the Ministry Maturing phase fall into two categories: (1) those who plateau at some level of ministry competency, and then show relatively little ongoing growth in ministry or spiritual development; and (2) those who are disciplined in ministry, limited in ministry, or set aside from it.

These two groups of leaders are in addition to those who drop out. A third termination pattern, the standard ministry boundary pattern, involves reflection on the meaning of ministry and God's involvement in it plus a major philosophical shift regarding the basis for ministry. The shift is from competency in *doing* to effectiveness flowing from *being*, and it comes as a result of the leader's reflection on God's involvement in his life and ministry.

In general, boundaries[9] represent a time of reflecting on the past, evaluating the present, and looking to future decisions in light of this reflection. This is especially true in the boundary between the Ministry Maturing phase and the Life Maturing phase because it is a subtle separation and primarily psychological. The transition may take place without change of ministry assignment, location, role, or other common changes associated with a major boundary transition.

In the shift from ministry as *doing* to a ministry as *being*, spiritual authority becomes the dominant power base. Boundary processing, which leads to the Life Maturing phase, may take several years.

SUMMARY

In the relational learning development stage, four major process items (the submission cluster) are used to develop a leader. These process items—authority insights, relational insights, ministry conflict, and leadership backlash—are used to bridge the first ministry problem, the authority problem. In this section we looked at two patterns: the five-stage authority pattern and the leadership backlash cycle. We identified the "ten commandments of spiritual authority" and a major leadership principle concerning authority.

We learned that in the discernment development stage a leader learns discernment in two major areas. The first deals with spiritual reality and the second with personal expansion. Discernment in the area of spiritual reality is learned through the spiritual warfare process item. A second problem (spiritual warfare) shows us that God also uses power items to teach leaders about spiritual warfare. These are the gifted power process item, the prayer power process item, the power encounter process item, and the networking power process item.

In the second area of discernment, personal expansion, we encounter a third problem, the plateau barrier. A leader needs to learn to discern God's challenges in order to continue to develop. God uses a cluster of process items—prayer challenge, faith challenge, and influence challenge—to teach the leader about the need for personal discernment. Two leadership principles—the prayer challenge principle and the faith challenge principle—have been identified, as was the faith challenge pattern. A final process item, ministry affirmation, was also discussed.

The fourth problem (ministry philosophy) was the final one in this chapter. It is important for a leader to develop a philosophy of ministry that embraces the lessons he has learned and then gives that leader a foundation for future decision making.

I closed with a discussion of the different ways the Ministry Maturing phase can end. It is necessary to discuss these terminations because not many leaders get beyond this phase. Entering the next phase depends on a successful evaluation of the Ministry Maturing phase.

The discernment stage is an important one because it embraces all the other stages of the Ministry Maturing phase. The process items and patterns described and the principles and warnings given should give spiritual insight to recognize God's involvement in the daily happenings of life and ministry. This, in turn, leads to confident expectation of His continued working and confident exercise of influence by the leader.

HOW ABOUT YOU?

As I described the four major functions toward which God works, perhaps you thought of incidents in your own ministry. The following questions are intended to encourage you to apply some of the insights to your own experience.

1. Consider again the five primary lessons the authority insights process item teaches:

- Submission to authority
- Authority structures
- Authenticity of power bases underlying authority
- Authority conflict
- How to exercise authority

Which of these five are found in the following examples?

- The centurion in Luke 7:1-10
- James and John in Matthew 20:20-28
- The friends of the paralyzed man at the healing in Luke 5:17-26
- Miriam and Aaron in Numbers 12:1-16

2. Give an illustration from your own life of an authority insights process item. Describe the incident and identify which of the five primary lessons you have learned. Share the details with some other person experienced in ministry.

3. Remember, the four major development stages of the Ministry Maturing phase are important not only for you to understand how God is developing you as a leader, but also to help you select and help emerging leaders in your ministry. Which of the following four stages do you think God is taking you through at this time? Is God giving insights for you personally or for you to use with emerging leaders in your ministry? Determine which stage is most important for you personally and which one is most useful for you in helping emerging leaders in your ministry.

- The entry stage
- The training stage
- The relational learning stage
- The discernment stage

CHAPTER 6

ONGOING LESSONS: GUIDANCE AND OTHER MULTI-PHASE PROCESSES

The Challenge/The Problem: The LORD went before them by day in a pillar of a cloud, to lead them the way; and by night in a pillar of fire, to give them light; to go by day and night. *(Exodus 13:21, KJV)*

Ken's voice quavered, and his eyes were misty. "I don't know what to do," he said as he discussed his situation with me. The mission with which he had been serving in the Indian Ocean had made a major philosophical shift. Ministries such as his, which were not directly related to church planting, would be phased out.

Missionaries involved in non-church-planting ministries would have three choices. If their ministry could be absorbed by some other church-planting mission then they could join that mission. Or perhaps they could be retrained and relocated in one of the church-planting ministries that would be opened up in Africa. Their last choice was to leave the mission field and return home to enter some other ministry. In any case, a number of missionaries were out of a job.

Ken had visited two of the newer church-planting fields in Africa to see if he could fit in. He shared with me two letters that he had received from these field leaders. Frankly, neither one looked promising to me. They didn't seem to take into consideration Ken's gift-mix, destiny, and leadership emergence to this point in his life.

Ken was committed to the mission field. He was on the verge of a life-changing decision. He was in his mid-thirties and had, Lord willing, at least another ten to twenty years of productive missionary service. What could I say to him? He clearly needed guidance.

Guidance[1] is an ongoing need in the life of a leader! Wouldn't it be nice if God would provide a cloud for Ken as He did for the nation of Israel in Exodus? Move when the cloud moves; stop when the cloud stops; go where the cloud goes. God does provide guidance, but in a fashion that challenges discernment, individual responsibility, and commitment.

Guidance is one of the crucial elements of leadership. The need for guidance occurs throughout a leader's lifetime, so process items referring to guidance do not restrict themselves to just one phase. They are ongoing processes. They occur in every development phase. There are other items that also occur throughout all development phases. For now I shall simply call them miscellaneous process items.

This chapter will discuss two classes of process items that occur throughout all development phases. I will discuss six guidance process items and four miscellaneous process items. The guidance items are relatively uncommon, except in the study of leaders' lives. I have selected four miscellaneous process items: literary items, word items, crises, and conflict. Guidance often comes through these, as well as through the ones I have defined as guidance items. However, they are general in nature and occur frequently in a leader's development.

GUIDANCE PROCESSING

A leader is a person with God-given capacity and God-given responsibility who influences a group of followers toward God's purposes for the group. The central element of this definition of a leader is his influencing toward God's purposes. Leaders must know how to get corporate guidance for the groups they are leading. How do they do that? That is the challenge of this chapter—to point out the guidance that God uses in developing a leader for this crucial aspect of leadership.

The basic guidance pattern is simple. A leader first learns about personal guidance for his own life. Having learned to discern God's direction for his own life in numerous crucial decisions, he can then shift to the leadership function of determining guidance for the group that he leads.

There are many books that deal with understanding God's guidance for personal decision-making. I will not duplicate that material. I assume that a leader is in fellowship with God and learning to hear His word through the written Word, the word ministry of others in the body of Christ, inner convictions from the Holy Spirit, and providential circumstances. I also assume that much guidance will come through *one's ongoing, obedient, daily walk with God*[2] as a leader meets with God in his devotional time and in personal study of the Word. In this section I am going beyond that. And I want to go beyond what is taught in most books about guidance. There are six major process items that are frequently used by God to heighten a leader's discernment for guidance:

- Divine Contacts
- Mentors
- Double Confirmation
- Negative Preparation
- Flesh Act
- Divine Affirmation

I will discuss each of these as I talk further about guidance.

Guidance development is complicated and delicate. God must teach a leader to discern guidance, without thwarting the leader's personal initiative. He does this while He is creating commitment to follow His guidance and teaching the leader to sense individual responsibility for making the decisions. This is not an overnight lesson. It takes place slowly through many process items over an extended period of time embracing several phases.

In 1964, Harold Dollar crossed my path at a church I was attending. He was God-sent. His challenge to me for discipleship changed my life forever, and he gave counsel concerning the next steps that I took in serving God. He was a divine contact.

I was almost finished with my doctoral work in missiology in 1979, when Chuck Kraft, another friend, was used by God to advise me in a major career decision. Not only did Chuck give advice, he paved the way for my next development phase.

Especially for younger emerging leaders, God frequently brings along wiser, experienced leaders who give timely advice. Two process items stem from this basic notion: the divine contact and the mentor. We need to understand these from a twofold perspective. We need to recognize divine contacts and mentors in our own lives, as we move through development phases where guidance is necessary. As we mature in our leadership, we need to recognize that God will use us as divine contacts and mentors for others.

Divine Contacts

At the right moment God brings just what is needed into the life of a developing leader to inspire, explain truth, or give direction. This could be a tract that challenges or explains some truth, a book that gives new perspectives, or a person who will be greatly used by God in that leader's life. The divine contact process item refers to the unusual way that God brings a person of significance into a leader's life at just the right time.

A *divine contact* is a person whom God brings to a leader at a crucial moment in a development phase in order to affirm leadership potential, to encourage leadership potential, to give guidance on a special issue, to give insights that broaden the leader, to challenge the leader toward God, or to open a door to ministry opportunity.

Barnabas was a divine contact for Paul in Acts 9:27, at a time when Paul could not get a hearing with the leaders in the church at Jerusalem. He opened the door by standing up for Paul and introducing him to those leaders. Peter was a divine contact for Cornelius in Acts 10. God sent him to speak so that Cornelius and his household could be saved. Cornelius perceived him as God's emissary. Paul was a divine contact for Timothy, Priscilla, Aquila, and a host of others. His entrance into their lives gave timely guidance that affected their lives and careers.

Divine contacts are often interwoven into the lives of leaders and will reappear at crucial moments. Sometimes the relationship is mutual and each helps the other along. This has certainly been the case between Harold Dollar and myself. Over the years God has brought our lives together at crucial times and each of us has been able to help the other. Harold was instrumental in my decision to leave the Bell Telephone Laboratories and go to Columbia Bible College in 1967. My wife and I invited Harold and Sharon to consider joining the West Indies Mission in 1972 and minister in Trinidad. God used Harold to introduce me to the In-Service Program of the School of World Mission. This was the start of my mid-career training, which eventually led to my doctorate and my present position with Fuller Theological Seminary.

Leaders, because of their ability to influence, need to recognize that they will often be divine contacts for others they meet. They should be especially sensitive to the Holy Spirit's use of them as divine contacts and recognize this special way of influencing. Sometimes divine contacts are unaware that God has used them at a special time in someone's life. Often a phrase or a message is a key at the right moment. Years later it may come to light how at a given moment someone was used especially as a divine contact. An awareness of the divine contact process item and how it works can be a major step forward in a leader's conscious ability to cooperate with God in using this with emerging leaders.

Mentors

God has given some people the capacity and the heart to see leadership potential and to take private and personal action to help the potential leader develop. That action usually becomes a form of significant guidance for the potential leader. *Mentoring* refers to the process where a person with a serving, giving, encouraging attitude, the mentor, sees leadership potential in a still-to-be developed person, the protégé or mentoree,[3] and is able to promote or otherwise significantly influence the protégé in the realization of potential. A *mentoring* process item refers to the process and results of a mentor helping a potential leader. The mentor is a special kind of divine contact, one who may offer prolonged help or guidance or be a stimulus for growth.

Barnabas mentored Paul. In Acts 11:25, Barnabas went out of his way to recruit Paul for the ministry at Antioch. Barnabas linked him into that church and co-ministered with him. Barnabas also mentored John Mark, a New Testament author. Even when Paul had given up on John Mark, Barnabas stood by him. John Mark became a gifted leader in his own right. We most likely would not have the gospel of Mark except for Barnabas's mentoring attitude.

Margaret Barber, an English missionary, mentored Watchman Nee through his early development. Her mentoring included informal apprenticeship and imitation modeling. Her wise counsel, knowledge of the Scriptures, and submissive spirit deeply affected him at an impressionable stage of his development. Much of what Nee accomplished in his ministry has its roots in the time of Margaret Barber's mentoring.

Over the past several years, I have observed several mid-career students from Burma who were studying with us at the School of Intercultural Studies. In probing into their life-histories and their guidance to Fuller, I found out that John Stott was their mentor sponsor.[4] He has found ways to send several emerging leaders for further training and other experiences that have broadened their sphere of influence.

Not everyone is suited to be a mentor. Mentors are people who can readily see potential in a person. They can tolerate mistakes, brashness, abrasiveness, and so on, in order to see potential develop. They are flexible and patient, recognizing that it takes time and experience for a person to develop. They have vision and ability to see down the road and suggest next steps that a protégé needs for development. And they usually have a gift-mix that includes one or more of the encouragement spiritual gifts: mercy, giving, exhortation, faith, and word of wisdom.

A mentor is someone who helps a protégé in some very practical ways: by giving timely *advice* that encourages the protégé; by *risking* his own reputation in backing the protégé; by *bridging* between the protégé and needed resources; by *modeling* and setting expectations that challenge the protégé; by *giving* tracts, letters, books, or other literary information that open perspectives for the protégé; by giving *financially*, sometimes sacrificially, to further the protégé's ministry; by *co-ministering* in order to increase the credibility, status, and prestige of the protégé; and by having the *freedom* to allow and even promote the protégé beyond the mentor's own level of leadership.

The emergent leader who has a wise mentor early on in those first ministry steps is fortunate. God's guidance through a mentor can be life-changing.[5] It can speed up the development process and set patterns that will last a lifetime.

Double Confirmation

Remember the opening scenario about Ken, the missionary, who was forced to find a new ministry? You may have wondered what I said to him. First, I must say that I had studied his personal life-history; therefore I had seen a number of patterns in his life, knew his gift-mix, and part of his ministry philosophy. I was able to talk with him about the future in terms of possible next development tasks that the Lord wanted to accomplish in his life. Apart from the general counsel I gave him, I also pointed out that in crucial decision times one could expect God to give certainty guidance. For example, the *double confirmation* process item refers to unusual guidance in which God makes His will clear by reinforcing it through more than one source.

Acts 9 tells of Paul's conversion. This was such a crucial event in the history of Christianity that God used a double confirmation to indicate its certainty. When Paul met the Lord Jesus on the road to Damascus, he saw a bright light that dazzled him, and he fell to the ground. As he did, he heard the Lord Jesus speak to him. Was this just self-delusion, or possibly hallucination? Acts 9:10-16 tells us that the Lord Himself told

Ananias what He had done to Paul. Ananias went, confirmed Paul's conversion, and laid hands on him to heal him of the blindness caused by the dazzling light. This crucial incident was doubly confirmed.

On a ministry trip I stayed in the home of a pastor named "Bill." As is my habit when staying with a leader, I did a short study of Bill's leadership. I ascertained his timeline and some of the major process items that stood out to him. During unstructured interviewing, I unearthed a double confirmation that exactly fits the classic pattern I will soon describe.

In connection with two fasting periods of some length, Bill was led to claim ground for God. He walked through neighborhoods and prayed about ground, families, streets, and so on. The passage that God used to convict Bill was Joshua 1:3, where God challenged Joshua by saying, "I will give you every place where you set your foot, as I promised Moses." It was during this time of experiential learning about possession that Bill attended a conference with his wife. Toward the end of the meeting the speaker began giving direct exhortations to people at the conference. He turned to Bill, pointed a finger at him, quoted Joshua 1:3, and said that God indeed wanted him to possess the land. The speaker had never met Bill prior to this. He had no knowledge whatsoever of Bill's situation. His word of confirmation was a great inspiration to Bill, who then made major decisions concerning taking next steps in his ministry.

The classic pattern for double confirmation involves four steps. First there is a crucial moment in the leader's ministry when a sure word from God is needed for direction. Second, God gives direction to the leader directly or indirectly. Third, God then confirms this direction through someone else. Fourth, God brings the two together in some unmistakable, sovereign way.

Double confirmation gives divine affirmation to an important decision and validates a leader's spiritual authority. It gives a renewed sense of destiny to the leader, while serving as a sign to outsiders as well as insiders.

Gideon's famous fleece incident (see Judges 6:36-40) is a double confirmation, although it is a somewhat unusual example.[6] Gideon wanted to make absolutely certain that God was leading him to deliver the people of God from the Midianites and Amalekites. He put a piece of wool on the ground and prayed that there would be dew on the wool but none on the ground. The next night he prayed that there would be dew all around the wool, but that the wool would be dry. God answered both of the prayers, and Gideon had his certainty.

In Acts 10:1-8, God gave Cornelius a vision in which He told him to ask Peter to come talk with him. God was also working with Peter by giving him a vision about the inclusion of Gentiles in the kingdom. Both were visited separately by God, and then they were brought together. This was a significant event for the expansion of Christianity. Gentiles were included in God's offer of salvation. In order for Jewish Christians to believe this, it took guidance such as God gave.

These were crucial times in the history of God's people and His work. Double confirmation is no light matter. It is not the normal guidance that God will use for the majority of decisions, but a leader who is confronted with a crucial decision can ask God to give double confirmation.

Negative Preparation

I almost hesitate to give this next guidance process item, because it offers the potential for a cop-out for those who are in situations they don't like. But I have seen it in the lives of many leaders and feel it must be mentioned, although it could be misinterpreted and misused.[7]

Someone has said that while it may appear that the grass is always greener on the other side of the fence, in fact, it is really brown on both sides of the fence. Negative preparation is frequently seen, particularly in boundary times between development phases. God often prepares some-one to accept the next steps of guidance by first allowing him to go through negative experiences during his present development phase. The negative experiences make the grass look greener, producing incentive to move on and seek the next thing God has. Without negative processing many would be satisfied to stay (and perhaps plateau), not moving on to develop, expand, and sense God's next steps.

Negative preparation involves God's use of events, people, conflict, persecution, and experiences that focus on the negative, in order to free a person from the present situation to enter the next phase of development with revitalized interest. The emphasis is not on escaping, but on release and on preparation to accept a new situation with an abandonment that would not otherwise be there.

Let me give two biblical examples of negative preparation. One, the pre-Exodus persecution made the Israelites open to Moses' leadership and promise of deliverance. After the immediate flight from Egypt, the Bible records that God did not take them directly to Philistia. If He had, they might have wanted to go back to Egypt when they saw the battles that lay ahead. Instead, He took them through the desert. At the end of this long and hard journey the Israelites were prepared for battle (see Exodus 13:17-18). Two, after struggling with barrenness, Hannah was willing to give Samuel into the Lord's service, which was God's means of raising up a prophet judge during a period of transitional leadership into the kingdom phase of Israel (see 1 Samuel 1).

Negative preparation process items may include: problems in a marriage relationship, a crisis in job or ministry, conflict with other Christian workers, dissatisfaction with one's inner life or present role, difficulties with children, tough living conditions, sickness due to climate-geographic conditions, isolation, and limiting restrictions that thwart sphere of influence development.

Let me reinforce what I said at the beginning of this process item. It is not to be used to escape from a situation that appears unpleasant to you. God may want to use the situation to mature your character, as described in James 1:2-4, and this should not be confused with the negative preparation item in which God wants to break you loose from a situation in order to move you on to something you might not otherwise choose.

The Flesh Act

Learning about guidance is not an overnight lesson. It takes place slowly, through experiencing many process items over an extended period of time embracing several phases. One such process item that is often repeated in an emerging leader is the flesh act, which gives him lessons about what not to do in the future. Experiencing this process item several times, maybe even numerous times, leads to discernment that can come in no other way. Emerging leaders need to learn to distinguish between presumptuous faith and God's situational word upon which faith can rely.

Learning to discern God's will can be a difficult process during trying times. Hindsight can be valuable as God teaches us to recognize His direction and guidance. The flesh act can be seen most clearly in those times when a leader presumes guidance and moves ahead of God. It also occurs when the leader has a part of God's guidance but not the complete picture (like knowing what but not when or how). The leader often tries to help God work things out.[8]

Flesh act refers to those instances in a leader's life when guidance is presumed and decisions are made either hastily or without proper discernment of God's choice. Such decisions usually involve human manipulation, which brings ramifications that later affect ministry and life negatively.

Genesis 16 records an example of a flesh act. God had promised Abraham and Sarah that they would bear a son and be parents to a nation. For over twenty years this promise from God was not fulfilled. Then Sarah made a plan. She sent her Egyptian maid, Hagar, to Abraham to bear them a child. Hagar conceived and bore Ishmael. This practice, though culturally acceptable in that era, was not God's plan. Later, in His own way, God did fulfill the promise. Negative consequences from this flesh act are still with us today.

Another flesh act that had corporate ramifications was the incident when Joshua made a treaty with the Gibeonites (see Joshua 9). He assumed that they had come from a far distance, but they were deliberately deceiving him and lived a short distance away. Joshua's reasoning probably went something like this: "What will it hurt if we sign a peace treaty with them? They live so far away that they will not be a threat to us." Verse 14 gives the telltale sign: "The men of Israel . . . did not inquire of the LORD." The Gibeonites were among the tribes that God had commanded Israel to destroy.

A close examination of Joshua's flesh act reveals some lessons that he learned in retrospect. Everyday affairs are fraught with things that are not what they seem. Also, when a leader follows hard after God, he can expect distractions to occur. He cannot presume to understand every situation but must evaluate each one in the light of the clear guidance he is following.

Hezekiah king of Judah entertained some messengers from Babylon and showed them all of his wealth and military equipment (see Isaiah 39). This seemed like a natural thing to do, but later Isaiah rebuked Hezekiah (see verses 5-8) with a word from the Lord that condemned his seemingly innocent action. The prophecy foretold a future time of disaster. Everyday affairs can lead to flesh acts if a leader is not alert and discerning in his actions. Seemingly minor decisions in daily life can affect major outcomes. Pride (wanting to show accomplishments, boast of possessions, and so on) can lead to flesh acts.

Reflection on the flesh act process item is not an exercise in negative thinking. It is a procedure through which God can sharpen a leader's discernment skills and strengthen his ability to recognize His guidance. As a leader reflects on guidance cases, his and others, he should look for lessons about the way God guides so that in the future he will be able to discern His direction more clearly.

Let me summarize the lessons I have identified thus far in the flesh act. *What*, *when*, and *how* are all important facets of guidance. Certainty on one and not the others often leads to presumption about the others and to a flesh act. Presumptuous faith assumes God will do something that He has not communicated and can lead to a flesh act. In major decisions, acting without consulting God often results in a flesh act. Failing to act and choosing a human alternative, instead of doing something God has pointed out, are also flesh acts.

Divine Affirmation

At least three times in the Lord Jesus' ministry one can observe the Father's divine affirmation. Matthew 3:17 describes the descent of the Holy Spirit in the form of a dove and a voice giving approval of Jesus. A similar voice of divine affirmation occurs on the Mount of Transfiguration (see Matthew 17:5). John 12:28 records divine affirmation again in the form of a voice from heaven, which was for the benefit of the disciples as well as for Jesus.

In a lifetime of ministry, there will be times when a leader will need reassurance from God that the ministry is relevant and worthwhile, and that his life is indeed counting toward God's purposes. This reaffirmation—usually the need for it is inward—will infuse new life into the leader. Occasionally, this affirmation is given outwardly as confirmation to followers that the leader does indeed have spiritual authority. The process item that describes this special approval from God is called divine affirmation. It is closely linked with spiritual authority. It is a guidance item, for without this special touch of God many leaders would be inclined to give up. But with it there is new life and a sense of keeping on with God's approval.

Divine affirmation is a special kind of experience in which God gives approval to a leader so that the leader has a renewed sense of ultimate purpose and a refreshed desire to continue serving God.

At the time when God called Abraham (see Genesis 12:1-3) and over the next twenty-five years, God gave divine affirmation to Abraham on a periodic basis. One significant experience was a symbolic vision that renewed Abraham's purpose (see Genesis 15). The vision also revealed a great truth of a unilateral covenant made between the Father and Son, which had eternal significance for Abraham's descendants.[9]

First Samuel 12:13-19 illustrates divine affirmation of Samuel's ministry with an external focus. Samuel's prayer for rain in the midst of the dry season was answered by God. The people saw that Samuel had spiritual authority; God was with him.

Divine affirmations have come through the sovereign arrangement of circumstances, an inner voice or other direct revelation, a dream, a vision, angelic visitation, a prophetic word, a miraculous sign, or a sense of God's blessing on a life as attested to by external testimony through Joseph in Genesis 39:2-3,21-23. Guidance to keep on doing what we are doing may often come in the form of divine affirmation. Leaders need to be aware of this form of guidance and to recognize the many ways through which God gives it.

MISCELLANEOUS MULTI-PHASE PROCESS ITEMS

There are other process items that can occur in several different development phases. These miscellaneous process items occur in conjunction with other process items to complement or supplement their force. All of the miscellaneous items discussed here often occur along with guidance items to reinforce the guidance, but do more than guidance processing. They provide growth stimulus both for inner-life growth and for ministerial growth for use with groups being led. The first two items, the literary and word items, are usually positive experiences. The last two, the crises and conflict process items, are related and are usually negative experiences, though positive lessons should be learned.

Literary

While reading the biography of Jim Elliot, I noticed how much he was helped by reading what others had written. One writer who influenced him deeply was Amy Carmichael, a missionary to India for fifty-five years. I began to read her works and saw that her biography revealed the same thing. She quoted many who had helped her. I began to look for this vicarious learning in the lives of others. Many great leaders were widely read and greatly helped by the experiences of others recorded in biographies and other works.

The *literary* process item refers to the means God uses to teach lessons to leaders for their own lives through others' writings. This ability to learn for one's own life from the lessons seen in the lives of others is vicarious learning. I am thankful that I came from a home where reading was stressed. When I was a little child, my mom used to read from *Egermeier's Bible Story Book* each afternoon as we took our naps. I well remember when she took me to the public library and helped me get my first library card. I learned to love reading early, but it was much later that I learned the value of it by seeing God speak to me through it. God has greatly used the literary process item in my own life.

Early in 1964, I began to read all of the China Inland Mission books—many of which were biographies. I can't tell you just how much God used those books in my life. I saw in *Hudson Taylor's Spiritual Secret* a man who was willing to take God at His Word and trust Him. The faith challenges that Hudson Taylor faced prepared me to receive faith challenges for myself. I could point out hundreds of literary items from which God has spoken to me. The hundreds of biographies I read formed the background for my study of leadership emergence patterns.

The intention of the literary process item is to achieve the ability to have God teach inner-life lessons through reading that can be applied to life and ministry. Many high-level leaders are known for reading widely and for their capacity to apply lessons to their own lives from what they read. The ability to do this often short-circuits the years it would have taken to learn the same lessons by personal experience.

The literary process item is suited to supplement almost any of the developmental tasks of Phase II through Phase VI. Information is available in Christian writings that deal with the whole spectrum of developmental tasks. Biographies of other leaders should be a regular part of a leader's literary diet.

Word

In Daniel 9, we see Daniel in a late phase of his leadership emergence. Daniel had been studying Jeremiah 27 and 29. These chapters tell of the end of the seventy years of captivity, when the Israelites called on God and sought Him. Reading this caused Daniel to fast, pray, and repent for his people. The Lord sent an angel with a special revelation that expanded

Daniel's perspective and brought on his prayer. This resulted in a faith challenge that Daniel accepted. God's answer was beyond Daniel's expectations.[10]

Philip's ministry to the Ethiopian eunuch changed his life forever (see Acts 8). The eunuch was reading Isaiah 53 when Philip came along and interpreted the Scripture for him. The eunuch believed what Philip said. God spoke through that passage, and the eunuch was converted.

An essential characteristic of leadership is the ability to receive truth from God. This is essential in building the power base for spiritual authority—the prime influence for a godly leader. It is also an integral part of a leader's methodology in getting guidance for ministry. Leaders greatly used of God have exhibited love for truth. They study the written Word to feed their own souls, as well as to help those to whom they minister. They are quick to discern God's truth in everyday life. They learn to hear the voice of God through the ministry of other people. One would expect God to develop a leader in his ability to appreciate truth, to cultivate habits of truth intake, and to obey truth.

A *word* process item is an instance in which a leader receives a word from God that affects significantly a leader's guidance, committal, decision making, personal value system, spiritual formation, spiritual authority, or ministry philosophy. This word varies in its major purpose depending on the phase in which it occurs. Word process items that occur prior to the Inner-Life Growth phase establish values. Word process items in the Inner-Life Growth phase will be word checks and will test and form character. In the Ministry Maturing phase word items will be used to build spiritual authority, for spiritual maturing, to reveal spiritual dynamics (as part of the normal exercise of word gifts), and to affect decision making and ministry philosophy. Word items are used throughout all phases for guidance.

Word gifts are those gifts that are specifically used by God to reveal and clarify truth about Himself and His purposes and to edify the believers and instill hope in them concerning God's present and future activity. Leaders are those who have word gifts. Word processing goes hand in hand with word gifts. Leaders can expect to have a great many word items throughout a lifetime. A major symptom of a plateaued leader is one to whom word items are infrequent.

Crises

The next two process items, the crises process item and the conflict process item, usually involve negative experiences.[11] It is most difficult to discern the working of God through these process items. God will cultivate sensitivity to His working in these experiences if a leader allows it and has a teachable spirit.[12]

Crises bring increased pressures due to threatening loss (of life, property, or way of life), conflict, perceived need of change, inner turmoil, sickness, persecution, the need to see God's character vindicated, or the need to have God's guidance or special intervention. These human situations are often used by God to test a leader and to teach him dependence on God. Crises will also teach the leader that God is the one who meets him in all of the major experiences of life with a solution that is tailor-made for him by God.

It is the ability to learn the sovereign lessons in crisis events that makes this process item important to the understanding of how a leader emerges. Crisis lessons will prove extremely valuable later in the Convergence phase. Crises process items are special intense pressure situations in life that are used by God to test and to teach dependence on God. Paul captures the benefit of this kind of processing when he says,

> Praise be to the God and Father of our Lord Jesus Christ, the Father of compassion and the God of all comfort, who comforts us in all our troubles, *so that we can comfort those in any trouble with the comfort we ourselves have received from God.* (2 Corinthians 1:3-4, emphasis added)

Paul later writes of beatings, stonings, being left for dead, shipwrecks, floods, and also attacks from robbers. See 2 Corinthians 11:21-29 for a listing and explanation of many of these crises.

Jephthah, one of the early judges, was a crisis leader. In Judges 10–11, his crises process items included: family conflict and ostracism, forced isolation, survival in a paramilitary band in a foreign country, the use of ministry power, a power encounter, an integrity check, and civil war. Crises prior to the Inner-Life Growth phase, as seen in the example of Jephthah, can develop inner character that is strong, independent, and that can be used in forceful leadership situations. Crises can drive one to God or away from Him. This frequently happens in the first two phases. Crises in the Ministry Maturing phase usually affect the relational and discernment stages and usually drive a developing leader more deeply into the heart of God. Crises are frequently a life-maturing process item.

Conflict

The conflict process item affects a leader in terms of spiritual or ministerial formation. Spiritual formation refers to development of the inner life of a person. Ministerial formation refers to the development of a person in ministry. Conflict is a preliminary form of a crises process item. When it occurs in the Ministry Maturing phase we call it ministry conflict, because the lessons learned tend to affect ministerial formation. The emphasis here is on the lessons learned by the leader, whether they affect spiritual or ministerial formation.

The *conflict* process item refers to those instances in a leader's life in which God uses conflict, whether personal or ministry related, to develop the leader in dependence upon God, faith, and insights relating to personal life and ministry. The prophet Jeremiah's life was filled with conflict processing, including both ministry conflict (various ministry tasks or assignments and the reaction to his ministry) and general conflict (affecting his self-image through persecution).

The majority of conflict process items will occur in combination with other items and will usually be the stimulus for learning. Some of the important combinations of conflict processing are with any of the following: ministry skills processing or ministry challenge or faith challenge or authority insights or structure insights or leadership backlash or isolation or guidance items. The things learned can include: the nature of conflict, ways to resolve or avoid conflict, ways to use conflict creatively, how to identify conflict with God's processing, and how to see conflict as the stimulus for other processing. The emphasis should be not just on the insights learned about conflict, but also on the intended development orchestrated by God in those conflict situations.

SUMMARY

Prior to this chapter I had been discussing process items phase by phase and pointing out the process items that occur in the Inner-Life Growth phase and the Ministry Maturing phase. In the next chapter, I will return to that pattern and discuss those process items that occur in the Life Maturing phase. I have interrupted that pattern of discussion because guidance process items and the miscellaneous process items have a lot to do with life maturing. I felt it would be easier to discuss that phase if you already knew about these important multi-phase process items.

PROBLEMS, PATTERNS, AND PRINCIPLES

The flesh act process item points out a basic guidance problem often seen in new leaders. I call it the patience problem. *Leaders tend to move ahead in major decisions before receiving a certainty word of guidance.* A certainty word would be some clearly understood sovereign guidance such as a double confirmation process item or an overwhelming consensus of regular guidance items. It is difficult to wait upon the Lord when there are pressures for a major decision. Sometimes leaders feel that something, maybe anything, is better than waiting.

A guideline that I use and see in the lives of others is that God's guidance to make a major change in a situation should be just as clear as His guidance that led into the situation. Waiting on the Lord is difficult. Further, the longer a leader waits, the fewer options he may have. Waiting does have its problems, and I can sympathize with those who want to go ahead and take action, but the flesh act process item points out that *what* and *when* and *how* are all necessary.

Leaders show a lack of balance by operating on partial knowledge, by manipulation of the situation, or by not balancing various guidance inputs. Normally, major decisions will see the convergence of God's voice in the heart (the emotional desires), God's voice in circumstances (providential factors), God's voice in the church (confirmation from mature fellow Christians in the local body in which we participate), and God's voice in the Word. It is this balance of elements that allows us to move with certainty. Of course, an overwhelming sovereign guidance process item—such as an unquestioned double confirmation process item alone—is enough to make a major decision, but there is safety in balanced confirmation. The problem can be stated this way: *Leaders tend to make decisions without a balanced cluster of guidance elements.*

Two guidance patterns are worth noting:

A leader learns via guidance process items to experience God's direction for his personal life that in turn builds confidence to discern guidance for groups being led.

A leader must learn to get guidance from God if he is to lead groups toward God's purposes. The leader first learns to know God's voice in terms of personal guidance. This is a step toward learning to discern guidance for the ministry situations in which a leader is placed.

God will confirm significant truth upon which a leader acts from more than one source in order to give credibility to leadership.

The double confirmation guidance process item is a special case of this long-standing biblical pattern. An examination of incidents throughout the Bible repeatedly points out this underlying pattern. The concept of this pattern has even wider application. It should especially be heeded by leaders with certain spiritual gifts. Some spiritual gifts need the cautions that come by using double confirmation. Apostleship, words of knowledge, words of wisdom, discernings of spirits, tongues, and words of prophecy serve as sources through which truth comes. To be credible, there needs to be outside or multiple confirmation when the gift is revealing truth from God that will affect others' lives. This axiom is frequently abused by strong leaders having these gifts.

I will list several principles that various leaders have found helpful concerning guidance. Some are suggestions to give perspective. Others are cautionary in nature.

1. Basic guidance will come through daily walking with God that involves word processing, obedience processing, sensing God's voice in circumstances, and God's voice via inner conviction of the Holy Spirit. This is the general rule of guidance.
2. Emerging leaders can expect to cross paths with mentors early on and be significantly helped by them in early development.
3. Unusual guidance is the exception to principle 1 and comes for crucial decisions. Such crucial decisions call for certainty guidance. Double confirmation, divine contacts, and other forms of direct sovereign intervention can be expected in these situations.
4. Mature leaders can expect to be used as divine contacts and mentors.

It is difficult to generalize for the miscellaneous process items, but the following five principles have proved helpful as suggestions and cautions:

1. Literacy is not a requirement for spirituality (stressing the literary process item seems to indicate this). But in countries where literary resources are readily available, God often greatly uses them to speed development of emergent leaders. Therefore, emerging leaders should cultivate reading skills and expect God to meet them in unusual ways through reading.
2. Biographies that reveal God's processing of leaders are a primary source for the literary process item.

3. Word process items are less frequent (if at all) with plateaued leaders.
4. Crises and conflict process items usually occur in conjunction with several other process items and signal the heightened importance of those other process items.
5. Crises and conflict process items provide rapid experiential training in maturity in both spiritual formation and ministerial formation.

More will be learned in a relatively short time with these process items than in a longer time with process items of less pressure.

HOW ABOUT YOU?

1. Identify a divine contact in your own experience. Which of the following functions did your divine contact accomplish?

   • To affirm leadership potential
   • To encourage leadership potential
   • To give guidance on a special issue
   • To give insights that broaden the leader
   • To challenge the leader God-ward
   • To open a door to ministry opportunity

2. I cautioned very carefully about the negative preparation item. Why do you think I did this? Express in your own words the problem about using this process item alone without confirmation from other balanced guidance elements. If you are unclear on this, talk to an experienced leader and have that leader reflect on the lessons learned through negative processing times.
3. See if you can identify a word process item from your own experience for each of the various aspects mentioned in the

word processing definition. Determine which of those significantly affected your

- Guidance
- Commitment to the Lord
- Leadership
- Decision making
- Personal value system
- Spiritual formation
- Spiritual authority
- Ministry philosophy

A leader who is growing will be continually seeing word process items in many of these categories.

4. Interview a mature Christian leader concerning the word process item in general. Seek to identify several illustrations that were important in the leadership emergence of that leader. Identify categories affected, such as those named under question 3. Note *one* of these process items and describe the incident, the source of the word process item, the function affected, and the results. You will find this exercise to be of great benefit to you. It should create in you a sense of expectation for your own life concerning word processing.

5. According to James 1:2-4, what is a major thing God wants to do in a leader through a crisis?

6. Paul suggests in 2 Corinthians 1:3-4 and 2 Timothy 3:10-11 how God uses crises process items in a leader's life. What principles concerning crises do you see in these passages?

CHAPTER 7

THE DEEPENING LESSONS: LIFE MATURING PROCESSES

The Challenge/The Problem: It was good for me to be afflicted so that I might learn your decrees. *(Psalm 119:71)*

Awake, north wind, and come, south wind! Blow on my garden, that its fragrance may spread abroad. *(Song of Songs 4:16)*

Praise be to the God and Father of our Lord Jesus Christ, the Father of compassion and the God of all comfort, who comforts us in all our troubles, so that we can comfort those in any trouble with the comfort we ourselves have received from God. *(2 Corinthians 1:3-4)*

Watchman Nee had given himself fully to the Lord to be used in ministry. Yet he was diagnosed with tuberculosis. He grew steadily weaker. Rest away from ministry in a better climate seemed only a temporary answer. It was the best he could do. He was isolated. He was alone with God. Why had this happened to him?

He determined to make the best of it. During the long months of isolation, he thought seriously about how God develops spirituality in a Christian worker and wrote a book detailing his findings. He discovered that part of the development of spirituality includes what happens when a person faces isolation. He came to see this as a special time of deep inner-life growth, designed by God for him. He had been set aside by God, and he recognized it.

Watchman Nee was healed (a faith act started the healing) from tuberculosis and went on in his ministry. The ending could have been otherwise. In fact, throughout his lifetime, Watchman Nee repeatedly faced times of isolation due to ministry conflict, sickness, discipline, and persecution. He saw the hand of God shaping him through these experiences.[1] This attitude should be imitated by leaders today.

Leaders face unexpected situations involving sickness, crises, and conflict. Few see these times as part of necessary training for effective ministry. Perhaps you are facing some unusual trying time in your leadership. How should you perceive what is happening to you? How should any leader understand these times? Can they be appreciated as leadership emergence? I believe that such experiences are used by God to deepen character. This premise underlies my thinking and comes from observations of the life histories of many leaders.

MINISTRY FLOWS OUT OF BEING

Throughout a leader's life, God works to deepen character as well as to develop ministry skills. Earlier, discussing transition into ministry, I pointed out how God works on foundational character development (primarily integrity) through integrity checks, obedience checks, and word checks. God produces faithfulness through ministry tasks and early assignments. The "Luke 16:10 little-big principle" describes the effect of faithfulness. Integrity and faithfulness are basic to leadership. But they are only the beginning.

God does not stop working on character after moving someone into leadership. God continues to form character throughout the ministry of a leader. This development does not focus on testing to enter ministry, but on the relationship with God. The qualities of love, compassion, empathy, discernment, and others are deepened. Such qualities differentiate between a successful leader and a *mature* successful leader. This deepening of character and of the leader's relationship with God overflows into ministry itself. A leader who has learned major maturity lessons exercises ministry with a new level of spiritual authority. Do you want this kind of ministry? Then you need to be open to God's means of developing you for it.

God uses a cluster of processing items to develop character, the maturity cluster.[2] This chapter describes three of the most common process items from this cluster—isolation, conflict, and crises—along with two maturity patterns found in many lives.

The major lessons of this chapter are:

- Mature ministry flows from a mature character.
- A mature character comes through difficult processing.
- Many leaders go through such processing without realizing the benefit of it.
- Spiritual authority is not a goal but rather a byproduct.

THE REFLECTIVE EVALUATION PATTERN

Leaders are often busy people. They are preoccupied with many facets of life and ministry. Often they do not notice that they are not growing, particularly in spiritual formation. God often breaks into the leader's life at this point. A pattern can be identified, as shown in table 7-1 following.

Table 7-1 The Reflective Evaluation Pattern – Five Stages

STAGE	STAGE DESCRIPTION
1	God initiates intense processing to gain the attention of the leader.
2	The leader is forced to do serious reflection about ministry, life, and ultimate reality.
3	The leader does an evaluation that results in formative thinking and commitment to growth measures learned in the processing.
4	The leader experiences a renewed determination to know God more deeply.
5	God blesses the commitment and the renewed determination by deepening the relationship between Himself and the leader.

If a leader refuses to see the hand of God in this intense processing but instead blames circumstances or people, or rationalizes away the processing, then this pattern may not develop. It is the purpose of this chapter to alert you to this pattern so that you may more readily gain from it and not just go through it.

THE UPWARD DEVELOPMENT PATTERN

The upward development pattern occurs throughout a leader's life. It is a spiral of growth in being and doing. In each *being* cycle there is an increased depth of experiencing and knowing God; and in each *doing* cycle there is an increased depth of effective service for God. The final result of the upward development pattern is a fusion of being and doing. One typical expression of this pattern might be:

1. Being—conversion or sense of awareness of salvation
2. Doing—leadership commitment
3. Being—inner-life growth
4. Doing—development and use of ministry skills
5. Being—ministry philosophy becomes life-based (John 15:5 reality)
6. Union life (being and doing fused)[3]

Other examples of being and doing in the upward development pattern could be given. But the basic idea is that growth in being results in a higher level of doing, which in turn brings out a need for increased maturity in being, and so on. Stages 5 and 6 do not come quickly. Time is involved. Miles Stanford points this out in discussing the maturity processing of a great number of spiritual giants from past years.

We might consider some familiar names of believers whom God obviously brought to maturity and used for His glory — such as Pierson, Chapman, Tauler, Moody, Goforth, Mueller, Taylor, Watt, Trumbull, Meyer, Murray, Havergal, Guyon, Mabie, Gordon, Hyde, Mantle, McCheyne, McConkey, Deck, Paxson, Stoney, Saphir, Carmichael, and

Hopkins. The average for these was fifteen years after they entered their life work before they began to know the Lord Jesus as their Life, and ceased trying to work for Him and began allowing Him to be their All in all and do His work through them. This is not to discourage us in any way, but to help us to settle down with our sights on eternity, by faith "apprehending that for which also we are apprehended of Christ Jesus, pressing toward the mark for the prize of the high calling of God in Christ Jesus," Philippians 3:12b.[4]

From God's perspective, what He does to move us forward in this upward development pattern is essential. He has a long-term goal in mind. It may not seem so essential to us, especially as it is happening. Further, that process most likely (from our perspective) will require much time.

ISOLATION

During the tremendous financial pressures that arose in China during World War II, Watchman Nee did an uncharacteristic thing. He began to devote some of his time to a commercial venture involving the manufacture and distribution of synthetic medical supplies. His brother was a trained chemist and provided the technical expertise. Watchman provided the business know-how. Nee trained his "apostles" (and at this time there were quite a few who were involved in evangelism and church-planting activities) as sales representatives of the company. Today they would be called bi-vocational workers.

There is some controversy over why Nee did this. There were rumors that he was collaborating with the enemy. He was accused of being bored with his ministry. He was accused of setting his hand to the plow and then turning back. He was seen as having violated his "faith" principles, that is, to trust God to supply for His work. At the height of this conflict and controversy, the main leaders in the mother church at which Nee preached and taught asked him to discontinue his preaching and teaching ministry at the church. Believers were shocked at this action and supposed that there were probably more serious reasons than had been given. Nee's testimony was tarnished. The elders did not clarify the issue. Nor did Nee.

He did not feel released from the burden of supporting workers. The company took more and more of his time. It became a successful company. During this time, Nee's giving to kingdom work was substantial, but he was set aside from ministry. He never defended his action nor sought to straighten out erroneous rumors. Several years later the elders came to Nee and apologized for their action. He was reinstated. But in the years that the processing went on, Nee was deeply tried as to his character.

As I studied Amy Carmichael's life with Reid and Van Dalen's analysis of it, I saw that isolation processing was a significant factor that deeply affected her leadership ability. Reid and Van Dalen identified several different kinds of isolation in her life, including one incident of isolation by self-choice, an experience forced by the missionary community, and one brought on by an accident.

Isolation by self-choice[5] is the least threatening of all isolation experiences. The person perceives some control over the situation. In 1890, Robert Wilson invited Amy to come to live with him in Broughton Grange where his estate was. He had been first a divine contact, then a mentor for her, and had quite an influence on her spiritual formation. He was quite old at this time and had only a relatively short time to live.

At the time, Amy was in the throes of her first ministry, with factory girls. This had helped Amy to discover apostolic gifts, teaching gifts, and mercy gifts and to use them in the early stages of their development. At first, Amy hesitated due to her feelings about leaving her ministry. Then she chose to come and serve Robert Wilson.

For three years, she was forced to be quiet and "sit at the feet" of others, such as Hudson Taylor, Theodore Monad, F. B. Meyer, C. A. Fox, and Robert Wilson himself. Wilson had an extensive network among Christian leaders who were influential at regional, national, and international levels. Amy was exposed to these leaders, saw them model Christian leadership, and heard their testimonies of what they had learned about God and ministry. Reid and Van Dalen comment on the effects of this isolation processing:

> This time of isolation from ministry prepared her for subsequent experiences when due to ill health Amy Carmichael was "laid aside." She grew in love for the Word and in her prayer life. An avid reader, Amy's life was also influenced by the writings of the scholars, preachers, missionaries and theologians of that era. She also became acquainted with the Quaker ways through Robert Wilson's influence. These influenced her life and ministry profoundly.[6]

Robert Wilson's mentoring, networking, and provision of literary materials during this isolation provided the stimulus for great growth, both in spiritual formation and in ministerial formation.

In 1895, Amy arrived in Bangalore, India, as a missionary with the Church of England Zenana Missionary Society. Her assignment was to serve as an evangelist to patients and their families at a mission hospital. The first year was lonely for her. Reid and Van Dalen describe the sense of isolation:

> The first year there was very lonely for her, and most difficult as Amy felt like "a fish out of water" [Houghton 1953:89] among other missionaries whose burdens and concerns were so unlike hers, but this year was part of her preparation for a life-work, too.[7]

This first year was one of isolation from the other missionaries in spirit and in ministry goals.[8] Though physically there, Amy was isolated psychologically from the missionary community to which she had been assigned. This created a deep loneliness that forced Amy to turn wholly to God — a habit that sustained her through many lonely times to come (as a result of death, disappointment, and physical weakness).[9]

In 1931, Amy had an accident in which her leg was broken and her ankle shattered. She was confined, for the most part, to her room. This time of isolation provided Amy with a quiet sanctuary. She spent much time in prayer. She wrote several books. A second accident in 1948 confined her to her room and bed entirely. For nearly twenty years Amy was in isolation processing. During these years, God provided the words of comfort that filled her books and letters, comforting those in pain and suffering. God also stimulated her to share the lessons she learned from her increasingly important prayer time.

One way that God forces a leader into reflective evaluation and into a "being" stage of the upward development pattern involves isolation. It is one of the most effective means for maturing a leader. Several times in a leader's lifetime, the leader may be set aside from his normal ministry. Causes may include crises, disciplinary action, providential circumstances (such as war, oppressive government action, illness), or self-choice. The thrust of the processing is on the recognition that the isolation is God's work and that it is a call to a deeper relationship and experience of God.

I define *isolation* process items as those in which a leader is separated from normal involvement, yet in the context in which ministry has been occurring, usually for an extended time, and experiences some aspect of relationship to God in a new or deeper way.[10] Isolation is often used by God to teach important leadership lessons that could not be learned while experiencing the pressures of normal ministry context.

Table 7-2 gives a number of examples of possible kinds of isolation that may occur during the Life Maturing phase and also gives possible resulting lessons.

Table 7-2 Isolation Processes — Kinds and Results

ISOLATION TYPE	LESSONS OBSERVED
Sickness	Dependence upon God Knowledge of supernatural healing Urgency to accomplish God's work Deepening of inner life through intercessory prayer
Prison	Dependence upon God Increased use of mental faculties, especially memory Submission to God's will Indirect influence through modeling and a widened intercessory life
Personality Conflict and Organizational Pressures	Submission to God Submission to spiritual authority Non-vindication of one's spiritual authority Value of others' perspectives Dependence upon God
Self-Choice for Renewal	New perspective on ministry Rekindled sense of destiny Power of prayer Inner convictions from Word Spiritual guidance
Self-Choice for Education, Training, or Transition	New perspective on ministry Rekindled sense of destiny Openness to new ideas and change Dependency upon the wider body of Christ Broadening through exposure to others

CONFLICT

In my travels, I have been particularly amazed at how much conflict there is in churches and in parachurch ministries. Leaders are constantly dealing with conflict. I would guess that most leaders spend the majority of their time and energy dealing with conflict. Here, I am focusing on conflict as a means of developing character.

The *conflict* process item includes those instances in a leader's life-history in which God uses conflict—whether personal or ministry related—to develop the leader's faith, dependence upon God, and insights relating to personal life and ministry.[11] Jeremiah's personal conflict items have to do with his self-image, the persecution he faced, and so on. His ministry conflict included the various tasks or assignments that he received and the reaction to his ministry.

Conflicts are complex situations that involve other process items as well. Through this processing, leaders learn lessons concerning:

- The nature of conflict
- Ways to resolve conflict
- Ways to avoid conflict
- Ways to creatively use conflict
- How to identify conflict with God's processing
- Conflict as the stimulus for other processing

For maturity purposes the most important thing learned is awareness of one's own character, its strengths and weaknesses. God will use conflict to point out areas of character needing modification, to point out or confirm areas of strength, or to point out areas of character entirely missing. Personal conflict can deal with inner fears, lack of self-image, fear of failure, guilt, and so on. The emphasis is not just on the insights learned about conflict, but also on the intended development of character orchestrated by God in those conflict situations.

Conflict, though fraught with negative implications, has its positive creative side, which is very important. Most leaders do not benefit from the positive side. Humanly speaking, it is bad enough to go through conflict processing. But it is even worse to go through it and not profit from it. Conflict is a common means for God to stimulate a leader in terms of the reflective and upward development maturity patterns.

CRISES

A crisis is a time of increased pressures due to numerous situations, such as:

- Threatened loss of life, property, or way of life
- Conflict of various kinds

- Situations requiring urgent change
- Inner turmoil
- Sickness
- The need to see God's character vindicated
- The need to have God's guidance or special intervention
- Persecution

These human situations are often used by God to test a leader and to teach him dependence on God. Consider the overall effect. A leader faces a major crisis. The leader sees that his only hope is in God. He experiences God in a new way in the crisis. He sees God as the One who can and does meet him in this major experience of life. Not only does God meet the leader in the situation, but He does so with a solution that is tailor-made for the leader.

The overall effect is a more confident leader. It provides a landmark experience that will affect this person's ability to lead others. His followers in turn sense a new spiritual authority in him. It is this ability to learn lessons in crisis events that makes this important to the understanding of leadership emergence. Learning lessons in these experiences is the goal. Spiritual authority is a most important byproduct.

Crises process items are those special intense pressures in human situations that are used by God to test and teach dependence on Him. A *life-crisis* process item refers to a crisis characterized by intense pressure in which the meaning and purpose of life are searched out, with a result that the leader has experienced God in a new way as the Source of life, the Sustainer of life, and the Focus of life.

Christians in general and leaders in particular react to crisis situations in one of two ways. Crisis processing either drives them deeper into the presence of God or drives them away from God. Identifying this process item will help you recognize its major function, drawing you into a deeper dependence on God both as your source of life and as your motivation to live and minister.

In 2 Corinthians 1:8-11, Paul describes valuable insights he learned about God and life, resulting from life crises:

> We do not want you to be uninformed, brothers, about the hardships we suffered in the province of Asia. We were under great pressure, far beyond our ability to endure, so that we despaired even of life. Indeed, in our hearts we felt the sentence of death. But this happened that we might not rely on ourselves but on God, who raises the dead. He has delivered us from such a deadly peril, and he will deliver us. On him we have set our hope that he will continue to deliver us, as you help us by your prayers. Then many will give thanks on our behalf for the gracious favor granted us in answer to the prayers of many.

Notice that Paul does not dwell on the process but on the deep lessons he learned from God in it. First, crises force a person to see the need for utter dependence upon God. Second, prayer is part of the process that God's people use to bring about deliverance. Finally, deliverance in answer to prayer should bring about a closure in which God is praised by those prayer participants.

In 2 Corinthians 4:7-12, Paul points out how this deepens one's understanding of God's power and of the leader as a channel of that power.

> We have this treasure in jars of clay to show that this all-surpassing power is from God and not from us. We are hard pressed on every side, but not crushed; perplexed, but not in despair; persecuted, but not abandoned; struck down, but not destroyed. We always carry around in our body the death of Jesus, so that the life of Jesus may also be revealed in our body. For we who are alive are always being given over to death for Jesus' sake, so that his life may be revealed in our mortal body. So then, death is at work in us, but life is at work in you.

Life and death situations certainly qualify, for they cause reflection on the deeper meaning in life and point to the possibility of the termination of life goals. These in turn drive one into deeper dependence upon God and the desire to do and be what God wants in whatever time remains. Life-crisis items are not limited to life and death situations. They can be any kind of crisis that causes reflection on ultimate purpose and a deepening of one's relationship with God, seeing that relationship as more important than any of life's attainments.

Recognition of a need for a deeper relationship with God and experiencing that relationship is central to this process item. The experience itself is a major power resource for spiritual authority.

SUMMARY

Quality leadership does not come easily. It requires time, experience, and repeated instances of maturity processing. Mature ministry flows from a mature character, formed in the graduate school of life. Ministry can be successful through giftedness alone; but a leader whose ministry skills outstrip his character formation will eventually falter. A mature, successful ministry flows from one who has both ministry skills and character that has been mellowed, developed, and ripened by God's maturity processing. Character formation is fundamental. Ministry flows out of being.

All leaders go through conflict, crises, and some isolation processing. You will too. But not all recognize its immense value for their long-term ministry. Will you? It is difficult to go through maturity processing even if you understand its positive long-term values; it is worse to go through it without this perspective. I hope you will desire to see the sovereign hand of God in it.

Spiritual authority is not a goal but rather a byproduct. It is a delegated authority that comes from God. It is the major power base of a leader who has learned God's lessons during maturity processing. Leaders have various power bases that give credence to their ability. Spiritual authority comes out of experience with God. A leader does not seek spiritual authority; a leader seeks to know God. Maturity processing enhances this desire to know God. Spiritual authority results from a leader's experience with God.

A leader cannot avoid maturity processing; it will come. A wise leader will benefit not only from direct personal experience, but will also benefit from vicarious learning. A perceptive leader learns to benefit from the maturity lessons of others. This greatly speeds a leader's development.

By understanding the purpose of maturity processing, its major patterns, and major process items, you should be able to perceive what God wants to do in your own life and in the lives of those you are influencing.

I want to close this chapter with a personal experience of maturity processing. It occurred over forty years ago. For about eight years I never shared it. It seemed too personal. But now enough time has gone by that I can share it without too strong an emotional bias. The process lasted for about a year. It was a complex situation that involved elements of conflict, crisis, isolation, and word processing. The isolation processing was the significant part of the processing.

I was on the executive leadership team of my mission. We were a close team that met weekly for prayer, sharing, and problem solving. We had been together as a team for several years. My role on the team, as I saw it, was that of creative facilitator. I constantly introduced new ideas and challenged the leadership. As I look back on it, I was sometimes pushy and maybe a bit abrupt and abrasive. I constantly analyzed situations and gave my solutions as if they were the only right ones. Frequently they were. (My opinion, of course!)

The group was led to an important decision concerning a new ministry direction for one of the group's members. It came as a result of a time set aside for praying and evaluating. In my mind that session was like the one described in Acts 13, where the Holy Spirit gave the word concerning Barnabas and Saul. I had felt that the Holy Spirit led us as a leadership team to that conclusion. The group as a whole felt the conclusion was right. This was a strong consensus decision. I saw it as solving a series of problems I had seen over the past several years.

Later that decision was reversed. I saw some inconsistencies in this. What bothered me concerned our ability as a team to discern the will of

God. It had seemed so clear. If we vacillated on this, then I didn't see how we could be certain on any future decision. How could we ever be certain that we as the top decision-making group in the mission were doing the right thing? My style of pushing on this issue probably lacked finesse (to put it mildly). I pushed hard for the original decision.

At a group meeting, one of the members admonished me strongly. He asked the group to remove me from the leadership team. I was totally surprised by this move. I had no warning of it. I had not been confronted privately first. I hadn't had an inkling that I was a problem to him, and in fact had been a problem to him for several years. What followed was a most distressful time for me. The discussion went back and forth.

Two items from that confrontive meeting stood out to me. I was accused of being very inflexible. There was a prophetic word (at the time I did not recognize it as that) that indicated that perhaps the mission did not have a position that would allow me to develop my potential. Perhaps I should move on. Both of these items struck me hard and caused me to have much meditation and reflection in the months that ensued.

The result was that I was removed from the executive leadership team. I was also taken off the board, which met annually. I was asked not to come into the office anymore, to give distance between myself and the group. I was told to work out of my home. I could continue my research, writing, workshops, seminars, and consulting on our fields; but I was banished from the office and from having any influence on the leadership team.

So I began to work out of my home. What hurt was that people in the office were not told of this nor was there any explanation to them. My wife continued to work in the office. It was hard on her. Everyone knew something had happened but did not know what. Of course, people may have imagined things that were much worse than the reality.

During this time I had been studying the life of Watchman Nee — his biography as well as his book on spiritual authority. I saw in this incident a lesson from God to teach me about submission to authority. I saw that spiritual authority was delegated from God. It was His responsibility to defend it. I saw how Watchman Nee had submitted on several occasions. He did not defend. I decided to take that approach, sensing that the Lord was teaching me.

At the same time we were studying Romans in our church. Just after the discipline incident, we came to Romans 6. The pastor's teaching was excellent as usual. The first hour of our service was given to worship and exposition of the Word; the second hour was given to application of what had been taught. Normally this meant breaking up into small groups to share.

That Sunday the pastor passed out small pieces of paper shaped like tombstones. On them were these words:

Here lies

August 14, 1977
. . . obedient unto death.

Figure 7-1 Personal Application Tombstone — Romans 6

Each of us was supposed to fill in his name, and then list what we felt God was pointing out in our lives to which we needed to die. We were told to write on the back if we needed more room. After we finished writing, we were to share what we had written. It was an emotional moment for me. I knew it was more than just an ordinary Sunday morning.

I sensed that God was pulling together what had happened to me and focusing it to teach me something important. I had been brought through the conflict and discipline. I had been forced to reevaluate my ministry and my past relationships at the office. I had done much thinking.

On the front I wrote in my name and the words "evaluation of life and ministry." As I was turning it over to write on the back, it came to me in a flash: *I was inflexible*. It was as if the Lord spoke to me Himself. I wrote on the back, "Die to the right to be right."

I shared with the church how God had met me and the important lesson I had learned. I have that tombstone in my Bible today. Occasionally, I get it out to remind myself. Every now and then my wife reminds me too, "Don't you have a tombstone somewhere that says you don't have to be right?"

That was a pivotal moment in my leadership emergence. I saw that my drive to analyze things and point out the "right action" had bothered the top Leader all along. That was a moment of freedom for me.

I still have a tendency to discern situations and arrive at analyses. I still have a tendency to feel I am usually right on assessing these situations. My giftedness as well as my experience and personality are all involved in this tendency. But I don't have to prove it to others. I don't have to continually correct people who say and do things that are different from what I think.

During the nearly twelve months of this isolation I became depressed. This is not a natural expression of my personality. In fact, it is the only time in my life that it has happened. It is uncharacteristic for me even to be discouraged. But the isolation and the apparent unfairness of the situation seemed to have this effect.

Each morning in my quiet time I read a sermon from George Morrison. His exhortive style that majors on encouragement and comfort spoke to me morning after morning. Finally, after about three months of his ministry, I came out of the depression. It was a tremendous experience for me that has helped me understand others who have tendencies toward discouragement and depression.

I never again worked in the mission office. This isolation experience was the major turning point for me. It deeply affected my personality. What were some of the lessons I learned?

First, I learned that God will vindicate spiritual authority. I never defended my action or even talked about the situation—except to my wife and to the person to whom I was accountable during the isolation period. Even in those conversations, I never attacked the group member who had admonished me. I did not complain about the decision. I saw this situation as something that God knew I needed. I was cast upon God in a new dependent relationship. God did vindicate my spiritual authority.

Second, the prophetic utterance given during the meeting proved to be true. About four years after this incident, God moved me into a new role. Some of what had happened was negative preparation to release me and free me for my new role. I would have never chosen the direction that opened to me if this processing had not occurred.

Third, I learned some organizational lessons. People in power usually win whether right on a given issue or not. I also learned that I needed to be taught about leadership style if I was to be a successful change agent in the future.

Fourth, I learned something about my character. I was a very flexible person as long as I was calling the shots. I had all kinds of creative ideas. But I was very inflexible when someone else differed from me. And it is on just such issues that flexibility is really measured. The statement that I was very inflexible proved to be true; but it took some hardy processing for me to see it.

I consider this experience to be the turning point in my leadership emergence. I thank God for the lessons He taught me in it. I can look back and see the providential weaving of many strands that led to that conflict, crisis, and isolation. The passage in Romans was the capstone to the entire process. A year of being set aside from ministry can be a painful thing, especially when your reputation is at stake. But what is a year compared to release for a more effective mature ministry in the future for as long as the Lord allows me to minister?

HOW ABOUT YOU?

Perhaps you have gone through some maturity processing but, at the time, didn't realize how much God intended it for developing you. The following exercises may help you reflect on some of these experiences and see afresh the hand of God in it.

1. Analyze several conflict process items as they relate to your experience. Perhaps previously you saw them only as problems and didn't realize that God was in them, working to develop you. This will help you reflect on these conflicts with new perspectives. Describe lessons that you can now see (faith, dependence upon God, revelation of insights about yourself, and so on).

2. Someone has said, "In a crisis, we are what we really are!" How we react in the crisis is often more important than our solving the crisis. A major crisis that David faced was the revolt of Absalom (see 2 Samuel 15:13–17:22). David, for all of his faults at this time of life, responded well. What was the major response of David in the crisis? (See Psalm 3 to pick up the inner-life response of David.)

3. Paul suggests how God uses crises process items in a leader's life (see 2 Corinthians 1:3-4; 2 Timothy 3:10-11). What principles concerning crisis do you see in these passages?

CHAPTER 8

INTEGRATING THE LESSONS OF LIFE: TOWARD A MINISTRY PHILOSOPHY

The Challenge/The Problem: Blessed is the man who finds wisdom, the man who gains understanding. *(Proverbs 3:13)*

John, William, and I were sitting in my living room discussing a ministry problem that was facing John. John had requested time to talk over some items that were bothering him in his church situation. His friend William had about four years of experience as a senior pastor. John had been a lay leader almost that long.

John's problem was common. There had been a recent transition in the church. The former head pastor had moved on to another ministry; a new pastor had since taken over. John had been involved in the church under the former pastor, who had communicated a sense of direction to the church. His vision for the church involved training young leaders and freeing those young leaders to serve in the church. He had articulated his vision and the reasoning behind it to the church. He was decisive, a risk taker.

John was growing in leadership skills. He had gained experience and skill while leading a small group. In fact, he had been assigned to head all small groups in the church. He had been in the church as long or longer than any of the present members.

The new pastor was not like the old one. He was very careful and deliberate. He was more cautious, but also indecisive. He was not likely to recognize innovative emergent leaders and free them for ministry. He did not communicate a clear vision to the church. People were no longer sure of the direction of the church. Folks who went to the pastor and asked for permission to do a specific kind of ministry did not get answers.

John was caught in the middle. He knew the old philosophy and operated under it. He saw that the new pastor was not operating under the former pastor's philosophy. People in the church frequently came to John for advice, when in his opinion they should have been going to the pastor. The new pastor had legitimate authority due to his position, but John was increasingly being recognized as the spiritual leader. As he described his situation, he asked me what he should do. He was frustrated, feeling the lack of direction. He didn't know what to say to the people who came to him for advice.

The problem was twofold. John did not want to usurp the spiritual authority of the pastor. What was he to do when people came to him who should have gone to the pastor? Under the former pastor the church had been clearly moving to carry out a plan (communicated as if it were God's plan) that reflected the ministry philosophy of the pastor. Under the present pastor people were not sure whether that old plan was still in effect.

I commented on the spiritual authority problem first. Before I could comment on the problem of indecisiveness, William interrupted. He had been carefully listening to John. He also knew the church and the new pastor. His comment showed wisdom beyond his young years.

William did not attack the indecisiveness directly. He pointed out that it was a symptom of a bigger problem. The new pastor did not have a clear philosophy of ministry. He had no framework in which to judge the requests that were coming to him from potential leaders. He pointed out that the former pastor did have a clear philosophy of ministry. When people had come to the former pastor with similar requests, he almost always saw immediately whether the proposed ministry fit with the philosophy of ministry of the church and the five-year plan that had been developed in line with that philosophy. If the ministry fit, even if it was new and different and not on the planning board, it would usually be given the green light. If it did not fit, the pastor would explain why he was turning it down. Sometimes it was a matter of timing; perhaps later it could be done. Sometimes it was a matter of not fitting. When that was the case, the former pastor would help the person find a church situation where that ministry would fit.

William had hit the nail right on the head. I mused to myself, "Would that all pastors had a clear understanding of their ministry philosophy, a framework through which they could screen ideas and make decisions." It is just such a framework that allows a leader to influence people toward God's purposes.

All leaders have a ministry philosophy. It flows out of their shared experiences with God. As leaders experience process items, whether in terms of spiritual formation (character building) or ministerial formation (ministry skills), they learn from them. These lessons form a growing reservoir of wisdom that leaders use in the future. Some lessons are more explicit; others are implicit.

I learned a number of important lessons in my early ministry processing. These lessons usually became pithy value statements. Because I valued these ideas, I began to develop principles that flowed from them, and I consciously developed life patterns and ministry patterns that were consistent with them.

A MINISTRY PHILOSOPHY [1]

In early one-on-one Bible studies I learned that I needed to apply what I was learning or I would forget it. *Use it or lose it!* arose out of this repeated learning experience. Later, after studying spiritual gifts, I saw that this desire to apply truth came not only from my personality but also from my spiritual gift of exhortation. This simple principle has shaped all of my ministry. A corollary of this, *Learn a little! Use it a lot!* expresses a balanced learning philosophy.

From early experiences with discipling and in small groups in my church in Reynoldsburg, Ohio, I saw that for me *ministry has to be personal.* I saw the power of small groups and the dynamic of one-on-one ministry. These ministry structures were life-changing. Yet not all people were willing to accept my personal ministry. I learned to be selective in those whom I discipled in-depth. From these insights I developed a further specific principle: *I will give as much as I can to one who chooses to have it.* If a person really wants my help I will be available to give it as long as he responds.

When someone had just made a personal decision for Christ, I learned to get that person to share it. *Expression deepens impression!* came out of these experiences. This principle was applied more broadly in my teaching. When people were forced to articulate what they were learning, they were taking a step of commitment toward what they were expressing.

Through parables, Jesus forced people to learn by engaging their minds. He did not hand teaching to them on a silver platter. I learned in home Bible classes that *truth discovered by the learner sticks longer.* Wherever I could, I would lead people toward truth but let them discover it.

Frank Sells imparted to me one of his ministry philosophy ideas: *Be as clear as the Bible is clear; nothing less, nothing more, nothing else.* This principle has forced me many times to back off from dogmatic statements or requirements.

Later, as I learned about organizational leadership, I discovered that *in a power conflict the leader with higher power will usually win regardless of rightness of issue,* and *a person convinced against his will is of the same opinion still.* Organizational change without ownership is treacherous.

I think you can get a feel for what I mean by value statements, principles, and underlying assumptions, which form a ministry philosophy. When I did identify a lesson and was able to put it into a concise statement, that lesson usually gained added significance and was applied more consistently and widely in my ministry.

Lessons learned in life situations become underlying assumptions that guide leaders. They become part of a ministry philosophy. All leaders operate from a ministry philosophy. Let me repeat. All leaders operate from a ministry philosophy. However, that philosophy may not be adequate, or it may be simplistic. It may be implicit and not explicit. Effective leaders can articulate much of their ministry philosophy.

The result of leadership emergence is a leader in whom God has developed character and ministry skills, who has learned some lessons in this processing, and who uses these lessons to shape his influence and to accomplish God's purposes. *Ministry philosophy* is the result of leadership emergence — the ideas, values, and principles whether implicit or explicit that a leader uses as guidelines for decision making, for exercising influence, or for evaluating ministry.

A growing awareness of one's ministry philosophy leads to more effective leadership. At lower levels of leadership the philosophy will be more simple and specific to the ministry situation. At higher levels[2] the philosophy will include general, umbrella-like guidelines, as well as specific guidelines.

One of the striking characteristics seen in effective leaders is their drive to learn.[3] They learn from all kinds of sources. They learn from Scripture. They are pressed by their situations to see new truth in the Scriptures and in the situations themselves. They learn about their own uniqueness. They build on the natural abilities they have. They acquire skills needed by the challenges of the situations they face. They learn to use their spiritual gifts. The processing, which I have been describing in the chapters leading up to this one, forms a major source of lessons for effective leaders with a learning posture. Let me state two observations about what I have seen in leaders who want to learn.

Effective leaders, at all levels of leadership, maintain a learning posture throughout life.

Effective leaders who are productive over a lifetime have a dynamic ministry philosophy that evolves continually from the interplay of three major factors: biblical dynamics, personal gifts, and situational dynamics.

I believe it is this ability to weave lessons into a philosophy that makes leaders effective. One strong indicator of leadership is a learning posture that reflects itself in a dynamic ministry philosophy.

Leaders must develop a ministry philosophy that simultaneously honors biblical leadership values, embraces the challenges of the times in which they live, and fits their unique gifts and personal development if they expect to be productive over a whole lifetime.

I'll first comment on the three dynamics involved in this statement.[4] Then I'll discuss the ministry philosophy evolutionary pattern, principles as the bedrock from which philosophy is drawn, and some overarching guidelines for ministry philosophy. Finally, I will define the concept of a leadership value and point out that expression of a ministry philosophy starts with concrete identification of some leadership values.

HONORS BIBLICAL LEADERSHIP VALUES

The Bible is the leadership anchor. As a Christian leader, above all else, I should be concerned that my leadership has something that is unique. While there are many things that are common with secular leadership, there should be this one difference: A Christian leader bases values, methodology, motivation, and goals on what God has revealed in Scripture. The Bible is the standard for evaluation of a Christian leader.

The Bible does not speak directly to all issues of leadership—when it does speak there is freedom. It often gives general ideas or specific examples from which a leader must be led by the Holy Spirit to applications. But it is always the tether and yardstick to which a Christian leader goes for fundamental guidance.

In the early stages, through specific word checks and general word processing, God will inculcate lessons and principles. These principles later become part of the leader's ministry philosophy. As the years go by, a growing leader will add other biblically derived assumptions and values so that there is a broad framework, even though implicit, that guides leadership.

These assumptions will affect relationships with followers, standards for ethical conduct, guidelines for evaluation of ministry, life goals, and a host of other issues. Most of these assumptions will be learned early in the ministry and will change very little over the years. Through maturity, ministry discernment, and destiny processing, new ones will be added and old ones clarified or modified slightly. Life's experiences give new perspective on the Scriptures and force one to see things not previously observed. Even the biblical element of a ministry philosophy is dynamic and changing over the years, though much less so than the leadership growth and gift development of the leader.

EMBRACES THE CHALLENGES OF THE TIMES IN WHICH THEY LIVE

There are three basal elements of leadership: leader, followers, and situation. A leader should learn from the changes involved in leadership. New ministry will change the followers. Even where the followers stay the same, relatively speaking, the current situation is always changing rapidly. The change in followers and situations brings with it new potential for learning. Lessons emerge. These life lessons will affect many assumptions crucial to the leader's philosophy. Frequently these lessons will have biblical implications. They will be grounded in assumptions previously learned from Scripture but now adapted to new situations. Often they will be new and will force more Scripture searching. This leads to new discovery of truth. Occasionally the new situation will not be covered by biblical revelation and will require Spirit-led confirmation either individually or through some part of the body of Christ. The challenge of the times forces a ministry philosophy to be a dynamic changing entity and not a static, perfect guideline for all times.

FITS A LEADER'S UNIQUE GIFTS AND PERSONAL DEVELOPMENT

A ministry philosophy must be tailored to fit each leader. The biblical values of a ministry philosophy can have much in common among many leaders. Leaders who have common situations will find much in common in their ministry philosophies. But that part of a leader's ministry philosophy that depends on the leader's own gifts will differ greatly from other leaders.

The giftedness set includes natural abilities, acquired skills, and spiritual gifts. Over the years, God refines an individual in the giftedness development pattern. This involves seeing the strengths of natural abilities and how they relate to ministry effectiveness. It involves identification and development of spiritual gifts, eventually recognizing a gift-cluster and roles that will best enhance that gift-cluster. It also involves the acquisition of skills that enhance both natural abilities and spiritual gifts and that are needed in available ministries. It is easy to see that a ministry philosophy will change as a leader discovers his own identity in terms of giftedness.

A ministry philosophy must be dynamic because it embraces dynamic elements. There is the core that changes relatively little. But there is a larger periphery, involving God's continued development of a leader. This learning involves dynamic elements that change with the leader's personal growth in the Word, in leadership, and in the ongoing discovery of giftedness.

In essence, one develops a ministry philosophy by seeing the lessons of life and applying them to ministry. Awareness of how the philosophy arises can be a step toward deliberate recognition, development, and use.

THE EVOLUTIONARY PATTERN

Ministry philosophy can be a complex subject. It has been helpful to use the following three-stage model as I study and evaluate how various leaders develop ministry philosophy.

- Stage 1: Osmosis—leaders learn implicit philosophy experientially

- Stage 2: Baby steps—leaders discover explicit philosophy through experience and reflection
- Stage 3: Maturity—leaders formulate and articulate their ministry philosophy to others along with their own retrospective reflection

Young leaders operate with an implicit philosophy derived from the sponsoring group of which they are a part. If you are a leader just starting out and you begin your ministry on a campus under the auspices of a parachurch organization, then the underlying ministry philosophy, whether known or not, will be imbibed by you as you fulfill the ministry tasks and assignments that come. Personal lessons, which affect ministry philosophy, are learned via critical incidents. Both ministerial and spiritual formation will be involved in these lessons. Positive lessons will reinforce assumptions, which then become part of the ministry philosophy. Negative lessons will create avoidance patterns. We use these lessons as we are given new ministry tasks and assignments.

Process items that involve particularly critical incidents cause us to think. We recognize that one of our assumptions is questionable or does not appear to work. We question and evaluate some of our implicit philosophy. One function of the reflective evaluation pattern (described in the preceding chapter) involves just such questioning. We see discrepancies between "what is" and "what ought to be" when we train others. We are often forced to see this, either by our own thinking as we design training, or by the people we train (who do not necessarily operate from the same assumptions). We discover some of the assumptions of our ministry philosophy. This leads to a better understanding as well as modification of our ministry philosophy. At this point, our ministry philosophy is represented by some explicit assumptions, although the majority are still implicit.

When a leader senses the need for more accountability, this leads to ministry evaluation, which in turn forces the process of identifying what motivates and controls ministry. The key ideas of this preliminary transition are control and accountability. The leader sees that direction for ministry needs to be specific and should be more controlled. Previous direction for ministry has been situationally controlled. Events have directed the emergence of a ministry philosophy. The ministry philosophy is increasingly becoming explicit

Toward the end of ministry, a philosophy emerges by looking back over a lifetime. Motivation for this involves passing on to others from what has been learned. This necessitates careful formulation.

This may seem very abstract to you now. Most people in positions of leadership are not philosophers but are doers. They want something to help them "do their ministry." Let me give you my practical guidelines for developing a ministry philosophy. Make the most of the lessons you learn as God develops you. Principles are the backbone of any philosophy. You don't need to have a systematic theoretical grasp of ideas for most specific direct ministry, just some principles that you can apply.

GUIDELINES FOR DEVELOPING A MINISTRY PHILOSOPHY

Here are three guidelines to help you develop a ministry philosophy:

1. Start by learning to identify principles.
2. Group principles into similar categories.
3. Look for obvious categories that are absent.

Most people probably only need to do step 1. Most lay leaders will need to learn only to identify principles and apply them directly to their ministries. But full-time leaders whose sphere of influence continues to expand and those who get involved in organizational leadership will need steps 2 and 3.

IDENTIFYING PRINCIPLES[5]

Principles refer to generalized statements of truth that are observations drawn from specific instances of ministry. Many principles of truth flow directly from the lessons in various process items. Reflect back to identify past lessons, and be more sensitive to current lessons. Start with a statement describing the lesson you see. Expect such beginning statements to be altered. When God is trying to teach me a lesson, He will do so through many means. Important lessons are usually repeated. From these repeated efforts I formulate and refine the lesson.

When I discover a value or principle, I see if it has biblical authority. If I find generalized teaching containing the principle, I feel more certain about applying it to my own life and asserting it as a leadership principle for others. I place principles on the certainty continuum:

Suggestions	Guidelines	Requirements
Tentative Observations		Absolutes
Very Little Authority -		Great Authority

Figure 8-1 Certainty Continuum

This continuum is based on two ideas: (1) Principles are observations along a continuum. (2) We can teach or use with increasing authority those principles that are further to the right on the continuum.

Absolutes refer to replicated truth in leadership situations across cultures without restrictions (for example, observable in all leadership situations). *Guidelines* represent truth that is generally replicated in most situations but not necessarily in all (observable in many). *Suggestions* refer to truth observed in some situations. *Suggestions* are the most tentative—use with caution. *Guidelines* are more firm and have evidence for broader application. *Absolutes* are principles that evince God's authoritative backing for all leaders everywhere. The Bible is the prime source for determining whether a statement is a suggestion, guideline, or absolute. The principle, *Be as clear as the Bible is clear*, underlies this continuum and forces me to see what the Bible actually says about lessons I learn in life.

GROUPING PRINCIPLES

When beginning to formulate a ministry philosophy, two major categories cover most possible statements. Some ministry philosophy statements deal with personal character development. Other ministry philosophy statements deal with actually doing the ministry. The ministry philosophy statements mentioned previously would fit under these two categories:

Category 1: Ministry Philosophy Applying to Character

- Use it or lose it!
- I will give as much as I can to one who chooses to have it.
- Be as clear as the Bible is clear; nothing less, nothing more, nothing else.

Category 2: Ministry Philosophy Applying to Doing the Ministry

- Use it or lose it!
- Ministry has to be personal.
- Expression deepens impression!
- Truth discovered by the learner sticks longer.
- Be as clear as the Bible is clear; nothing less, nothing more, nothing else.
- In a power conflict the leader with higher power will usually win regardless of rightness of issue.
- A person convinced against his will is of the same opinion still.

Some statements will apply to both of these categories (for example, *Use it or lose it!*). They affect character as well as ministry. As you look at principles, values, and lessons that God has taught, you may identify more than just two categories. Grouping is a helpful first step toward integrating a ministry philosophy.

LOOK FOR OBVIOUS CATEGORIES THAT ARE ABSENT

For those who have leadership responsibilities other than direct ministry, additional categories may be helpful.[6] The following list may point out areas in your ministry philosophy that either need beefing up or need to become more explicit. These items apply to higher-level leadership with responsibilities beyond direct ministry. These leaders are responsible for the generic leadership functions. These functions can be helpful categories for identifying principles.

Table 8-1 Eight Generic Leadership Functions

FUNCTION	TOPIC LABEL OF GENERIC LEADERSHIP FUNCTION
1	Motivation Toward Vision
2	Leadership Selection and Training
3	Decision Making
4	Crisis Resolution[7]
5	Routine Problem Solving
6	Coordinating with Superiors
7	Coordinating with Peers
8	Coordinating with Subordinates

Function 1 deals with the central task of leadership—getting guidance from God and motivating followers toward that vision. Your track record in guidance processing (see chapter 6) will be a helpful source of ministry philosophy principles fitting that category.

A major responsibility of leadership is recognition of rising leaders, their selection, and development. The Bible has a lot to say concerning this category. Process items dealing with the ministry training stage (see chapter 4) will be a helpful source for philosophy statements.

Leaders regularly face decisions. Discernment processing, seen in the ministry phase, will be the single most helpful source of philosophy for this important function (see chapter 5 for details).

Functions 4 and 5 are similar. Conflicts and crises teach a leader lessons of life that aid in performing these functions (see especially chapter 5).

Functions 6, 7, and 8 deal with relationships. Most leaders face repeated disappointments in this area. Lessons from discernment and relationship processing form the basis for a ministry philosophy (see especially chapter 5).

PASTOR JOHNSON

At the beginning of this chapter, I discussed a case of difference in pastoral leadership—a former pastor with an explicit ministry philosophy contrasted with an implicit one. I went to the former pastor, Johnson, after this discussion, and interviewed him. He explained to me how he had developed his initial ministry philosophy. First, he derived a purpose statement, which described what he felt was the purpose of the church. He pointed out that he had imbibed much of the philosophy of ministry from the movement of which he was a part (see stage 1, osmosis). Following is his statement of the purpose of the church:

> We are to be working for God as He establishes His kingdom through the teaching, preaching, proclaiming, and testifying about His kingdom. This will be accomplished if we not only speak His words, but also do His works. We are to be the extension of Jesus to the world. We need to maintain an attitude of service and give the Holy Spirit the freedom to move and empower and release us into ministry. The power of God should be evident in our people and church to such an extent that we are witnesses to both the unchurched (through evangelism) and to the churched (through renewal).[8]

He took that as an overarching statement and developed principles that would be important to such a church.

Table 8-2 Pastor Johnson's Eight Ministry Philosophy Principles

#	STATEMENT
1	The Holy Spirit is the administrator of the church.
2	The supernatural power of God can accomplish more than the combined fleshly efforts of sincere Christians.
3	Relationships are essential. Relationship to God is our chief goal. Relationships with one another provide the intimacy and accountability which the Holy Spirit uses to mold us.
4	Every believer has a special place in the body of Christ and it is vital that everyone be in their place. Some people are more visible but not necessarily more essential. God builds the church and places people where they need to be.
5	People must be free to be themselves. Each person needs to be loved where they are.
6	There has to be room for failure. Where there is no failure, there is no growth. There needs to be an attitude of risk taking.
7	We take seriously the Great Commission (Matthew 28:18-20). We are to be people who are sent into all the world to preach the gospel of the kingdom.
8	Because we are such an experientially oriented church we need especially to be constantly grounding our ministry in the Word of God.[9]

This led him to identify and label some priorities, or further statements of ministry philosophy.

Table 8-3 Pastor Johnson's Ministry Vision Statements (Five-Year Plan)

LABEL	STATEMENT IN VALUE LANGUAGE
1. Worship	We must continually develop ways to express our adoration, praise, and thanksgiving for all that God has done for us. Worship should be a reflection of our relationship to God.
2. The Word	We need to know and understand what the Scriptures teach. The Scriptures provide the models and the guidelines for our lives and ministry.
3. Fellowship	We are to provide a loving, sensitive, supportive, and healing environment through relationships.
4. Training Ministry	We are to be an equipping center. We are to be training and activating the people of God for service.
5. Sending	We are to be a people who "go forth." We are to be active in sending forth laborers into the harvest both here and around the world.[10]

Pastor Johnson then showed me a statement of vision, a five-year plan for the church, which flowed from these philosophical statements. This twenty-nine-page document contained statements that brought out the uniqueness of this church.

Pastor Johnson had a framework that he could use to evaluate potential ministries suggested by emerging leaders. His philosophy also led him to expect that these ministries would emerge. His values, priorities, and vision gave him a framework for decision making. They were developed over a four-year period in the context of ministry. At first they were implicit in the ministry. They then became explicit as the church planned for its future.

WARREN WIERSBE

I first met Warren Wiersbe in a seminar in Cedarville, Ohio, when I was an assistant pastor in a Baptist church. His seminar was titled "Send Us a Pastor Who Reads." That seminar showed me the importance of a leader maintaining a learning posture. It also affirmed my desire to study biographies of leaders. He shared examples from his own literary processing. The seminar exposed us to his reading habits, the great books he had read, the kinds of books a pastor ought to have in a library, and many great ideas that were to be gained.

Pastor Wiersbe was superb, ministering to pastors and sharing some of the books and ideas that had been used in his life. He modeled a learning posture for us. It was clear to me why his ministry had such depth. What he learned was continually being fed back into his ministry. I knew immediately that he was a wise man with a solid ministry. I was not surprised when, seventeen years later, his article in *Leadership* carried insightful ideas about a philosophy of ministry. That article, "Principles Are the Bottom Line," is one of the very best that has been printed in that magazine.

In the article, Wiersbe gave a broad philosophical statement that has guided him in all of his ministry. Using that statement he described principles that guided him in his ministry, forming the bedrock of his ministry philosophy. (Wiersbe uses the word *principle* like I use *absolute* on the certainty continuum.) His principles apply to Christian leadership in general as well as pastoral leadership.

Wiersbe was stimulated to think about principles by a poem given in one of his seminary classes:

Methods are many,
Principles are few.
Methods always change,
Principles never do.[11]

His meditation on this led him to look for principles (or absolutes). *Develop a ministry that is based on absolutes.* He evaluated his own and other ministries on the basis of underlying absolutes, as well as on the basis of the success of the ministry. It kept him from "fad" chasing. Means and methods may be good, but Wiersbe went beyond them.

I learned never to adopt a method until I understood the principle behind it.[12]

With this basic attitude, Wiersbe began to minister and to identify absolutes for ministry as he went. He wrote his article as a retrospective reflection on this process. I have captured the gist of his observations in the table that follows. The ten statements were worked over and reworded to make them apply generically. (The labels are my own, and I have listed these principles in my own words.)

I am sure that Pastor Wiersbe had many day-to-day principles such as the ones I shared from my own life. I am also sure that each of them was evaluated in terms of these ten overarching statements.

These two examples give the framework around which leaders have developed their ministry philosophies. Pastor Johnson portrays a ministry philosophy that is moving from stage 1 to stage 2 in the ministry evolutionary pattern. Wiersbe illustrates movement toward a stage 3 ministry philosophy.

Table 8-4 Wiersbe's Principles Adapted to Include Value Language

LABEL FOR PRINCIPLE	SIMPLE STATEMENT OF VALUE/ PRINCIPLE
1. Character	A leader must recognize that God's work of developing character in him is foundational, for effective ministry flows out of being.
2. Ministry	A leader must serve, for the nature of ministry is service — first of all to the Lord and then to those we lead.
3. Motivation	Ministry must fundamentally be motivated by love for those being ministered to and not by gain nor duty nor giftedness.
4. Sacrifice	Leaders must recognize that effective ministry will require sacrifice.
5. Authority and Submission	A leader must first learn submission to authority; it is essential in order to exercise authority properly.
6. Ultimate Purpose	A leader ought to know that God must receive the glory in the leader's life and work.
7. Dynamic Balance	A leader must grow in and effectively use the basic tools of the Word and prayer.
8. Faithfulness and Capacity	A leader must strive for faithfulness in ministry with a result in an increase of his capacity for ministry.
9. Spirit Empowered	Ministry must be empowered by the Holy Spirit.
10. Modeling Principle	A leader should recognize that Jesus is the supreme model for ministry.

MINISTRY PHILOSOPHY AS A GRID[13]

These two examples show the importance of a ministry philosophy as a guidance framework for a leader. Some of them might be suggestive to you. If, in fact, God develops a leader over a lifetime and if, in fact, He teaches lessons concerning character and ministry, then it follows that identifying and using these lessons is crucial to God's purposes for that leader.

Read again the statement I have been working on during this chapter.[14]

Leaders must develop a ministry philosophy that simultaneously honors biblical leadership values, embraces the challenges of the times in which they live, and fits their unique gifts and personal development if they expect to be productive over a whole lifetime.

I want to suggest a minimum approach to fulfilling this leadership value statement. Rather than get overwhelmed with the idea of doing a full-blown ministry philosophy, start by writing up any of your basic ministry principles as leadership value observations[15] — that is, by using leadership value language. Let me explain what I mean by leadership value language.

TWO DEFINITIONS NEEDED FOR CAPTURING ONE'S IMPORTANT LEADERSHIP CONVICTIONS

Different authors use the concept of values differently. Let me define how I am using value.

Definition 1

A *leadership value* is an underlying assumption that affects how a leader perceives leadership and practices it.

The leadership conviction, when identified and written out (using value language), moves to the status of an explicit leadership value.

Definition 2

An *explicit leadership value* is a statement of commitment by a leader to some insight concerning his leadership/ministry which is written in the format of a first-person commitment to the statement and uses one of three auxiliary verbs to endorse the commitment: should, ought, must, in that emphatic order.

The strength of the commitment is shown by which modal auxiliary verb — *should* or *ought to* or *must* — is used.

THE FORMAT — THREE POSSIBILITIES

- I *should* . . . plus the commitment statement (*possible* value for others)
- I *ought to* . . . plus the commitment statement (*strong guideline* others must consider)

- I *must* . . . plus the commitment statement (*will* apply to most leaders; nearing an *absolute*)

Let me illustrate by giving some examples. Here are six explicit leadership value examples from my personal spiritual DNA list[16] along with a parenthetical (explanation/rationale, why I hold the value). Note I have already taken them out of the first person (my value) and applied them to leaders in general. But you can be sure that I am personally committed to each of these values.

Table 8-5 Six Clinton Spiritual DNA Leadership Values

VALUE LABEL	STATEMENT OF VALUE
Value 1. Intimacy	A leader must seek intimacy with God in terms of beingness, for ministry flows out of being.
Value 2. Developmental Mindset	A leader ought to have a developmental mindset, for God is a God who develops people. Leaders ought to be developing emerging leaders from those they minister to.
Value 3. Growing in the Word	A leader must continually be developing in terms of his grasp of God's Word, for God's Word is His foundational revelation of Himself and His purposes.
Value 4. Obedience Track Record	Over a lifetime, a leader must walk in obedience to God, for obedience is the key to knowing God's will for a life.
Value 5. Growing in Christlikeness	Over a lifetime a leader must be transformed into the image of Christ by the power of the Holy Spirit, for a major goal of God's is transformation of an individual toward Christlikeness in terms of the leader's uniqueness.
Value 6. Gifted Power	A leader should minister with gifted power, for the essential ingredient of leadership is the powerful presence of the Holy Spirit in the life and ministry of the leader.

In my ML524: Focused Lives class at Fuller Seminary, I have my students do a section of their paper titled "Values Section," which includes a timeline and their ten most important explicit leadership values learned thus far. The following, table 8-6, is one student's 10 Top Explicit Values.[17] Notice how all three modal auxiliary verbs occur. Note also his explanation of the value. This is an extended table continued over several pages.

Table 8-6 Value Section, Student Paper in ML524: Focused Lives Class

FOUNDATIONS 1979–1999 (20 YEARS OLD)	DECADE OF 20S TO 30 1999–2009 (30 YEARS OLD)
V1: 1987–1992 Learning Posture	V6: 1999–2006 Networking to Connect and Empower
V2: 1987–1996 Genuine Interest in People and Cultures	V7: 2000–2003 Small Groups as Leadership Training Outlets
V3: 1991–present Ministry Pioneering Through Risk	V8: 2000–present Active Listening
V4: 1994–2004 Mentoring Toward Life Change	V9: 2001–2004 Relational Leadership
V5: 1997 Attitude of Surrender	V10: 2008 Family as Ministry

Value 1: I *must* at all times maintain a *learning posture*.

Explanation: Many leaders feel that they have attained sufficient aptitude in their skill repertoire to "do the job" and stop learning. Yet, a lack of personal development can plateau and even disempower a leader, rendering him less effective, if not useless. In my ministry, I must maintain a constant desire to develop in my abilities and seek to learn something new in every possible circumstance. By reminding myself that being an effective leader is about lifelong personal development, I will be less prone to conceit, apathy, and pride.

Value 2: I *must* take genuine *interest in people and other cultures*.

Explanation: The key to understanding people and their culture is showing genuine interest in them. If my interest is insincere, I will jeopardize my ability to develop friendships, adapt to unfamiliar circumstances, and effectively minister to my surroundings. I must therefore never allow myself to forget the inherent value that people and therefore their culture possess.

Value 3: In pioneering new ministry expressions, I *ought to* take *risks*.

Explanation: Taking risks is part of doing ministry, in particular when it involves pioneering new ministry expressions. While I must always seek to discern the directing of God's Spirit, there will be times when He remains silent or purposely unclear. In times like these, I must invoke my gift of faith and continue to press forward, even at the risk of personal failure. After all, I am a (developing) pioneer, and my job will undoubtedly entail making decisions based on an outcome I cannot yet foresee. I must remember at all times that God is in control.

Value 4: I *should* use one-on-one *mentoring to change people's lives.*
Explanation: People are commonly most transparent in intimate settings. When given a safe and inviting environment, they are prone to open up and share their hearts, in particular when it involves a person with whom they have developed a relationship of trust and respect. It is in these places where I am best able to challenge and develop individuals toward life change. I should therefore find people who desire to make a kingdom contribution and seek to mentor them in such a way that their lives are permanently redirected.

Value 5: Everything I do *must* flow out of an *attitude of surrender.*
Explanation: Ministry flows out of being. Leaders whose lives are unconditionally surrendered to God's purposes are His most effective tools. If I am to be useful to God, I must constantly evaluate whether there are any strongholds in my life that are keeping me from such surrender. Because distractions creep into our lives so subtly and often go undetected, I must allow others to call me out when they detect deviation.

Value 6: I *should* use my *networking skills to connect* people with each other and thereby *empower* them toward a more effective ministry.
Explanation: Networking is a great way of empowering leaders. Because I will be limited in my ability to develop and resource certain leaders, being in relationship with those whose gift-mix is more fitting will help me to pass on these leaders to them. I should therefore seek to continue developing relationships with people from around the globe, and I must be willing to hand off mentorees when others can train them more appropriately.

Value 7: I *should* use *small groups to train developing leaders.*
Explanation: Small group settings can provide wonderful leadership development opportunities. Because the level of responsibility is limited

and the scope of potential failure manageable, I should regularly allow budding leaders to take charge in small group settings as a means of growing in their leadership abilities. I should also seek to debrief the experience with them, encouraging and redirecting them toward progress.

Value 8: I *ought to* be an *active listener*.
Explanation: Active listening helps guide a conversation toward an intended outcome. By asking good questions, making comments when appropriate, and exemplifying an overall attitude of interest and concern, I can help direct a mentoree toward a set of desired results, for example, insight, clarity, or direction. I ought to therefore adopt a conversational style in which all of these elements can be encompassed. My priority should be listening, with giving advice or providing personal insight taking the proverbial back seat.

Value 9: I *ought to* lead from *relational and not positional leadership*.
Explanation: People have always and will always follow me based primarily on relationship. While there will be instances in which I will have to exercise authority based on rank, I should seek to keep such instances at a minimum. Human dysfunction provides enough opportunity for dissention, and I will be able to most effectively counter squabbles within a highly relational framework. I should therefore make people feel valued and taken seriously at all times.

Value 10: I *must* remember that my *family life will be the key component of my ministry*.
Explanation: The way I lead my family will determine the way I lead in public ministry and will serve as evidence for my integrity as a leader. In fact, my family will be *the* key component of all that I do. Unless my family life (as far as it depends on me) is healthy, I have no business leading others. I must therefore prioritize my family over anything else I do in ministry, paying careful attention to my wife and children's physical and spiritual well-being. I should also seek to encourage others

to do likewise by both example and direct challenge.

See appendix B, where I give a list of materials that I have written giving illustrations of explicit leadership values. Most people will learn to do explicit leadership values by simply observing a large number of explicit leadership values done by others. The materials in appendix B give just such a large number of explicit leadership values.

CONCLUSION

I believe that most leaders can list ten important explicit leadership values. Start there. Read through the many illustrations of explicit leadership values that I refer to in the materials listed in appendix B. Just reading these examples will probably suggest to you your own ten top explicit leadership values. I wish I had known value theory when I interviewed Pastor Jeff for his story (see the Introduction). I would love to see his "commitments" to leadership principles, written in leadership value language. So then, if you can, do a full-blown ministry philosophy as I have described it in this chapter. But if you cannot, at least do your Top Ten Explicit Leadership Values.

HOW ABOUT YOU?

1. What are some of the most important lessons God has taught you personally concerning your leadership character? Define two of these in terms of an explicit leadership statement, a commitment to the lesson that was learned. Use one of the three modal auxiliary verbs to reflect it as a suggestion, guideline, or absolute for you in ministry.

2. What are some of the most important lessons that God has taught you concerning your ministry? Define two of these in terms of an explicit leadership statement, a commitment to the lesson that was learned. Use one of the three modal auxiliary verbs to reflect it as a suggestion, guideline, or absolute for you in ministry.

CHAPTER 9

ACCEPTING THE LESSONS OF LIFE: THE LEADERSHIP CHALLENGE

The Challenge/The Problem: When he saw the crowds, he had compassion on them, because they were harassed and helpless, like sheep without a shepherd. Then he said to his disciples, "The harvest is plentiful but the workers are few. Ask the Lord of the harvest, therefore, to send out workers into his harvest field." *(Matthew 9:36-38)*

The Challenge/The Solution: "Come, follow me," Jesus said, "and I will make you fishers of men." *(Matthew 4:19)*

The things you have heard me say in the presence of many witnesses entrust to reliable men who will also be qualified to teach others. *(2 Timothy 2:2)*

THE NEED: MORE AND BETTER LEADERSHIP

In this chapter, I want to suggest three challenges that apply to leaders. These challenges stem from the need for leadership in Christian work. Everywhere I go I hear, "We don't have enough trained leadership." This may mean, "We don't have full-time leaders who have been to seminary." I disagree somewhat with that thinking. We don't need only full-time leaders. Also, formal training will not solve the problem. But the essence of the statement is true: Leaders who are equipped are needed.

The need grows particularly crucial now for two reasons. First, in numerous Western parachurch organizations, particularly those with international ministries, there are a number of older leaders who have been influential in Christian thought and activity for some time. They will leave the scene in the next ten years. There are many rising young leaders but seemingly few middle-age leaders to fill the gap until these young leaders mature. Second, in many places in the Third World the church is growing so fast it outstrips its leadership. How can leadership be trained to fill this rapidly increasing need? To echo Jesus' sentiment (see Matthew 9:37): The workload is great. There is need for leadership, equipped for the multitude of tasks facing leaders in Christian work. The perspectives given in this book can help us to raise up leaders to fill the gaps more sensitively and effectively, and in less time.

I want to suggest three final challenges. Those who have studied the leadership ideas of this book and have seen some truth in these ideas have a responsibility to use this truth. I will state these challenges then explain each in more detail:

Challenge 1:   When Christ calls leaders to Christian ministry He intends to develop them to their full potential.[1] Each of us in leadership is responsible to continue developing in accordance with God's processing all our life.

Challenge 2:   A major function of all leadership is that of selection of rising leadership. Leaders must continually be aware of God's processing of younger leaders and work with that process.

Challenge 3:   Leaders must develop a ministry philosophy that simultaneously honors biblical leadership values, embraces the challenges of the times in which they live, and fits their unique gifts and personal development if they expect to be productive over a whole lifetime.

PERSONAL LEADERSHIP

The leadership lessons shared in this book have been based on the assumption that God is in the business of cultivating leaders and intervening in their lives to develop them for His purposes. Jesus still calls people to follow Him and to influence many others. My studies of those in the Scriptures whom God has used as leaders to accomplish His purposes lead me to a working definition of a leader.

A *leader*, as defined from a study of biblical leadership, and for whom we are interested in tracing leadership development, is a person (1) with God-given capacity *and* (2) with God-given responsibility to *influence* (3) a specific group of God's people (4) toward God's purposes for the group.

The *God-given capacity* denotes giftedness — spiritual gifts and natural abilities and skills.[2] This giftedness is inherent in the leader. The *God-given responsibility* includes not only a burden for the work, but also a sense of accountability before God for that work. My studies in giftedness, particularly the permanence of gifts (see Romans 12; Ephesians 4) and the stewardship parables (see particularly Luke 19, the pounds; Matthew 25, the talents), have led me to the conclusion that leaders have capacities that must be developed and used.

Romans 12:3-7 is particularly instructive. Its thrust is on evaluation and qualitative use of gifts. We are admonished to assess our gifts. The daily sacrifice that is the outworking of that commitment (see 12:1-2) will involve understanding giftedness.

In verse 3, "grace given me" contains a metonymy (a figure in which one word is substituted for another to which it is linked by some relationship, like cause for effect).[3] "Grace" is substituted for "gifts," meaning gifts given by grace. Paul's spiritual gifts were grace gifts. The translation of this in the New English Bible ("the gift that God in his grace has given me") confirms my view on this metonymy. Paul is saying that by the gifts that were given him he can assert truths about spiritual gifts with authority.

"In accordance with the measure of faith" in verse 3 contains the other critical metonymy. This figurative phrase qualifies how we are to use our spiritual gifts. *Measure* is referring to capacity; *faith* is the metonymy standing for "gift that we exercise by faith." Every person should exercise his gift according to the capacity of faith God has given with the gift. The passage goes on to point out that each will have a different capacity. Each should evaluate and use his gifts to the capacity for which God intended.

Therefore, each of us as leaders is expected to assess our spiritual gifts and our abilities and to use them to capacity. Each is unique. Another's success is not our standard. Bigger is not better, nor is a greater sphere of influence. If God has endowed me to be a lay leader, wonderful. I certainly don't want to be a full-time leader, if that is the case. If God has endowed me with potential to be a national leader, then I don't want to plateau as a lay leader. We should be what God intends us to be.

We can develop as persons using spiritual gifts and natural abilities right up to the level of potential that God intends.[4] Skills that enhance our gifts and abilities should be learned and used. Knowledge that will make us more effective in our use of gifts should be sought. If we do not do so, we will have to account to God. And we will have to account for what we actually did, whether or not we developed to the potential that God intended. Hebrews 13:17, James 3:1, and the judgment passages certainly make it clear that leaders are accountable for their influence.

In order to review our lives and assess God's processing, we need to evaluate where we are, and thus encourage ourselves to continue to develop. Let me repeat the challenge:

When Christ calls leaders to Christian ministry He intends to develop them to their full potential. Each of us in leadership is responsible to continue developing in accordance with God's processing all our life.

The perspectives I have shared can help you to perceive where you are in your own development, to more clearly evaluate it, and to sense

God's hand in it. This in turn will make you operate in tandem with God's developmental purposes. This is the most important challenge. Unless we experience God's ongoing development we will not be able to help others develop their leadership capacity. How are you doing in your development as a leader? Be all you are meant to be as God's leader!

RISING LEADERSHIP

A major function of all leadership is the selection of rising leadership. I don't mean picking young people to send off to Bible college or seminary, but rather observing those God is selecting and processing, and then finding ways to enhance their development. Awareness of early symptoms and processing concepts can mean that you can much more efficiently advise and mentor emerging leaders. You can point them to informal and nonformal training that you know can move them along in several of the developmental patterns. In each ministry God is developing leaders and followers. As leaders we must work with God to recognize leadership gaps and to fill them with emerging leaders.

Paul points out that faithfulness is a key ingredient in the selection of emerging leaders. That ingredient is at the heart of the early testing patterns and the foundational ministry pattern. That is why it is to your advantage to recognize those key early selection and developmental patterns: the testing-negative remedial, testing-positive expansion, foundational ministry pattern, like attracts like gift pattern, and giftedness drift. Process items like the destiny items, ministry task, ministry challenge, ministry skills, training progress, and giftedness discovery should be very familiar to you. All the guidance items, but particularly divine contact and mentoring, should be in your tool kit as you seek to help emerging leaders move along in their development.

Look at people in your ministry with leadership selection eyes.[5] Be continually asking yourself such questions as, "Where is this person in his development?" "What could I do to help him see how God is processing toward leadership?" "Is God using me as a divine contact in this situation?" "Can I possibly be a mentor or trainer for this person?" Remember Goodwin's expectation principle: *A potential leader tends to rise to the level of genuine expectancy of a leader he respects.*[6] Make sure you are a respected leader. Make sure you know followers well enough to spot emerging leaders. And make sure you are giving challenges that stretch, yet are reachable.

The leadership gap will never be met unless all leaders begin to take to heart Paul's admonition to Timothy (see 2 Timothy 2:2). That means each should take an active interest in developing leaders. How are you training leaders for your ministry? Are your efforts helping fill the leadership gap? Or are you making the gap wider? As the Lord admonished: Pray for emerging leaders in your ministry. Then do what is needed with them when He answers.

> A major function of all leadership is that of selection of rising leadership. Leaders must continually be aware of God's processing of younger leaders and work with that processing.

MINISTRY PHILOSOPHY

Leaders with good ministry philosophies usually finish well. The discernment function, the fourth major developmental stage of the Ministry Maturing phase, is crucial to effective leadership. Leaders must be able to see God working in events and people and in situations around them. They must recognize God's work in their own lives. A discerning leader is a leader with a solid ministry philosophy. The ministry philosophy pattern is essential for effective leadership that will carry through to the end.

Not all leaders finish well. I have observed four patterns concerning the response of leaders to processing in the ministry development phase. These patterns include:

1. Dropouts—quite a few
2. Plateaued leaders—the majority of leaders[7]

3. Disciplined — a few

4. Those who continue to grow and finish well — some

The challenge is to finish well, as the apostle Paul did. We need to reverse the number of leaders in patterns 2 and 4. Without a clear ministry philosophy, few leaders will be in pattern 4.

Ministry philosophies will be as diverse as there are leaders. We cannot copy a successful leader's philosophy and simply put it into our situation. The ministry philosophy of a leader must arise out of that leader's leadership emergence. It must fit the lessons learned by that leader, growing out of the unique processing that God has for that leader. It must fit that leader's giftedness development pattern. It must fit the situation in which God places that leader. It will follow the destiny processing of that leader.

There are, of course, values in the Bible concerning leadership ethics and styles, ends and means, and the overarching attitude of servant leadership that apply to all leaders. We can, of course, profit greatly from studying the ministry philosophies of leaders whom God has greatly used. However, the vast majority of values learned will be unique to a leader because of unique situations. That is, each situation will force a closer scrutiny of Scripture for truth that fits that situation.

A ministry philosophy does not have to be explicitly stated in propositional statements, though that is very helpful. But it has to be there and has to give integration to a leader's ministry. Notice especially concepts 3 and 4 of my leader definition:

> A *leader*, as defined from a study of biblical leadership, and for whom we are interested in tracing leadership development, is a person (1) with God-given capacity *and* (2) with God-given responsibility to *influence* (3) a specific group of God's people (4) toward God's purposes for the group.

If the Lord were to make a statement to us, looking not only at the leadership gap but also at the present leaders, He might rephrase Matthew 9:36-38 as I have done:

When He saw the leaders, He was filled with dismay, because so many quit, so many were set aside, and so many were plateaued and directionless. They had lost their zest for leading. They had no clear philosophy or direction in their leadership. They were leaderless leaders. Then He said to His disciples, "The harvest is plentiful, but the leaders with clear direction are few. Ask the Lord of the harvest, that He will send forth knowledgeable, discerning, and direction-oriented leader-laborers into His harvest."

The central task of leadership is *influencing God's people toward God's purposes*. This objective will not be maintained over an entire lifetime without an adequate ministry philosophy.

Leaders must develop a ministry philosophy that simultaneously honors biblical leadership values, embraces the challenges of the times in which they live, and fits their unique gifts and personal development if they expect to be productive over a whole lifetime.

Wouldn't it be wonderful if ten or fifteen years from now the Lord Jesus could rephrase Matthew 9:36-38 in the following way?

When He saw the immensity of the work and the multitudes to be reached, He was not disheartened but was moved with joy because many leaders were meeting those needs and were continually raising up new leaders to meet the tremendous leadership challenge. He said, "Thank the Lord of the harvest, for He is giving harvest leaders, and they are leaders with direction and purpose."

How is God developing the discernment function in you as a leader? If you and I accept the third challenge and pass on its intention to emerging leaders in our ministry, we may well hear my second revision of Matthew 9:36-38.

SUMMARY

The leadership gap is enormous. There is a great need for effective leadership. In my opinion, the three challenges I have given get at the heart of the problem. Each leader personally must be what God wants him to be. Each leader must be involved in raising up other leaders. Leaders must be in tune with God's purposes for them. Leadership emergence theory can be a great help in all three of these challenges.

When I began my own pilgrimage into the study of leaders' lives, I was challenged by the following biblical admonition. I began the book with this challenge. Now I give it again, but as a final challenge.

The Final Challenge

Remember your leaders, who spoke the word of God to you. Consider the outcome of their way of life and imitate their faith. Jesus Christ is the same yesterday and today and forever. *(Hebrews 13:7-8)*

When I first read these verses, two questions used to come to mind. The first question is how do I "consider the outcome of their way of life"? The second is how do I "imitate their faith"? I hope this book has shown that processes in the development of the lives of these great leaders are the same processes that God uses to develop leaders today. We can count on Jesus Christ, who is the same yesterday, today, and forever. The same ways He taught in the past apply to you and me today. The same Jesus Christ who enabled those leaders to live lives of faith will enable you and me to live a life of faith today. He is both the source and the reason for our study of leadership.

Leadership evolves and emerges over a lifetime. In fact, leadership is a lifetime of God's lessons. I trust that you, too, will accept the challenge of Hebrews 13:7-8 and that you are now much better equipped to do it than I was when I started.

A FINAL STERN WARNING

I am going to close with a rather stern warning. Hear it well! In endnote 12, chapter 6, I made the following statement. I am going to quote the whole endnote because it points strongly to my final warning.

Endnote 12

I have labeled this with special sensitivity. I call it a *sovereign mindset*. A *sovereign mindset* is a way of viewing life's activities so as to see and respond to God's purposes in them. Paul is the New Testament exemplar in the Church Leadership Era for demonstrating a sovereign mindset. Paul had a leadership value: He sought to always see God's hand in his circumstances as part of God's plan for developing him as a leader. I generalize this leadership value and apply it to all leaders.

Here is my wording:

Label: Sovereign Mindset Value

Statement of the Leadership Value: Leaders Ought to See God's Hand in Their Circumstances as Part of His Plan for Developing Them as Leaders. I have written a leadership article on this topic – "Sovereign Mindset." This article occurs in all of my New Testament biblical leadership commentaries. A leader who does not have a sovereign mindset *will probably not finish well.* This leadership value is a must.

Note that phrase: *will probably not finish well.*

FEW LEADERS FINISH WELL

In my comparative studies of biblical leaders,[8] I gave four observations. The first one surprised me.

- Observation 1. Few leaders finish well.
- Observation 2. Leadership is difficult.
- Observation 3. God's enabling presence is the essential ingredient of successful leadership.
- Observation 4. Spiritual leadership can make a difference.

In this research, I saw that thirteen of forty-nine Bible leaders who had data indicating their finish, finished well. That means that only one out of three or four finished well. This was my first evidence concerning leaders not finishing well. This led me to further study to answer the following questions:

- What exactly does finishing well mean (in other words, What are the characteristics of finishing well)?
- What are the barriers to finishing well?
- What are the enhancements to finishing well?

See appendix C, where I will give you some of my initial answers to these important questions.

But let me finish this section on a more hopeful note, rather than just a stern warning. In the Preface to the Revised Edition I made this closing statement, and I quote it again.

I am hopeful that leaders who are more aware of God's lifetime of shaping activities will finish well and *at a higher percentage* than we now see.

I hope by now, having read in this book how God shapes a leader over a whole lifetime, you are getting that *sovereign mindset*. And that you can quote with Paul,

Being confident of this, that he who began a good work in you will carry it on to completion until the day of Christ Jesus. (Philippians 1:6)

MAY YOU FINISH WELL.

OBSERVATIONS ON LEADERSHIP SELECTION

I indicated in chapter 9 that leadership selection is a major responsibility of leadership. In my comparative study of leaders who have finished well, I have identified seven major leadership lessons. Let me list them. But note especially lesson 5, emphasized in bold.

Lesson 1	Effective leaders view present ministry in terms of a lifetime perspective.
Lesson 2	Effective leaders maintain a learning posture throughout life.
Lesson 3	Effective leaders value spiritual authority as a primary power base.
Lesson 4	Effective leaders who are productive over a lifetime have a dynamic ministry philosophy.
Lesson 5	**Effective leaders view leadership selection and development as a priority function in their ministry.**
Lesson 6	Effective leaders see relational empowerment as both a means and a goal of ministry.
Lesson 7	Effective leaders evince a growing awareness of their sense of destiny.

This appendix will give some help concerning lesson 5. It will give suggestions on how to select emerging leaders early on.

Below I list some principles that I have identified in comparative study of early stages of many leaders. I then follow these principles with some implications that I feel grow out of the principles.

TEN EMERGENCE PRINCIPLES AND IMPLICATIONS

You will recall that a *principle* is a generalized statement of truth that is an observation drawn from specific leadership acts, God's use of process items with leaders, analysis of ministerial formation, analysis of spiritual formation, and other leadership emergence analyses that describe patterns applicable to other leaders in other situations.

Hundreds of principles have been suggested by leaders who are analyzing their own lives. While many principles could be given here that are common to many leaders, I have chosen to list and discuss just ten that deal primarily with leadership emergence and selection. Then I will follow with some implications flowing from these ten.

Six Principles Involving Personal Orientation

1. **Word Orientation.** An appetite to learn the Word of God (shown by a person's response to the ministry of Bible teachers and self-initiated study projects) is a good indicator of an emerging leader.
2. **Application Orientation.** A person who readily applies Scripture to his life in response to word checks, obedience checks, and integrity checks is likely to emerge as a leader.
3. **Righteousness Orientation.** A hunger for righteousness, a desire for personal integrity, and frequent process items dealing with these issues are good indications of an emerging leader.
4. **Specific Prayer Orientation.** A potential leader prays specific prayers for his ministry and sees specific answers to prayer in such a way as to increase faith and expand the kinds of specific requests.

5. **Guidance Orientation.** A potential leader will learn personal guidance lessons that serve as springboards for learning group guidance.

6. **Self-Starter Orientation.** Leadership emerges at lowest levels in self-initiated projects, ministry tasks, and experiences with God.

Four Principles Involving Relationships with Leaders

1. **Like Attracts Like Gift Principle.** Frequently a gifted potential leader is attracted to a like-gifted leader who mentors him toward developing gifts.

2. **Modeling Attraction Principle.** Frequently a potential leader is attracted to a leader who uses modeling as a means of influence.

3. **Expectancy Principle.** A potential leader responds to genuine expectancy challenges from an older leader whom he admires (Goodwin's expectancy rule).

4. **Divine Contact Principle.** God often brings one or more significant persons, divine contacts, across the path of an emerging leader at opportune movements to perform some necessary mentoring, which spurs him to develop leadership capacity.

NINE IMPLICATIONS FROM THE PERSONAL ORIENTATION PRINCIPLES

1. Leaders need to be aware of indicators of those who have an appetite for the Word (such as having a marked Bible, ordering and using CDs, buying Bible study books, attendance at Bible studies, producing of written studies, and so on).

2. Leaders should make available Bible study materials and other resources that can be used to build skills and good Bible study habits.

3. Leaders should personally challenge potential leaders and lend or otherwise provide Bible study materials and resources to them.

4. Leaders need to be good listeners and know followers well, if they are to find out how Scripture is being applied in the lives of potential leaders.

5. Leaders need to provide potential leaders with adequate opportunity to testify concerning God's work in integrity checks, word checks, and obedience checks, and other processing focused on righteous living.

6. Leaders need to model a prayer life that demonstrates specific prayer requests and answers.

7. Leaders need to specify how they get guidance for the groups they lead and to encourage emerging leaders to seek guidance in the same way for their initial ministries.

8. Leaders must raise awareness of needs, challenge potential leaders concerning those needs, and release those potential leaders to solve them.

9. Leaders need to be aware that those who often engage in self-initiated projects do so to correct the status quo and often do so in an abrasive way.

NINE IMPLICATIONS FROM THE RELATIONSHIP PRINCIPLES

1. Leaders should recognize that those emergent leaders with gifts like their own frequently will be drawn to them. Informally a leader should be testing close followers for similarities to his gift-mix.

2. Leaders should model their use of a gift with an explanation of early indicators of the gift and of how the gift can be developed.

3. Leaders who use modeling as an important means of influence are demonstrating spiritual authority, which is a main reason potential leaders are drawn to certain leaders.

4. Leaders who use modeling should recognize they can play a vital part in moving potential leaders along the spiritual authority development pattern.

5. Leaders should be familiar with the spiritual authority development pattern and be prepared to have stimulating exercises and tasks that move potential leaders along it.

6. Leaders need to assess potential emerging leaders accurately for giftedness (natural abilities, spiritual gifts).

7. Leaders must challenge potential emerging leaders with appropriate challenges—too great can discourage them, too little will not stretch them.

8. Leaders should seek to cultivate an awareness of destiny in emerging leaders based on abilities, spiritual gifts, and destiny process items.

9. Leaders must be aware that God will often use them as divine contacts in the lives of emerging leaders. Hence leaders need to be thoroughly aware of the divine contact process item and mentoring process item.

Many other implications could be suggested. But these will give an idea of how a principle should engender some action from a leader if it is to be used. Leadership selection is a crucial function of all leadership. These emergence principles and resulting implications could form a base upon which a leader builds a ministry philosophy concerning leadership selection.

In addition to these principles, I want to point out the importance of the testing cluster for leadership.

IMPLICATIONS OF THE TESTING CLUSTER

The testing cluster consists of the major inner-life process items—word check, integrity check, and obedience check—along with the transitional testing item, ministry task. This cluster provides the backdrop from which emergent leaders are identified. Both the positive-testing expansion pattern and the negative-testing remedial pattern are very important in understanding God's use of the testing cluster.

1. Leadership selection is a major ongoing responsibility of leadership.
2. The testing cluster and testing patterns should be an ongoing part of a leader's thinking when counseling potential leaders.
3. Word checks are indicative of possible word gifts and should suggest ministry tasks and informal word training that can be further used to confirm leadership potential.

ANNOTATED LIST OF MATERIALS DEALING WITH MINISTRY PHILOSOPHY

Below I list my attempts to get at and articulate ministry philosophy concepts. This involves a number of items over a thirty-year stretch. I have done the most work on articulating the notion of a leadership value. I am convinced that if a person identifies his top ten leadership values (see below for *ML524 Values Reader*, in which five top students in my 2009 class identified their top ten values) and learns to pass them on there is great gain. Writing a full-blown ministry philosophy is probably beyond the ability of most leaders. Listing their top ten leadership values is possible for 70 percent of all leaders. And the best way to do that is to read a lot of explicit leadership values others have described. The following materials give lots of explicit leadership values as examples to help you identify your top ten leadership values.

Table B-1 Research Papers Dealing with Ministry Philosophy/Leadership Values

LABEL / PAGES	YEAR	WHERE AVAILABLE	WHAT IT DOES
Chapter 8, *The Making of a Leader* / 19 pages	1988	First edition, *The Making of a Leader*	• Points out the need for a ministry philosophy • Describes the threefold steps that a basic ministry philosophy develops
Position Paper: "A Personal Ministry Philosophy — One Key to Effective Leadership" / 70 pages	1992	www.bobbyclinton.com (website, Resource Store)	• Unpacks the following statement: Effective leaders who are productive over a lifetime have a dynamic ministry philosophy • Gives nineteen Pauline leadership values in value language drawn from 2 Corinthians • Introduces the three major variables of a ministry philosophy: Blend, Articulation, and Focus • Gives the ministry philosophy diagram with its seven basal elements • Distinguishes gift-driven values and other derived values
"Passing On My Heritage" / 69 pages	2000	www.bobbyclinton.com (website, Resource Store)	• Gives six foundational values in value language format • Gives three design paradigms • Lists my ten commandments of teaching, which are "must" values for me as a teacher

LABEL / PAGES	YEAR	WHERE AVAILABLE	WHAT IT DOES
"Value Driven Leadership" / 73 pages	2009	www.bobbyclinton.com (website, Resource Store)	• Defines leadership value and then explicit leadership value • Explains the three emphatic modal auxiliary verbs used in an explicit leadership value (should, ought to, must) • Gives my six personal explicit spiritual DNA leadership values; values for all five philosophical models modeled by Jesus (Servant Model [six values], Steward Model [eight values], Harvest Model [eight values], Shepherd Model [thirteen values], Intercessor Model [eight values]); nine macro lessons (values) seen in Jesus' ministry; sixty-two Pauline leadership values seen in 2 Corinthians (nineteen), 1 Timothy (nine), 2 Timothy (ten), 1 Corinthians (eight), Philippians (twelve), Philemon (four); Samuel Brengle's eight spiritual formation values; thirteen ministerial formation values; six strategic formation values; A. J. Gordon's ten critical leadership values; Morgan's fourteen values about the Bible and Bible study; Clinton's six values associated with Bible-centered leadership; Clinton's eighteen teaching values; many leadership values from Hankin's Latino Mentoring; many mentoring values from Feiker
ML524 Values Reader / 16 pages	2010	www.bobbyclinton.com (website, Resource Store)	• Explores fifty leadership values: Top Ten Leadership Values from five students in the 2009 ML524: Focused Lives class

ANNOTATED LIST OF MATERIALS DEALING WITH FINISHING WELL

I first discovered the notion of finishing well when I was reflecting on my first eight years of teaching ML530: Lifelong Leadership Development at Fuller Seminary. This was further stimulated when I wrote in 1989 the position paper "Listen Up Leaders! Forewarned Is Forearmed!" Table C-1 is a record of my continual study and presentation of finishing well information. Appendix D contains further findings.

Table C-1 Research Papers Dealing with Finishing Well

LABEL	YEAR DONE/ PAGES	WHERE AVAILABLE	WHAT IT DOES
Position paper: "Listen Up Leaders!"	1989/ 22 pages	www.bobbyclinton.com (website, Resource Store)	Four major observations seen: Observation 1. Few leaders finish well. Observation 2. Leadership is difficult. Observation 3. God's enabling presence is the essential ingredient of successful leadership. Observation 4. Spiritual leadership can make a difference. Thirteen of forty-nine Bible leaders who had material indicating their finish, finished well. This was my first evidence concerning finishing well. This led me to further study: • What exactly does finishing well mean (in other words, What are the characteristics of finishing well)? • What are the barriers to finishing well? • What are the enhancements to finishing well?
Position Paper: "The Mantle of the Mentor — An Exhortation to Finish Well"	1993/ 26 pages	www.bobbyclinton.com (website, Resource Store)	This was a plenary address given at the 1993 International Foursquare Convention in Louisville, Kentucky. Using Elijah's famous passing of the mantle to Elisha as a springboard, this talk exhorts leaders to finish well and pass on the mantle of a life well lived as a legacy to the next generation of leaders. The talk addresses the issue of *Finishing Well as a Leader*. Three scenarios illustrate the idea that relatively few leaders finish well, some of the barriers to finishing well, some things that can be done to finish well, and the characteristics of a leader who finishes well. This was the first time I put in print: characteristics, barriers, and enhancements to finishing well.

LABEL	YEAR DONE/ PAGES	WHERE AVAILABLE	WHAT IT DOES
Position Paper: "Finishing Well – The Challenge of a Lifetime"	1994/ 24 pages	www.bobbyclinton.com (website, Resource Store); *Clinton's Biblical Leadership Commentary*, Vol. II and other biblical leadership commentaries	Plenary address given to a 1994 leadership forum at Estes Park, Colorado, sponsored by Interest Ministries. Four scenarios introduced cases of a bi-vocational worker, an evangelistic parachurch worker, two church planters, and a pastor. The ideas – finishing well characteristics, enhancements, and barriers – were seen in the cases. An application sheet challenged the listeners to evaluate how they were doing toward finishing well.
Leadership Article: "Finishing Well – Six Characteristics"	1999/ 3 pages	www.bobbyclinton.com (website, Resource Store); *Clinton's Biblical Leadership Commentary*, Vol. II	Identifies the six characteristics seen comparative in leaders who finish well: vibrant relationship, learners, Christlike character, convictions, legacies, and destiny. See appendix D for this paper.
Article: "Finishing Well – Six Major Barriers"	1999/ 2 pages	www.bobbyclinton.com (website, Resource Store); *Clinton's Biblical Leadership Commentary*, Vol. II	Identifies the six major barriers seen comparative in leaders who did not finish well: finances, abuse of power, inordinate pride, sexual misconduct, failure in family issues, and plateauing. See appendix D for this paper.
Leadership Article: "Finishing Well – Five Enhancements"	1999/ 3 pages	www.bobbyclinton.com (website, Resource Store); *Clinton's Biblical Leadership Commentary*, Vol. II	Identifies the five factors helping leaders finish well: perspective, renewal, disciplines, learning posture, and mentoring. See appendix D for this paper.

THREE PAPERS ON FINISHING WELL

What does it mean to finish well? See "Finishing Well—Six Characteristics."

What are the barriers to finishing well? See "Finishing Well—Six Major Barriers."

What are the enhancements to finishing well? See "Finishing Well—Five Enhancements."

This appendix has three short papers summarizing my findings about these three questions. These papers were first published in *Clinton's Biblical Leadership Commentary* in 1999.

FINISHING WELL – SIX CHARACTERISTICS
Introduction to Research on Finishing Well

In 1989, in an article titled "Listen Up Leaders! Forewarned Is Forearmed!" I summarized my research on biblical leaders with the following opening comments.

A repeated reading of the Bible with a focus on leadership reveals four crucial observations fraught with leadership implications:

Observation 1. Few leaders finish well.[1]
Observation 2. Leadership is difficult.

Observation 3. God's enabling presence is the essential ingredient of successful leadership.

Observation 4. Spiritual leadership can make a difference.

And what is true of biblical leaders is equally true of historical and contemporary leaders.[2] It is the first observation to which this article speaks. Identifying the fact that few leaders finish well was a breakthrough warning for me. This led to further study. Why do few leaders finish well? What stops them? What helps them? *What does it mean to finish well?* This article answers this last question by identifying six characteristics of those finishing well.

Six Characteristics

Comparative study of effective leaders who finished well has identified six characteristics. While there may be other characteristics that I have not seen, certainly these are important ones. Not all six always appear, but at least several of them do in leaders who finish well. Frequently, effective leaders who finish well will have four or five of them seen in their lives. And some, like Daniel in the Old Testament and Paul in the New Testament, demonstrate all of them. What are these six characteristics of those finishing well?

Characteristic 1. They maintain a personal vibrant relationship with God right up to the end.

Example: Daniel is the classic Old Testament leader who exemplifies this. In the New Testament, Peter, Paul, and John all demonstrate this. See their last writings — the tone, the touch of God, the revelation from God, and their trust in enabling grace for their lives.

Characteristic 2. They maintain a learning posture and can learn from various kinds of sources — life especially.

This characteristic is also one of the enhancement factors for finishing well.

Example: Daniel is the classic Old Testament leader who exemplifies this. See Daniel 9 for a late-in-life illustration of one who continues to study and learn from the Scriptures. Paul and Peter are the classic New Testament leaders with a learning posture (see 2 Timothy 4:13; 2 Peter 3:18).

Characteristic 3. They manifest Christlikeness in character as evidenced by the fruit of the Spirit in their lives.

Example: Daniel is the classic Old Testament leader who exemplifies godliness (see the summary references to him in Ezekiel 14:14,20). In the New Testament, note the evidence of character transformation in Paul's life (see 2 Timothy 2:24; and an illustration of it—the book of Philemon). These were men who over a lifetime moved from strong personalities with roughness in their leadership styles to strong personalities with gentleness in their leadership styles.

Characteristic 4. Truth is lived out in their lives so that convictions and promises of God are seen to be real.

Example: Joshua's statement about God's promises never having failed him in his closing speech demonstrates this characteristic of someone believing God and staking his life on God's truth (see Joshua 23:14). See the many aside truth statements that Paul weaves into his two letters to Timothy. See his famous stirring convictions echoed in Acts 27:22-25.

Characteristic 5. They leave behind one or more ultimate contributions.

In a study on legacies left behind by effective leaders who finished well, I have identified the following thirteen categories of lasting legacies as shown in table D-1.

Table D-1 Categories of Lasting Legacies

CATEGORY	EXPLANATION
1. Saint	A model life that others want to emulate
2. Stylistic Practitioners	A ministry model that others want to emulate
3. Family	Promote a God-fearing family, leaving behind children who walk with God, carrying on that godly heritage
4. Mentors	Extensive personal ministry; end product is changed lives
5. Public Rhetoricians	Extensive public ministry; end product is changed lives
6. Pioneers	Start new works for God; end products are new churches, new movements, and new works for God
7. Crusaders	Those who correct wrongs; end products are changed institutions, societies, and so on that reflect justice, fairness, and so on
8. Artists	Those who introduce creative ways of doing things; end products are whatever is created as well as a model for how to do things differently
9. Founders	A special category of pioneer who starts a new Christian organization; end product is the organization
10. Stabilizers	Those who can work in churches, movements, and other organizations to improve them and keep them alive and consistent; end product is a revitalized and efficient organization
11. Researchers	Those who find out why things happen the way they do in Christian endeavor; end product is an understanding of the dynamics of things that can help others in Christian work
12. Writers	Those who can capture ideas in writing in order to help others in Christian work; end product is the writing that is produced
13. Promoters	Those who can motivate others and inspire them to use ideation, to join movements, and so on; end product is people committing themselves to new ventures

Examples: Daniel's ultimate contributions include: saint, mentor, writer, and stabilizer. Paul's ultimate contributions include: saint, mentor, pioneer, crusader, writer, and promoter.

Of course, in addition to these standard categories there are also unique legacies that leaders also leave behind. These have to be described individually for each leader.

Characteristic 6. They walk with a growing awareness of a sense of destiny and see some or all of it fulfilled.

A *sense of destiny* is an inner conviction arising from an experience or a series of experiences in which there is a growing sense of awareness that God has His hand on a leader in a special way for special purposes.

Over a lifetime a leader is prepared by God for a destiny, receives guidance toward that destiny, and increasingly completes that destiny. No biblical leader who accomplished much for God failed to have a sense of destiny, one that usually grew over his lifetime.

Examples: An awareness of destiny was revealed through Joseph's dreams and his saving of the embryonic nation, Moses' saving of the nation, and Paul's vision to take the gospel to the Gentiles.

Conclusion

The classic example in the Old Testament of a good finish is Daniel, who manifests all six characteristics. The classic example in the New Testament other than Christ is Paul. There are gradations of finishing well. Some finish well but do not quite have all six characteristics or there is a lesser intensity on one or the other major characteristics. This list of characteristics is probably not complete. Others may not agree totally with them. In that case, they should at least provide an alternate list. But these are certainly evident in many leaders who have finished well.

FINISHING WELL – SIX MAJOR BARRIERS
Introduction to Research on Finishing Well

In 1989, in an article titled "Listen Up Leaders! Forewarned Is Forearmed!" I summarized my research on biblical leaders with the following opening comments.

A repeated reading of the Bible with a focus on leadership reveals four crucial observations fraught with leadership implications:

Observation 1. Few leaders finish well.
Observation 2. Leadership is difficult.

Observation 3. God's enabling presence is the essential ingredient of successful leadership.

Observation 4. Spiritual leadership can make a difference.

And what is true of biblical leaders is equally true of historical and contemporary leaders. It is the first observation to which this article speaks. Identifying the fact that few leaders finish well was a breakthrough warning for me. This led to further study. Why do few leaders finish well? *What stops them?* What does it mean to finish well? What helps them? This article answers the second question by identifying six major barriers to finishing well.

Six Barriers to Finishing Well

Comparative study of effective leaders who finished well has identified six barriers that hinder leaders from finishing well. It takes only one of them to torpedo a leader. But frequently a leader who fails in one area will also fail in others. What are these barriers? We can learn from those who didn't finish well. We can be alerted to these barriers. We can avoid them in our own lives. Proverbs 22:3 tells us,

Sensible people will see trouble coming and avoid it, but an unthinking person will walk right into it and regret it later. (GNT)

Let me share with you six barriers to finishing well that I have identified. We need to look ahead in our lives and not walk right into these barriers. We need to avoid being entrapped by them.

Barrier 1. Finances — Their Use and Abuse

Leaders, particularly those who have power positions and make important decisions concerning finances, tend to use practices that may encourage incorrect handling of finances and eventually wrong use. A character trait of greed often is rooted deep and eventually will cause impropriety with regard to finances. Numerous leaders have fallen due to some issue related to money.

Biblical Examples: Old Testament: Gideon's golden ephod; New Testament: Ananias and Sapphira.

Barrier 2. Power—Its Abuse

Leaders who are effective in ministry must use various power bases in order to accomplish their ministry. With power so available and being used almost daily, there is a tendency to abuse it. Leaders who rise to the top in a hierarchical system tend to assume privileges with their perceived status. Frequently, these privileges include abuse of power. And they usually have no counterbalancing accountability.

Biblical Example: Uzziah's usurping of priestly privilege.

Barrier 3. Pride—Which Leads to Downfall

Pride (inappropriate and self-centered) can lead to a downfall of a leader. As a leader there is a dynamic tension that must be maintained. We must have a healthy respect for ourselves, and yet we must recognize that we have nothing that was not given us by God and He is the one who really enables ministry.

Biblical Example: David's numbering.

Barrier 4. Sex—Illicit Relationships

Illicit sexual relationships have been a major downfall both in the Bible and in Western cultures.[3] Joseph's classic integrity check with respect to sexual sin is the ideal model that should be in leaders' minds.

Biblical Example: David's sin with Bathsheba.

Barrier 5. Family—Critical Issues

Problems between spouses or between parents and children or between siblings can destroy a leader's ministry. What is needed are biblical values lived out with regard to husband-wife relationships, parent-children relationships, and sibling relationships. Of growing importance in our day is the social base profiles for singles in ministry and for married couples.

Biblical Examples: David's family; Ammon and Tamar; Absalom's revenge.

Barrier 6. Plateauing

Leaders who are competent tend to plateau. Their very strength becomes a weakness. They can continue to minister at a level without there being a reality or Spirit-empowered renewing effect. Most leaders will plateau several times in their lifetimes of development. Some of the five enhancement factors for a good finish will counteract this tendency (perspective, learning posture, mentors, disciplines). There again is a dynamic tension that must be maintained between leveling off for good reasons (consolidating one's growth and/or reaching the level of potential for which God has made you) and plateauing because of sinfulness or loss of vision.

Biblical Example: David in the latter part of his reign just before Absalom's revolt.

Conclusion

Forewarned is forearmed. There are many other reasons why leaders don't finish well — usually all related to sin in some form. But at least the six categories are major ones that have trapped many leaders and taken them out of the race. Leaders who want to finish well, Take heed!

FINISHING WELL — FIVE ENHANCEMENTS
Introduction to Research on Finishing Well

In 1989, in an article titled "Listen Up Leaders! Forewarned Is Forearmed!" I summarized my research on biblical leaders with the following opening comments.

A repeated reading of the Bible with a focus on leadership reveals four crucial observations fraught with leadership implications:

Observation 1. Few leaders finish well.
Observation 2. Leadership is difficult.

Observation 3. God's enabling presence is the essential ingredient
of successful leadership.

Observation 4. Spiritual leadership can make a difference.

And what is true of biblical leaders is equally true of historical and contemporary leaders. It is the first observation to which this article speaks. Identifying the fact that few leaders finish well was a breakthrough warning for me. This led to further study. Why do few leaders finish well? What stops them? What helps them?

Five Enhancements

Comparative study of effective leaders who finished well has identified five commonalities. Not all five always appear in leaders who finish well but at least several of them do. Frequently, effective leaders who finish well will have four or five of them seen in their lives. What are these enhancements?

Enhancement 1. Perspective

Effective leaders view present ministry in terms of a lifetime perspective.[4] We gain that perspective by studying the lives of leaders as commanded in Hebrews 13:7-8. I have been doing intensive study of leaders' lives over the past thirteen years. Leadership emergence theory is the result of that research. Its many concepts can help us understand more fully just how God does shape a leader over a lifetime.[5]

Enhancement 2. Renewal

Special moments of intimacy with God, challenges from God, new vision from God, and affirmation from God both for personhood and ministry will occur repeatedly to a growing leader. These destiny experiences will be needed, appreciated, and will make the difference in persevering in a ministry. All leaders should expectantly look for these repeated times of renewal. Some can be initiated by the leader (usually extended times of spiritual discipline). But some come sovereignly from God. We can seek them, of course, and be ready for them.

Most leaders who have been effective over a lifetime have needed and welcomed renewal experiences from time to time in their lives. Some times are more crucial in terms of renewal than others. Apparently in Western society the mid-thirties and early forties and mid-fifties are crucial times in which renewal is frequently needed in a leader's life. Frequently during these critical periods discipline slacks, there is a tendency to plateau and rely on one's past experience and skills, and a sense of confusion concerning achievement and new direction prevail. Unusual renewal experiences with God can overcome these tendencies and redirect a leader. An openness to them, a willingness to take steps to receive them, and a knowledge of their importance for a whole life can be vital factors in profiting from enhancement 2 for finishing well. Sometimes these renewal experiences are divinely originated by God and we must be sensitive to His invitation. At other times we must initiate the renewal efforts.

Enhancement 3. Disciplines

Leaders need discipline of all kinds. Especially is this true of spiritual disciplines. A strong surge toward spirituality now exists in Catholic and Protestant circles. This movement combined with an increasingly felt need due to the large number of failures is propelling leaders to hunger for intimacy. The spiritual disciplines are one mediating means for getting this intimacy. Such authors as Eugene Peterson, Dallas Willard, and Richard Foster are making headway with Protestants concerning spirituality.[6] Leaders without these leadership tools are prone to failure via sin as well as plateauing.

I concur with Paul's admonitions to discipline as a means of ensuring perseverance in the ministry. When Paul was around fifty years of age he wrote to the Corinthian church what appears to be both an exhortation to the Corinthians and an explanation of a major leadership value in his own life. We need to keep in mind that he had been in ministry for about twenty-one years. He was still advocating strong discipline. I paraphrase it in my own words.

> I am serious about finishing well in my Christian ministry. I discipline myself for fear that after challenging others into the Christian life I myself might become a casualty. (1 Corinthians 9:24-27)

Lack of physical discipline is often an indicator of laxity in the spiritual life as well. Toward the end of his life, Paul is probably between sixty-five and seventy years old; he is still advocating discipline. This time he writes to Timothy, who is probably between thirty and thirty-five years old. Again, I've paraphrased this in my own words.

> Instead exercise your mind in godly things. For physical exercise is advantageous somewhat but exercising in godliness has long-term implications both for today and for that which will come. (1 Timothy 4:7-8)

Leaders should from time to time assess their state of discipline. I recommend in addition to standard word disciplines involving the devotional life and study of the Bible other disciplines such as solitude, silence, fasting, frugality, chastity, and secrecy. My studies of Foster and Willard have helped me identify a number of disciplines that can habitually shape character and increase the probability of a good finish.

Enhancement 4. Learning Posture

The single most important antidote to plateauing is a well-developed learning posture. Such a posture is also one of the major ways through which God gives vision.

Another of the seven major leadership lessons is *Effective leaders maintain a learning posture all their lives.* It sounds simple enough but many leaders don't heed it. Two biblical leaders who certainly were learners all their lives and exemplified this principle were Daniel and Paul. Note how Daniel observed this principle. In Daniel 9, when he is quite old, we find that he was still studying his Bible and still learning new things from it. And he was alert to what God wanted to do through what he was learning. Consequently, Daniel was able to intercede for his people and become a recipient of one of the great messianic revelations. Paul's closing remarks to Timothy show he was still learning. "And when you come don't forget the books, Timothy!" (2 Timothy 4:13, my paraphrase).

There are many nonformal training events available such as workshops, seminars, and conferences covering a variety of learning skills. Take advantage of them. A good learning posture is insurance against plateauing and a helpful prod along the way to persevere in leadership. An inflexible spirit with regard to learning is almost a sure precursor to finishing so-so or poorly.

Enhancement 5. Mentors

Comparative study of many leaders' lives indicates the frequency with which other people were significant in challenging them into leadership and in giving timely advice and help so as to keep them there. Leaders who are effective and finish well will have from ten to fifteen significant people who came alongside at one time or another to help them. Mentoring is also a growing movement in Christian circles as well as secular.

The general notion of mentoring involves a relational empowerment process in which someone who knows something (the mentor) passes on something (wisdom, advice, information, emotional support, protection, and linking to resources) to someone who needs it (the mentoree, protégé) at a sensitive time so that it impacts the person's development. The basic dynamics of mentoring include attraction, relationship, response, accountability, and empowerment. My observations on mentoring suggest that most likely, any leader will need a mentor at all times over a lifetime of leadership. Mentoring is available if one looks for specific functions and people who can do them (rather than an ideal mentor who can do it all). God will provide a mentor in a specific area of need for you if you trust Him for one and you are willing to submit and accept responsibility.

Simply stated, a final suggestion for enabling a good finish is find a mentor who will hold you accountable in your spiritual life and ministry and who can warn and advise so as to enable you to avoid pitfalls and to grow throughout your lifetime of ministry.

Conclusion

A leader ought to want to finish well. I never give this warning: "few leaders finish well" and this challenge: "do you want to finish well?" without an overwhelming response. "Yes, I do!" leaders will say. "Then heed these five factors," I tell them. Proactively take steps to get these factors working in your life. Finish well!

NOTES

Preface

1. The School of World Mission, now called the School of Intercultural Studies (SIS), is part of Fuller Theological Seminary. ML530, "Leadership Emergence Patterns," is one of several courses in the leadership concentration. This concentration focuses on leadership theory, including selection, training, curriculum, organizational dynamics, and leadership research. At the time of the first writing of this book, I had been researching and teaching on leadership for six years. At the time of this revision, I have retired after thirty years of research and teaching on leadership at Fuller. Much of my writing flowing from my research can be obtained from my website, www.bobbyclinton.com. See the Resource Store.

2. These studies are individual case studies that deal with specific leaders. They use the patterns and processes discussed in this book as perspectives to stimulate discovery of God's shaping activity in these lives. The vast majority of these case studies are of contemporary leaders. Though in the minority, there are a number of leaders from numerous cultures validating the notion that leadership emergence theory as seen in this book does apply to leaders of other cultures. There are also a number of studies validating God's shaping activities of female leaders.

3. My definition is more complex than I have indicated. In an introductory leadership theory course, I have defined leadership as a dynamic process over an extended period of time in various situations in which a leader, utilizing leadership resources and by specific leadership behaviors, influences the thoughts and activities of followers toward accomplishment of aims usually mutually beneficial for leaders, followers, and the macro context of which they are a part. A biblical leader is defined as a person with God-given capacity and God-given responsibility to influence a specific group of God's people toward His purposes for the group. Of particular note, leaders as defined in this book are those who will give an accountability for their leadership (see Hebrews 13:17).

Notice that the definition embraces both males and females. Throughout the book I frequently use the masculine pronoun when I am describing some leadership aspect. I am using it generically to mean he or she, his or her, and so on. Unfortunately, English, unlike Haitian Creole, does not have an inclusive pronoun that means both he/she or him/her.

4. In the leadership concentration at the School of Intercultural Studies, we view five leadership levels along a continuum on which we identify five types: A, B, C, D, and E. Two thresholds help distinguish points on the continuum. Threshold 1 is the point differentiating full-time Christian leaders fully supported from non–fully supported leaders. Threshold 2 is the point along the continuum distinguishing fully supported Christian leaders who have direct ministry functions (preaching, teaching, evangelizing) from those who have indirect ministry functions (directing, training, setting strategy, and so on). Type A and B leaders have not crossed threshold 1. They are not fully supported, and they are primarily involved in direct local ministries. Type C leaders have crossed threshold 1 but not 2. They are primarily involved in direct ministry functions. Type D and E leaders have crossed threshold 2. They are primarily involved in indirect ministry, though from time to time they do direct ministry.

5. I have not dealt with all the processes and patterns in this book but have been selective. In this book I deal with four development phases of the generalized timeline, which I define in chapter 2. These phases are common to type A, B, C, D, and E leaders. In addition, I focus on those process items that are common to all of the levels of leadership. Additional material is available on type C, D, and E leaders. There are process items other than these given in chapters 3, 4, 5, 6, and 7 of this book. These additional concepts are discussed in the manual titled *Leadership Emergence Theory* available in PDF in my Resource Store at my website, www.bobbyclinton.com, or in hard copy from the Fuller Theological Seminary Bookstore. While most of the case studies researched dealt with full-time, paid Christian leaders, it should be noted that in the earlier stages of their development they were not "full-time, paid Christian workers." Those shaping activities will apply to younger emerging leaders whether or not they become full-time, paid workers. The findings of this book do apply to both lay leaders and full-time paid Christian workers.

6. Of particular interest to Christian leadership is character formation. The term *spiritual formation* is used in the leadership concentration at the School of Intercultural Studies to designate the transformation process whereby a leader's inner character is developed. It is defined as the development of the inner life of a person of God so that the person experiences more of God, reflects more God like characteristics in personality and in everyday relationships, and increasingly knows the power and presence of God in ministry. This should be the bottom line of any development or training. We also deal with two other formations: ministerial formation (shaping that leads a person to develop effective ministry) and strategic formation (guidance toward ultimate contribution focusing on God's life purposes for the leader). See my manual *Strategic Concepts—Clarifying and Living a Focused Life*, available in the Resource Store on my website.

Introduction: Who Needs These Lessons Anyway?

1. This book treats double confirmation in depth (chapter 6), but the other three concepts are only briefly touched on in various portions of the book. Double confirmation is one of the shaping activities grouped under *certainty guidance*. For an in-depth study on guidance, see the PDF position paper "Various Inputs on Guidance—A Compendium," available in the Resource Store on my website.

2. A focused life is defined as a life dedicated to exclusively carrying out God's unique purposes through it, by identifying the focal issues—that is, the *life purpose, effective methodology, major role*, and *ultimate contribution*, which allow an *increasing prioritization* of life's activities around the focal issues and results in a *satisfying life* of being and doing. Accomplishments of life purposes are what is meant by ultimate contribution. See my manual *Strategic Concepts That Clarify a Focused Life*, available in the Resource Store on my website; an entire chapter is devoted to ultimate contribution.

3. *Giftedness set* describes the influence capacity elements of a leader. These include spiritual gifts, natural abilities, and acquired skills.

4. A *focal element* in a giftedness set refers to the dominant influence element, either spiritual gifts, natural abilities, or acquired skills, that dominates the ministry efforts of a leader. For some leaders, spiritual gifts will dominate ministry; for others, natural abilities or acquired skills will dominate.

5. *Pre-service* refers to training that is given prior to the leader's actual use of the training in full-time ministry. It is training that hopefully trains for the future, not the present. There is a fairly significant dropout of pre-service-trained leaders after about four or five years of ministry. See my manual *Leadership Training Models*, which describes a-service, pre-service, in-service, and interrupted service training. Interrupted service training is probably the most effective.

6. This organization's top leaders were males. They held a quasi-restricted view of women as leaders. Women could minister in teaching and evangelism to children but could not exercise leadership over adult males. The organization had no middle-level roles for leaders (either men or women). Their top leaders formed a small staff, who handled administrative details like salary and benefits. The majority of the organization was doing grassroots ministry like Mary. See my leadership commentary *1 and 2 Timothy: Apostolic Leadership, Picking Up the Mantle*, in which I deal with the concept of gender and leadership gifts in an article titled "Gender and Leadership." I hold that women can indeed have leadership gifts. See also Henry Mintzberg's Five Essential Organizational Structures described in his book *Structure in Fives: Designing Effective Organizations*, which describes the missing structures this mission needed. Mintzberg's five structures include: Strategic Apex (partially done); Middle Line (missing); Operating Core (of which Mary was a part); Technostructure (missing); and Support Staff (partially done). Mary should have been moved to the middle line where she could develop other Operating Core employees to do what she had learned to do.

7. Effective organizational leadership molds roles to enhance convergence factors (giftedness, experience, spiritual maturity, geographic location, effective influence-mix). In doing this, they will best meet the needs of developing an individual and fulfilling organizational functions. Convergence in the simplest terms means a time of maximum ministry productivity. Convergence roles not only free up a leader from doing ministry for which he or she is not gifted or suited but also put to use the best that the leader has to offer. Life Maturing and Ministry Maturing peak together during this period. The organization does not have the structure — a middle line — that Mary needs in order to expand her role.

8. I discuss this particular point, making decisions that concern both the organizational needs and the person's needs, in a leadership article titled

"Leading with a Developmental Bias," available in the Resource Store on my website.

9. In chapter 8, I will suggest that as a beginning effort at ministry philosophy, a leader ought to identify some important leadership values. These can be passed on readily to emerging leaders. I am sure Pastor Jeff has many important and valuable leadership values that would help a young emerging leader. More on this later. I, myself, have done this. I have captured a number of my leadership values that I want to pass on in an important position paper, "Passing On My Heritage." See my website Resource Store, where this position paper is available.

10. See my 457-page manual *Leadership Emergence Theory: A Self-Study Manual for Analyzing the Development of a Christian Leader*, available at my website Resource Store.

Chapter 1: A Letter to Dan, the Intern

1. This internship is a specialized training model in which there is guided training in on-the-job experience with particular focus on spiritual formation, in-service activity, and continuing dynamic reflection. The intern is assumed to have prior teaching and thus seeks to add experiential learning. He is guided in this experiential learning by the supervisor, who must ensure that spiritual formation, in-service activity, and dynamic reflection take place. See my self-study manual *Leadership Training Models*, available in the Resource Store on my website. See especially chapter 8 for a detailed explanation of the internship model and its eight essentials.

2. The supervisory role is crucial to the success of an internship. In most internships there should be training at four levels: for supervisors (pre-training), for the intern, for those administering the program, and for those who make up the context in which the intern will work. In this case, the supervisor (an extremely busy person for whom this internship was a very low priority) was not performing up to par. See my manual *Leadership Training Models*, chapter 8, page 129, essential 3, for seven skills demanded of a supervisor.

3. *Gift-mix* is a term coined by Dr. C. Peter Wagner—a church growth theorist—in his book *Your Spiritual Gifts Can Help Your Church Grow*. It describes the set of spiritual gifts a leader demonstrates in his ministry. Usually leaders demonstrate more than one spiritual gift in their ministries. The point I am making here is that the identification of

personality traits or natural abilities in leaders who have manifested known gifts suggests that perhaps there is a correlation between certain personality traits and certain kinds of gifts. I make an attempt to present this in the book *Unlocking Your Giftedness: What Leaders Need to Know to Develop Themselves and Others*. Natural abilities may be reflected in a spiritual gift; that is, a spiritual gift may relate to or be based on a previously recognized natural ability. The Holy Spirit releases the gift through the individual in such a way that his natural ability is enhanced with the power of the Spirit.

4. *Informal training* is a technical term taken from leadership training models theory. Training can be categorized under three broad headings: formal, nonformal, and informal. Informal training models are defined as those non-programmatic models that make deliberate use of life-activities for closure training. See my manual *Leadership Training Models*, chapter 9, which deals with informal training.

5. *Imitation modeling* is a technical term taken from leadership training model theory that usually refers to informal training models in which the person learns primarily by observing a role model and imitating skills, values, and attitudes.

6. *Informal apprenticeship* refers to that category of informal training model that is an in-service training model in which the teacher, called the master, imparts attitudes, knowledge, and skills to a learner, called the apprentice, in the context of actual ministry. In an informal apprentice-ship, the learning may not be directed or accounted for as is the case in a formal apprenticeship. See my manual *Leadership Training Models*, chapter 9, which deals with this informal training model.

7. *Mentoring* refers to a low-key informal training model where a person with a serving, giving, encouraging attitude (the mentor) sees leadership potential in a still-to-be-developed person (the protégé or mentoree) and is able to promote or otherwise significantly influence the protégé toward the realization of leadership potential. I list eight major ways that I have observed mentors helping protégés. This letter is an instance of mentor-ing. I was performing a mentoring function for Dan. See *Connecting: The Mentoring Relationships You Need to Succeed* by Paul Stanley and me for a popular treatment of mentoring. See also *The Mentor Handbook: Detailed Guidelines and Helps for Christian Mentors and Mentorees*, written by me and my son, Dr. Richard Clinton (available at my website Resource Store).

8. *Formal training*, one of three broad categories of training models, refers to training that takes place in institutions set up to offer programmatic instruction leading to degrees or other recognized closure incentives. See my manual *Leadership Training Models*, chapter 7, which deals with the Formal Mode—especially centralized models.

9. *Self-study growth projects* are a form of low-accountability informal training model. Growth projects are defined as self-directed learning projects where an adult learner is motivated to learn something and does so via learning activities that lead to some specific and attainable goal. See my manual *Leadership Training Models*, chapter 9, page 149, where I define a growth project.

10. *Nonformal training*, another of the three broad categories of training models, refers to organized, non-programmatic, functional training that has as its end product skills and knowledge that can be immediately applied to practical ministry aims. See my manual *Leadership Training Models*, chapter 8, where I describe carefully and differentiate between two popular nonformal training models: seminars and workshops. I also describe conferences, convocations, and congresses, pointing out the similarities and differences.

11. See chapter 11, "Development Toward What?" in the book *Unlocking Your Giftedness*, where in the introduction I give a table with six distinctions between the fruit of the Spirit and the gifts of the Spirit.

12. Though I do define *integrity check* briefly in this letter, I give a much more detailed explanation of how God uses it in chapter 3, "Foundational Lessons."

13. *Sphere of influence* is a technical term used in leadership emergence theory to mean the people being influenced by a leader and for whom a leader will give an account to God.

14. See Isobel Kuhn, *Green Leaf in Drought* (Singapore: Overseas Missionary Fellowship, 1981), which is a biography of an Overseas Missionary Fellowship missionary and is replete with process items. These four principles are called Andrew Murray's "Formula for Trial" and were derived from his sermon titled "Anchors to Throw Out in a Time of Testing," based on Acts 27:28-29 (see page 70 in Kuhn's book).

15. See Miles J. Stanford, *Principles of Spiritual Growth* (Grand Rapids, MI: Zondervan, 1975). This was first published as *The Green Letters*. Later the *Back to the Bible* radio program printed it in booklet form as *Principles of Spiritual Growth*.

16. Here is the quote: "A student asked the President of his school whether he could not take a shorter course than the one prescribed. 'Oh yes,' replied the President, 'but then it depends upon what you want to be. When God wants to make a oak, He takes a hundred years, but when He wants to make a squash, He takes six months'" (Stanford, 6–7).

17. I would be remiss if I didn't mention one of the best resources on isolation. Shelley G. Trebesch, one of my PhD students at Fuller, wrote a booklet titled *Isolation: A Place of Transformation in the Life of a Leader.* This little manual is worth its weight in gold. Almost every leader at one time or another will face being set aside from ministry—the basic notion of isolation. This booklet shows what leaders face when set aside from ministry for various reasons, such as sickness, persecution, discipline, crises, self-choice, and so on. The manual gives patterns and proper attitudes to face these experiences as leaders develop toward maturity in their leadership. Isolation is one of the deep processing items all leaders should schedule for. This manual has been a top seller and has been used as a very important supplemental text in courses dealing with lifelong development. It describes what is probably the most common deep processing a leader faces. It is available from the Fuller Theological Seminary Bookstore.

Chapter 2: The Basis for Lessons: The Big Picture

1. I have studied several of A. W. Tozer's writings. The most helpful to me personally were *The Knowledge of the Holy: The Attributes of God: Their Meaning in the Christian Life* and *The Pursuit of God.* I studied *A. W. Tozer: A Twentieth Century Prophet,* by David James Fant Jr., when I did my leadership emergence study of Tozer's life.

2. My major source for my leadership emergence study of Dawson Trotman's life was Betty Lee Skinner's book *Daws: The Story of Dawson Trotman, Founder of The Navigators* (Grand Rapids, MI: Zondervan, 1974).

3. My initial training in discipleship, while still an electrical engineer with Bell Telephone Laboratories, was along Navigator lines. A group of Navigator contacts were working at Lockbourne Air Force Base just outside Columbus, Ohio. I went through the Topical Memory System and read and heard *Born to Reproduce* and *The Need of the Hour.* The Hand Illustration for balanced intake of the Word and the basics of The Wheel Illustration became mine in those early years of training. The

wider fellowship with The Navigators took place at Lake Wawasee in Indiana, where we made a yearly trek to meet with others from the Great Lakes Region, then under the auspices of Jack Mayhall. I have kept up my contacts with The Navigators through the years.

4. I have read and profited from almost all of Watchman Nee's writings. *The Normal Christian Life* has been a great help, especially with illustrations, in my own ministry concerning union life. While I do not always agree with Nee's exegesis, I still admire the tone of his life. I have repeatedly studied *Against the Tide: The Story of Watchman Nee*, Angus Kinnear's biography of Nee. It was the major source for my leadership emergence analysis of Watchman Nee.

5. *Union life* is a phrase that I use to refer both to the fact of the spiritual reality of a believer joined in spirit with the resurrected Christ and the process of that union being lived out. Various slants on this doctrine go by different names, such as the exchanged life, the deeper life, the victorious life, and the normal Christian life. Today there is a movement whose voice is the magazine *Union Life*, which also seeks to expose this truth. While agreeing with its major purpose and its inspirational stories, I do not always agree with all its teachings. Union life is one of the crucial factors that come together in Phase V, Convergence. I have an important leadership article on union life in several of my New Testament biblical leadership commentaries—notably Philippians, which contrasts Paul's right-brain teaching via modeling of seven characteristics of union life and his left-brain teaching of union life as logically developed in the book of Romans.

6. *Spiritual authority* enables a leader to influence followers through persuasion, modeling, and moral expertise. In short, it is delegated authority from God that is foundational to a leader's influence with his followers. I define spiritual authority in two ways: its essence and its origin—that is, how one gets it. Essentially, spiritual authority is the right to influence, conferred upon a leader by followers, because of their perception of spirituality in that leader. Spiritual authority can also be described in terms of how a leader gets it. Spiritual authority is that characteristic of a God-anointed leader, developed upon an experiential power base (giftedness, character, deep experiences with God), that enables him to influence followers through persuasion, force of modeling, and moral expertise. I have a leadership article in my New Testament biblical leadership commentaries titled "Spiritual

Authority: Six Characteristics." See especially my commentary on Philemon, which shows how Paul very carefully uses spiritual authority.

7. The essence of leadership is influence. *Power base* refers generally to credibility or the source from which a leader derives authority to influence followers.

8. In my biblical leadership commentaries, especially *Habakkuk — Hope for a Leader in Troubled Times, Jonah — Seeing God's Perspective*, and *1, 2 Samuel*, I include a special leadership article titled "God's Shaping Activities," in which I evaluate the various processing items seen in the shaping activity. I have done this for Habakkuk, Jonah, David, Saul, Samuel, and other characters in the books of 1 and 2 Samuel. In doing this, I am demonstrating that leadership emergence theory concepts are biblical.

9. Warren Wiersbe, "Principles," *Leadership* 1, no. 1 (Winter 1980): 80.

10. Here I am giving a simplified timeline. In formal leadership emergence case studies, we do an overview chart that has the timeline along the horizontal axis. The vertical axis along the left margin of the paper is broken up into categories that allow for detailed information concerning God's processing to be recorded.

11. I am implying by this that two persons, both trained in methods of leadership emergence theory and doing independent studies on the same leader, would probably not agree totally on identification of development phases and sub-phases. But their differing perspectives would both be helpful in seeing leadership processes and principles in the development of the leader.

12. This retroactive advantage is seen very clearly in the lives of Joseph and Jephthah in the Old Testament and Barnabas and Paul in the New Testament.

13. Wiersbe has captured the spirit of what I am trying to say concerning the total impact of God's developmental task for these first three phases. Let me refer to his quote, which includes Phillips Brook's insights as well: "God makes a worker, then he uses that worker to make a work. Phillips Brooks was right when he defined preparation for the ministry as 'nothing less than the making of a man' (or the making of a woman — Brooks would agree with that). No matter what kind of ministry God gives to us — preaching, teaching, counseling, supervising, encouraging — we can never give to others what we do not have ourselves. To ignore character is to abandon the foundation of ministry" (Wiersbe, 80).

14. Convergence is a significant and complex concept. We have identified as many as eleven factors that can converge. Convergence as described in Phase V is absolute—a large number of factors converging. Some aspects of convergence, labeled mini-convergence, occur along the way in other phases.

15. Organizations often promote people into roles that do not utilize their dominant gifts, major experiences, or personality characteristics.

16. Apparent "early deaths" such as Trotman's, at least as viewed from the human perspective, would be a case in point. Watchman Nee's imprisonment would be another. These kinds of events must be viewed providentially. God's purposes in such processing are much more important than any Convergence or Afterglow ministry would have been.

17. It is a real joy to see a leader in Afterglow. I have been around two such leaders: Elmer Thompson, who founded the West Indies Mission, now called World Team; and Donald McGavran, the father of the church growth movement. I have observed the Afterglow phases of these men and have noted their influence. I have gained greatly from the privilege.

18. My last ten years have been a specialized study of leaders finishing well. My findings occur in the manual *Strategic Concepts That Clarify a Focused Life*. In that manual, I do identify developmental tasks that are part of Afterglow. I give numerous observations and suggestions about what a leader ought to do in Afterglow ministry.

19. Daniel Levinson's work *The Seasons of a Man's Life*, published by Ballantine in 1978, is an insightful book that has been helpful to me in my research on leadership development. Levinson seeks to identify development phases in adult males, using psychology and related social sciences as the theoretical base. His work builds on earlier works of Freud and Jung. I have found in Levinson's work much similarity to my own. This has given me external confirmation of my approach to leadership development studies. Levinson is using an age/grade approach to boundaries, where I use specific boundary items. I also attempt to categorize process items, where he describes them specifically. I am studying change in sphere of influence because I am concentrating on leaders, while Levinson is looking at adult males in general. And finally, I am looking at divine development toward leadership, not just development inwardly due to psychological growth or externally due to social influences.

20. I have summarized these process items from information given by Skinner in her account of Trotman's life. See pages 31–32. Note that I

use the words *check* and *test* to describe these challenges. A test or check comes after a conviction, to test or check up on the sincerity of that conviction.

21. Skinner, 70.

22. Skinner, 70.

23. Skinner, 75–76.

24. Reproduction by addition is when one person seeks to lead as many people as he can to the Lord. Multiplication is when one person seeks to lead a person to the Lord and then build into that one the heart and skills to lead others to the Lord and in turn to train them to repeat the process. If the pattern continues, there is a geometric progression that multiplies rapidly.

25. My convictions on this come from my understanding of a biblical leader as being a person with a God-given capacity and a God-given responsibility to influence a specific group of God's people toward His purposes for the group and from my biblical study on spiritual gifts and leadership accountability. I discuss this point in much more detail when I give the first challenge in chapter 9.

26. Sphere of influence refers to the totality of people being influenced and for whom a leader will give an account to God. The totality of people can be further refined to mean individuals or groups of people being directly influenced and for which a leader has direct responsibility and those people who are indirectly influenced by that leader. In leadership emergence theory, I use three major categories to describe the areas in which sphere of influence is measured: direct personal influence, organizational influence, and indirect influence.

Chapter 3: Foundational Lessons: Inner-Life Growth Processes

1. Warren Wiersbe, "Principles," *Leadership* 1, no. 1 (Winter 1980): 81–82.

2. A biblical leader is a person with a God-given capacity and a God-given responsibility to influence a specific group of God's people toward God's purposes. This chapter identifies *testing* processes that focus on the first two concepts, "capacity" and "responsibility." Chapters 4 and 5 identify processes that focus on ministry in general and specific groups in particular. Chapter 6 identifies processes that focus on the last concept, "toward God's purposes." In each of these chapters, the thrust is toward formation of a person along the lines of this definition.

3. *Webster's New Collegiate Dictionary*, 10th ed., s.v. "integrity."

4. The lists of traits in 1 Timothy 3:1-13 and Titus 1:5-9 are used somewhat idiomatically. The basic pattern is a generic summary trait that is umbrella-like, followed by specific items that clarify what is meant locally by that generic trait. In Titus 1:5-9, verse 6 gives the generic and then gives specifics, and verse 7 repeats again for emphasis the generic followed by about eleven specific items in verses 7-9. In 1 Timothy, the first trait list gives the generic in verse 2 followed by about twelve items. It then repeats the generic for emphasis in verse 7 using different phraseology. In Timothy, a similar pattern occurs for the second list. The thrust of the meaning of the generic statements in both the Titus and Timothy lists is integrity. See Charles H. Kraft, *Christianity in Culture: A Study in Dynamic Biblical Theologizing in Cross-Cultural Perspective* (New York: Orbis, 1979), 322–327; see also Burton Scott Easton, *The Pastoral Epistles* (London: SCM Press, 1948), 197–202.

5. A testing pattern is easily identified in the use of integrity checks, obedience checks, and word checks. It is threefold: (1) the test comes; (2) the test is seen and responded to; (3) the results of the test happen. For a positive test the threefold pattern is: (1) the test comes; (2) the leader sees it and responds to it appropriately; (3) God expands the leader in some way. For a negative test the threefold pattern is: (1) the test comes; (2) the leader does not see it or does not respond appropriately; (3) God gives remedial training—another test (or, worse still, sets the leader aside). Expansions are often delayed after the passing of the check. Joseph went through an integrity check with Potiphar's wife and saw just such a delay. He spent several years in prison before the expansion was realized. The example of Daniel shows an almost immediate expansion. This is apparently something God frequently does to encourage younger emerging leaders. King Saul is the exemplar for negative testing. Note that the demotion came fast as to proclamation (Samuel jumped on him quickly and gave the announcement of God's setting aside of King Saul), but it took years to work out in life. I discuss this further in this chapter.

6. I illustrate most of these kinds in the examples in this chapter. One notable exception is the prophecy of persecution integrity check. It is illustrated in Paul's strong desire to go on to Jerusalem in spite of advice to the contrary. The most dramatic urging was Agabus's prophecy (see Acts 20:22-23; 21:4,10-13).

7. Patricia Reid and Norma Van Dalen, "An Abiding Work-Leadership Development Study of Amy Carmichael" (unpublished research paper, Pasadena, CA: School of World Mission, 1985), 24–25.

8. Carlton Booth, *On the Mountaintop* (Wheaton, IL: Tyndale, 1984), 32.

9. Booth, 33.

10. Note the testing pattern — (1) the test comes; (2) Saul chooses to respond inappropriately by disobeying the clear word given him; (3) the resulting response happens. Here Saul is divinely set aside. The outworking of this divine discipline will take time but the result is already certain. Apparently the normal pattern after failure of an integrity check is repeated testing or discipline as described in Hebrews 12:7-12. Repeated failure may of course lead to being set aside. Saul was a leader in a transition era. His act would have consequences for thousands. Therefore, the discipline is more strict and immediate.

11. I cannot remember for certain but believe it was my friend Skip Gray of The Navigators who used the illustration of the rubber knife. I have often been reminded, when facing a question of obedience, to consider whether the knife in my hand is a rubber one.

12. In this chapter, I have not illustrated willingness to be used in ministry, willingness to right a continued wrong, and learning about possessions. However, in chapter 2 the illustration of Dawson Trotman giving his testimony is an illustration of a ministry obedience check. The Barnabas obedience check in Acts 4:32-37 illustrates the giving obedience check. The righting of a continued wrong usually involves financial restitution.

13. In musing with God over this issue, Nee told God, "It is not necessary to confess to others a sin of the mind." God said, "Yes, that's right, but your situation is different." This illustrates an important leadership principle, the Moses principle. In the case of leaders God often demands higher standards of obedience. This is due to the influence leaders have on followers. (See the incident in Numbers 20. Note especially the severity of the punishment both to Moses and Aaron in verse 12. See verse 8 for the obedience checks and verse 11 for Moses' failure.)

14. Watchman Nee and K. H. Weigh, *Watchman Nee's Testimony: A Unique Public Testimony* (Hong Kong: Church Book Room, 1974), 62–64.

15. In chapter 2, endnotes 6 and 7, I defined spiritual authority and power base. I am implying a direct correlation between a person's understanding, personal use of, and ministry of the Word to others with spiritual

authority. I have yet to prove this conclusively but indications of my present research are that a necessary correlate of spiritual authority is in-depth maturity in the Word of God.

16. In my own teaching on spiritual gifts, I have found it helpful to recognize three generic functions and to group the gifts according to these generic functions: power gifts, love gifts, and word gifts. These three categories recognize crucial functions that must occur in corporate situations. They are closely related to, but not identical with, the Pauline formula describing corporate traits of churches: faith, love, and hope. The power gifts demonstrate the authenticity, credibility, power, and reality of the unseen God. The word gifts clarify the nature of this unseen God and His demands and purposes. They communicate about and for this God. The love gifts manifest God in practical ways that can be recognized by a world around us that needs love. There is overlap in the clusters; that is, some gifts occur in more than one cluster. The primary word gifts are teaching, prophecy, and exhortation. Secondary word gifts include apostleship, evangelism, and pastoring. Tertiary word gifts include word of wisdom and faith. I have yet to see a leader (who has identified his gift-mix) who doesn't have a word gift. See my manual *Unlocking Your Giftedness: What Leaders Need to Know to Develop Themselves and Others.* It is available in hard copy from the Fuller Theological Seminary Bookstore or in PDF from the Resource Store on my website, www .bobbyclinton.com.

17. Angus Kinnear, *Against the Tide: The Story of Watchman Nee* (Wheaton, IL: Tyndale, 1985), 53.

18. Kinnear, 81–82.

19. Betty Lee Skinner, *Daws: The Story of Dawson Trotman, Founder of The Navigators* (Grand Rapids, MI: Zondervan, 1974), 30.

20. Reid and Van Dalen, 23–24.

21. Early integrity checks, obedience checks, and word checks seem to have long-term significance. That is, emergent leaders are often more pliable during the Inner-Life Growth phase so that process items occurring in the early development stage set guidelines for all of life. This chapter has implied this several times particularly in the examples from Nee, Carmichael, and Trotman. This highlights the necessity for recognizing potential leaders early and for instilling foundational principles during this formative stage.

Chapter 4: Second Lessons: Ministry Maturing Processes – Part I

1. Mentor, master, and supervisor are technical terms in leadership training model theory. A *master* is an expert who is associated with an apprentice and teaches his expertise to that apprentice until he can reproduce it. A *supervisor* is a person who oversees an intern (someone who has had some training and now wants to put it into practice) and meets periodically to review the intern's progress. A *mentor* is a facilitator who may have casual or in-depth contact with a potential leader. The effect of the mentor is to move the potential leader along through a variety of means.

2. It was a ministry task in that Barnabas's yet undeveloped apostolic gift was tested. It was apostolic in that the work at Antioch was to be evaluated for its authenticity. Barnabas had gone through the word processing of Peter concerning the Cornelius incident. He knew Gentiles were accepted by God. Now he would use that new knowledge to assess whether the Antioch Gentiles were indeed "true Christians" and accepted by God. Apostolic functions with new works include evaluation, correction, formative decision making, and leadership establishment. Barnabas was involved in all of these functions. This apostolic ministry task would fit about midway on the ministry task continuum. I have three leadership articles explaining apostolic ministry: "Apostolic Functions"; "Apostolic Functions: Comparison of Titus and Timothy"; "Apostolic Giftedness: Multiple Gifted Leaders." All three of these are in my biblical leadership commentary, *1 and 2 Timothy: Apostolic Leadership, Picking Up the Mantle.* This is available in PDF at my website Resource Store. Or it is available in hard copy from Fuller Theological Seminary Bookstore.

3. There is a resurgence in continuing education for missionaries and ministers in our day. Interrupted in-service training for formal training and shorter stints for nonformal training are certainly becoming more popular as ministers and missionaries recognize they cannot afford to plateau. Training progress items and ministry skills items occur well into the latter part of the ministry maturing processing. This is a healthy thing. At the School of Intercultural Studies we have categorized training as a-service, pre-service, in-service, and interrupted in-service using the criteria of time/ministry context. In terms of learning motivation, sensed relevancy, and immediate application of skills and knowledge learned, by far the most effective is the interrupted in-service.

4. Symptoms of the plateau barrier include: (1) no enthusiasm for leadership selection (a major function of leadership: recognition of emerging leaders and helping them in early training functions); (2) no personal growth projects (ministry skills and training progress items are relatively infrequent, if at all); (3) lack of interest in basal formation aspects (interaction with the Word, prayer, and special personal times alone with God); (4) a tendency to take the "easiest way" in conflict situations; (5) the fourth aspect of a leader — influencing God's people toward God's purposes — is not reflected in the leader. A major symptom is a noticeable lack of God's processing for development's sake and an increased processing for discipline or for limiting the leader's influence. This means that those aspects of convergence and life-maturing process items that overlap the Ministry Maturing phase and shift the leader into the Life Maturing phase are conspicuously absent or not perceived by the leader. I write more on this plateau barrier in the next chapter where I talk about the challenge cluster that seeks to bridge this barrier.

5. I am indebted to Bob Edwards, one of my students, who suggested the label gift-cluster in a short presentation he made to the leadership emergence class in the fall of 1986. The definition and inclusion in the giftedness development pattern are my own thinking, but the name and essential idea were his.

6. See *Barnabas: Encouraging Exhorter — A Study in Mentoring* by Laura Raab and Bobby Clinton available in PDF at my website Resource Store or in hard copy from Fuller Theological Seminary Bookstore.

7. This is an illustration of Goodwin's Expectation Principle, which suggests that a potential leader tends to rise toward the level of genuine expectancy of an established leader who is respected by the potential leader. This is an excellent leadership selection principle that requires discernment and reaps superior results. See also note 6 of chapter 9.

Chapter 5: Second Lessons: Ministry Maturing Processes – Part II

1. *Power base* refers to the source of credibility, power differential, or resources that enables a leader to have authority for influencing followers. This could be made up of any of the power-mix power forms. *Power-mix* is a term describing the combination of power forms — force, manipulation, authority, persuasion — that dominate a leader's influence in leadership acts during a given point of time in a development phase. The authority form has sub-forms of coercive authority, induced

authority, legitimate authority, competent authority, and personal authority. Spiritual authority is a special hybrid power form falling under both authority and persuasion. Leaders must have spiritual authority as the undergirding power form although, to fulfill the leader definition, they will need other power forms in combination with spiritual authority. I have written a basal paper on power forms—based on Dennis Wrong's typology. See Dennis Wrong's book *Power: Its Forms, Bases, and Uses.* This paper titled "Influence, Power, and Authority" appears in all of my New Testament biblical leadership commentaries —for example, *1 and 2 Corinthians: Problematic Apostolic Leadership.* In this paper, I clearly show that spiritual authority is a hybrid form having some authority elements and some persuasive elements.

2. In the Life Maturing phase, a leader recognizes that he ministers out of what he is. "Being" not "doing" is the primary power source—that is, the spiritual authority power resource par excellence. Of course, "doing" is important and is concomitant with "being."

3. To say it in a more optimistic way, God has some lessons to teach me, and He will go to the necessary means in order for me to learn those lessons. Therefore, I should approach conflict knowing that God may have some formative lessons for me.

4. "Success often brings with it unforeseen results that may negate the gains of the success." In change dynamics theory, we utilize this maxim: "In implementing changes we rarely solve a problem; we usually exchange one set of problems for another." Leadership backlash expresses these ideas but focuses on what God teaches the leader in those situations.

5. A leader's experience with each of the power items usually has with it a twofold pattern. Power pattern 1 is the "temporary acquisition" pattern. Power pattern 2 is the "confident usage" pattern. The "temporary acquisition" pattern is as follows: (1) not aware of or at least have no need, (2) recognition of need, (3) situation forces seeking, (4) insightful moment when God meets the leader with the particular power item, and (5) return to normal status. The "confident usage" pattern is as follows: (1) constantly aware of need for power, (2) insightful moment when God prompts usage of power, followed by (3) confident acceptance of power item by faith, and (4) God's channeling of the power situation. Power items describe the "insightful moments" when God meets the leader to meet the

situation's need. Usually the temporary acquisition pattern is repeated several times before a leader begins to move in power pattern 2. It is not clear how closely these power items are correlated to power gifts. Apparently, some leaders not manifesting power gifts regularly move in terms of the power items as well as those who have power gifts that stimulate use of pattern 2.

6. This is an illustration of a "corporate word check." The group of believers as a whole was being tested for its response to God's Word. It responded. Expansion resulted, as seen in Acts 13 (sending Paul and Barnabas). This church became a Gentile center for missions. Sometimes churches and parachurch organizations are stymied in their growth. Failed corporate word checks or obedience checks may well be the reason.

7. It is interesting to note that most great visions or purposes or destinies that giants in the faith accomplished were discovered in prayer (a prayer challenge) or were confirmed and moved upon in faith prayer. If we feel a paucity in vision, might we not first see if God has or wants to process us via the prayer challenge?

8. Change of influence was given in chapter 2 as a major way of determining a different developmental sub-phase or phase in a leader's timeline. Influence-mix is the concept that aids in understanding and cataloging a change of capacity to influence. Both kind (whether direct, indirect, or organizational) and degree (extensiveness, intensiveness, or comprehensiveness) in various combinations will most likely change as a leader moves from each development phase to the next.

9. Since writing *The Making of a Leader*, I have done extensive research on boundaries. Because each leader will go through three or four major boundaries over his lifetime, it is important that a leader knows about boundaries. Getting perspective on boundaries will help a leader pass through the boundary with minimum stress or trauma. Boundaries have three phases: entry, evaluation, and exit. Each of these three phases has special meaning for the leader going through them. See my position paper "Boundary Processing—Looking at Critical Transition in Leaders' Lives," available in the Resource Store on my website.

Chapter 6: Ongoing Lessons: Guidance and Other Multi-Phase Processes

1. I was greatly helped by a professor at Columbia Bible College, Frank Sells, who gave me a paradigm for discerning personal guidance. I have

worked further with this paradigm and since taught it and other things I learned about personal guidance to many of my classes. In 2010, I summarized all that I have learned and taught about guidance in a compendium/position paper titled "Various Inputs on Guidance — A Compendium." This forty-five-page position paper is available in the Resource Store at my website. These concepts have helped many.

2. One should recognize, however, that the biblical thrust in guidance is moral guidance and not decision-making guidance. In this chapter, I am basically talking about decision-making guidance. The six major process items I will describe are not usually part of any teaching on guidance as seen in the literature.

3. In *The Making of a Leader*, I usually use the term *protégé* when describing the person being helped. However, later when Paul Stanley and I co-authored our mentor text *Connecting*, we used the term *mentoree*. I have also seen the term *mentee* used for describing the person being helped. Stanley and I identified a mentoring continuum with different mentoring types functionally identified (those to the left are more directly involved with the mentoree; those toward the right have less personal contact with the mentoree): Discipler, Spiritual Guide, Coach, Counselor, Teacher, Sponsor, Contemporary Model, Historical Model, Divine Contact. See our book *Connecting: The Mentoring Relationships You Need to Succeed in Life*.

4. John Stott was a sponsor, promoting the careers of these Burmese leaders by financially investing in them and by backing them with credible references.

5. By calling your attention to this process item, I am hoping to stimulate you to be a mentor for emerging leaders. I'll say more on this in my final chapter, when I give the second challenge, on leadership selection.

6. The example of Gideon's fleece is a double confirmation process item in its functional intent, not in its form. The functional intent is to obtain certainty guidance, which is exactly the thrust of the double confirmation process item.

7. James 1:2-4 is the antidote against copping out. It shows that there can be preparation that appears negative to a person going through it but that has very positive benefits in formation of character. This differs from the negative preparation process item. Both will build character. But the negative preparation process item will ingrain a "release attitude" so that the person being processed can be free to embrace a new ministry that

would probably never have been considered without the negative preparation process item.

8. A biblical study of guidance (the apostle Paul is the classic case study) shows that three elements are important to guidance: *what*, *when*, and *how*. Some of these may be given fully, others partially, and all may be revealed progressively over time. The flesh act process item relates to making a decision based on partial information and presuming the other items.

9. This is a symbolic vision given in Genesis 15:1-21. Galatians 4 helps to unlock the eternal significance of the symbols—the "smoking firepot" and the "blazing torch" passing between the sacrificial carcasses (Genesis 15:17).

10. Daniel was concerned about the sins of his people. God showed Daniel in a great messianic vision how He intended to deal with the whole sin question.

11. I will discuss these two process items again in a later chapter, where I will emphasize maturity processing. Here I am emphasizing learning for ministry, there learning for character formation.

12. I have labeled this *special sensitivity*. I call it a *sovereign mindset*. A sovereign mindset is a way of viewing life's activities so as to see and respond to God's purposes in them. Paul is the New Testament exemplar in the Church Leadership Era for demonstrating a sovereign mindset. Paul had a leadership value: He sought to always see God's hand in his circumstances as part of God's plan for developing him as a leader. I generalize this leadership value and apply it to all leaders.

    Here is my wording:

    Label: Sovereign Mindset Value.

    Statement of the Leadership Value: Leaders Ought to See God's Hand in Their Circumstances as Part of His Plan for Developing Them as Leaders. I have written a leadership article on this topic—"Sovereign Mindset." This article occurs in all of my New Testament biblical leadership commentaries; it can also be purchased individually in the Resource Store on my website. A leader who does not have a sovereign mindset *will probably not finish well*. This leadership value is a must.

Chapter 7: The Deepening Lessons: Life Maturing Processes

1. Nee demonstrated that special sensitivity toward God's shaping processes, which I called in a chapter 6 note the *sovereign mindset*.

A *sovereign mindset* is a way of viewing life's activities so as to see and respond to God's purposes in them. It often takes a paradigm shift to move from "Why me?" kinds of questions to "What are you shaping in me through this?" kinds of questions.

2. The maturity cluster includes the following process items: destiny revelation, word items, literary items, contextual items, guidance items, life crisis, isolation, and spiritual authority discovery. All of these work on the major development task of life maturity. That task involves moving a leader to develop spiritual authority as the major power base. Spiritual authority is based on an experiential power base. That is, a leader's power resources for spiritual authority primarily depend on his experiential knowledge of God. Not all these process items are described in this book.

3. See endnote 5, chapter 2, where I describe *union life*. See also my article "Union Life," available in the Resource Store on my website and in many of my New Testament biblical leadership commentaries. This is the ultimate "being" for my oft-repeated statement that *"Ministry flows out of being!"*

4. Miles J. Stanford, *The Green Letters: Principles of Spiritual Growth* (Grand Rapids, MI: Zondervan, 1975), 7–8.

5. Frequently, mid-career students at the School of World Mission (now SIS) are in isolation processing. They illustrate isolation by self-choice. The time becomes a boundary transition to a new development sub-phase or phase. The isolation processing allows evaluation of past ministry and gives renewed hope for future ministry.

6. Patricia Reid and Norma Van Dalen, "An Abiding Work-Leadership Development Study of Amy Carmichael" (unpublished research paper, Pasadena, CA: School of World Mission, 1985), 33.

7. Reid and Van Dalen, 8.

8. This is a special kind of isolation process item. It is a case of psychological isolation primarily due to a different ministry paradigm. Carmichael was physically present with other missionaries and had a missionary assignment, but she was isolated psychologically from them in that her perspectives were so different from theirs.

9. Reid and Van Dalen, 39.

10. In my position paper "Isolation Processing: Learning Deep Lessons from God," available in the Resource Store on my website, I make the following comment: "More than 90% of leaders will face one or more

important isolation times in their lives. Most do not negotiate these times very well. Knowing about them and what God can accomplish in them can be a great help to a leader who then faces isolation." I go on to close this paper with five proactive suggestions for profiting from isolation. See also Shelley Trebesch's 1997 booklet, a basal work, *Isolation: A Place of Transformation in the Life of a Leader* (available at the Fuller Theological Seminary Bookstore).

11. I have already mentioned conflict in chapter 6 when I talked about multi-phase processing. The process item described here is the same. But here, I am pointing out the focus of maturity coming from that conflict. In chapter 6, I was focusing on lessons learned for ministry itself.

Chapter 8: Integrating the Lessons of Life: Toward a Ministry Philosophy

1. Chapter 8 (first written in 1988) was my first attempt to articulate what a ministry philosophy is and first steps at how to derive one. Since then I have written or compiled further works dealing with specific aspects of ministry philosophy. See "Appendix B: Annotated List of Materials Dealing with Ministry Philosophy." My last efforts have been to help leaders identify their top ten explicit leadership values.

2. See endnote 5 of the Preface, which explains what I mean by levels of leaders. I do not in any way intend to indicate that higher or lower is better or worse, simply different and requiring different leadership functions. Here I am simply indicating that higher-level leaders will have both general categories of guidelines as well as specific guidelines. The lesser levels will have identified specific guidelines but not yet generalized them to higher categories.

3. This is often indicated by repeated occurrences of the literary process item that was discussed in chapter 6 under the miscellaneous process items (multi-phase process items). I have verbalized this observation as one of my seven major leadership lessons: *Effective leaders maintain a learning posture throughout life.*

4. One would tend to think that a ministry philosophy would be unchanging. In other words, we find some principles and assume that they never change. While this is true with some core principles, the thrust of this chapter is how ministry philosophy is dynamic and changes over a lifetime because of continual learning from the Bible, learning from life, learning about one's giftedness, and learning from ministry experience.

5. In my booklet *Leadership Perspective* (chapter 5), I develop the whole concept of identification and confirmation of principles in much more depth than given here. In that treatment I give six assumptions underlying derivation of principles, a certainty screen for analyzing biblical principles, and an applicability screen. I also talk about truth drawn from sources other than the Bible. Such a treatment is beyond the scope of this book.

6. In terms of leaders who are on certain leadership levels, types A and B are usually most concerned with direct ministry. Types D and E are usually most concerned with indirect ministry. For them these additional functions are extremely important. Type C leaders are usually more direct than indirect but both apply. (See again endnote 5 of the Preface for explanation of levels.)

7. Crisis resolution is a form of decision making and a form of problem solving, but it differs in that decision making and problem solving can become rather routine. Hence, you can adapt styles to these regular occurring leadership functions. When a crisis comes unexpectedly, most likely you will revert to a reflexive style that will be a major function of your personality. Crisis leadership acts are aperiodic rather than recurrent.

8. Dr. J. Robert Clinton, "Interview Notes with Pastor Johnson" (unpublished research notes of interview, August 1987).

9. Clinton, "Interview Notes."

10. Clinton, "Interview Notes."

11. Warren Wiersbe, "Principles Are the Bottom Line," *Leadership* 1, no. 1 (Winter 1980): 80.

12. Wiersbe, 80.

13. I have not mentioned the powerful effect that worldview has on shaping one's ministry philosophy. I am assuming that this book will be used primarily by leaders with a Western worldview. Discussing ministry philosophy for non-Western cultures would require a very different chapter indeed.

14. I am writing this section in 2011 along with my revised version of *The Making of a Leader*. In retrospect, I have seen that few leaders will really develop in detail a ministry philosophy. So in this last section I am going to suggest as a minimum that a leader ought to identify at least some important leadership values. I will define a leadership value in terms of format of leadership value language.

15. This was what I meant way back in the Introduction when I said, "I am

sure Pastor Jeff has many important and valuable leadership values that would help a young emerging leader." I went on to point out that I have done that. I have captured a number of *my leadership values* that I want to pass on in an important position paper titled "Passing On My Heritage." See my website Resource Store where this position paper is available. In this final section of chapter 8, I am suggesting that a leader should identify at least a set of leadership values that are important—and pass them on to others.

16. These six spiritual DNA values come from my position paper, "Passing On My Heritage," available in my website Resource Store. See appendix B.

17. I received permission from the student to use this example.

Chapter 9: Accepting the Lessons of Life: The Leadership Challenge

1. Not all Christian leadership theorists agree with the concept of a call. The leadership commitment process item is the process item that deals with this issue. I did not define this in chapter 4 where it would normally fit simply because of space limitation. I selected those process items that most fit the larger audience of the book. The *leadership commitment process item* is a destiny process item, either an event or process, that culminates in an acknowledgment from a potential leader to God of willingness to be used in ministry in whatever way God chooses, with the recognition that the ministry is from God and that accountability must go to God. When leaders sense this process item their leadership is transformed drastically.

2. Remember, as I have stated before: The giftedness set includes spiritual gifts, natural abilities, and acquired skills. Leadership development involves expansion in all three of these areas. Natural abilities can be supplemented with skills. Giftedness discovery occurs over a period of time and also can be supplemented by skills. The thrust of this point is the concept of accountability for developing potential.

3. See my manual *Figures and Idioms*, which deals with definition and rules for interpreting metonymies (available in the Resource Store on my website).

4. Some writers on spiritual gifts would differ about developing a gift. They would argue that a believer does not own a gift. I define a spiritual gift as a God-given unique capacity to each believer for the purpose of channeling a Holy Spirit–empowered ministry through that believer, either for a momentary situation or repeatedly over time. A gift is non-vested if it

appears situationally and cannot be repeated at will by the person. Such a gift does not carry with it responsibility for development nor accountability for use over time. A gift is vested if it appears repeatedly in a person's ministry and can be repeated at will by the person. Such a gift carries with it responsibility for development and accountability for use over time. Apparently, gifts fluctuate over the life of a believer. Primary gifts are those vested gifts that are currently being demonstrated as a significant part of the gift-mix. A secondary gift at one time was a vested gift but is now not demonstrated as part of the current gift-mix. A gift is tertiary if it has been or is a non-vested gift or if it was necessitated by "role" in the past and is not now viewed as vested. When I speak about developing to one's full potential, I am thus focusing on primary (vested) spiritual gifts. See Dr. J. Robert Clinton and Dr. Richard W. Clinton, *Unlocking Your Giftedness: What Leaders Need to Know to Develop Themselves and Others* (Altadena, CA: Barnabas Publishers, 1993), available in the Resource Store on my website.

5. Recognizing emerging leaders at their earliest point of rising to leadership is a special interest of mine. I am noting principles and implications drawn from my research that deal with this special function of leadership selection. Appendix A lists the early emergence observations and implications that I have identified to date.

6. I first saw this in Bennie Goodwin's booklet *The Effective Leader*, produced by InterVarsity. I have altered the wording slightly to fit my broader concept of leadership.

7. Because of the rapid pace of change in our society, a leader who has plateaued is not stationary but is actually declining.

8. See my position paper "Listen Up Leaders!" where I introduce these four observations.

Appendix D: Three Papers on Finishing Well

1. There are around eight hundred or so leaders mentioned in the Bible. There are about one hundred who have data that helps you interpret their leadership. About fifty of these have enough data for evaluation of their finish. About one in three finished well. Anecdotal evidence from today indicates that this ratio is probably generous. Probably less than one in three are finishing well today.

2. At the time of this article, I had studied nearly 1,300 cases with about fifty Bible leaders, perhaps one hundred historical leaders, and the rest

contemporary leaders. The findings for enhancements and barriers generally hold true.

3. This is probably true in other cultures as well, though I do not have a database to prove this.

4. This is one of seven major leadership lessons derived from comparative studies. See my article "Leadership Lessons — Seven Major Lessons Identified."

5. My findings are available in a lengthy, detailed self-study manual titled *Leadership Emergence Theory*, which I privately publish for use in classes and workshops. In addition, my latest research is available in position papers at my website Resource Store.

6. See my section on spiritual guides and the appendix on the disciplines in *The Mentor Handbook*. See also "Spiritual Disciplines and On-Going Leadership." Both of these are available at my website Resource Store.

GLOSSARY

absolute convergence. A phrase describing the merging of major **convergence factors** (giftedness, role, influence mix, upward dependence) and minor convergence factors (experience, geography, prophecy, destiny items, personality shaping, etc.), maximizing a leader's effective capacity to influence at a given point in time.

afterglow phase. A term used to label the sixth development phase of the **generalized timeline**. Synonym: celebration.

apostleship or **apostleship gift.** One of the leadership gifts that is part of the **word gift-cluster** (a secondary word gift); refers to a specific leadership capacity in which one exerts influence over others so as to establish new local churches and new works needed to enhance the spread of Christianity and to guide those new works in their foundational stages.

authority insights process item. A **process item** describing God-given lessons about authority and its use in exercising influence; especially those lessons leading to use of **spiritual authority** as a primary power form.

authority problem. A major problem normally faced by all leaders at one time or another (sometimes repeatedly), usually in the early or middle **ministry maturing sub-phases**, in which an emerging leader learns to submit to the authority of other leaders; it is the spirit of submissiveness that is crucial in the problem. One who is to later exercise authority without abusing it must learn submissiveness. The authority problem is the occasion for this important lesson.

balanced guidance problem. A guidance problem identified with the tendency of leaders to make decisions without a balanced cluster of guidance elements and sources. What, when, and how are the major elements in guidance; sources include circumstances, inner, believers, and revealed Word. These elements and sources may use any of the **guidance factors**.

boundary. *See* **boundary time**.

boundary events. Significant experiences that happen during a **boundary time** and influence its outcome.

boundary item. A special **boundary event**, that is, an identifiable **process item** during a **boundary time** that can be correlated significantly to the transition process of the leader from one phase to the next.

boundary time. An indefinite period of time embracing the transition experiences a leader goes through in moving from one **development phase** (or **sub-phase**) to another. Synonym: boundary.

bridging guidance pattern. The growth pattern describing how God teaches a leader lessons of personal guidance as a bridge to corporate guidance.

celebration. *See* **afterglow phase**.

certainty continuum. A horizontal line on which is depicted principles as suggestions, guidelines, and absolutes—in that order. The principles can be used with more certainty as they are identified to the right on the continuum. *Suggestions* refer to truth observed in some situations. Suggestions are the most tentative—use with caution. *Guidelines* are more firm and have evidence for broader application. *Absolutes* are principles that evince God's authoritative backing for all leaders everywhere.

challenge cluster. A group of **process items** that cluster together around the **discernment function** and focus on expanding a leader's personal development and ministry accomplishment. Includes process items such as **prayer challenge, faith challenge, influence challenge, divine affirmation**, and **ministry affirmation**.

conference. A technical term in leadership training models theory describing a short **nonformal training model** that groups leaders (usually type D or E) together for plenary sessions, **seminars**, and **workshops** dealing with major themes important to Christian workers.

confirmation pattern. A guidance pattern that reflects the repeated instances of God's confirmation of significant truth upon which a leader acts because of God's use of more than one source to confirm guidance and give credibility to leadership.

conflict process item. Instances in a leader's life in which God uses conflict, whether personal or ministry related, to develop the leader in dependence upon God, faith, and insights relating to personal life and ministry.

continuum. *See* **certainty continuum**.

convergence factors. The generic category label embracing the dominant **process items** in the **convergence phase** and the elements of convergence. The major convergence elements include: **giftedness set**, role, **influence-mix**, and upward dependence. The minor convergence elements include such things as special opportunity, experience, geography, prophecy, **destiny process items**, personality shaping, etc.

convergence phase. A term used to label the fifth development phase of the **generalized timeline**.

crises process item. **Process items** that refer to special intense pressure situations in life, which are used by God to test and to teach dependence on Him.

destiny process items. Significant acts, people, or providential circumstances or timing that hint at some future or special significance to a life and add to an awareness of a sense of destiny in a life. Usually these items are grouped into three kinds: destiny preparation, destiny revelation, and destiny fulfillment.

development phase. A period of time along a leader's **timeline** that is integrated around a **development task** and characterized by a concentration of like **process items**, a relatively stable **influence-mix**, and marked by **boundary items** at its initiation and close.

development tasks. The central thrusts of processing in a given **development phase**; that is, the direction or intent of God's efforts in changing (exposing, enlarging, or initiating) a leader's influence capacity in a development phase.

direct influence. One of the three domains of a **sphere of influence**, which indicates the totality of people being influenced face to face. *See also* **indirect influence** and **organizational influence**.

discernment function. The fourth **development task** described in the **ministry maturing phase**, which has to do with capacity to perceive, learn, and assimilate lessons about ministry, so as to form a ministry philosophy that informs future leadership efforts.

discipleship. The process of developing a believer. A disciple is described as a committed believer who increasingly is dependent upon Christ as life, who communicates with God, who uses his gifts to minister to God and others, and who relates to and depends upon others in the body of Christ in order to live a life that is both personally satisfying and meaningful to God's kingdom.

divine affirmation process item. A special kind of guidance experience in which God gives approval to a leader so that the leader has a renewed sense of ultimate purpose and a refreshed desire to continue serving God. Divine affirmations have come in the following forms: sovereign arrangement of circumstances, an inner voice or other direct revelation, a dream, a vision, angelic visitation, a prophetic word, a miraculous sign, and a sense of God's blessing on a life as attested to by external testimony (see Joseph in Genesis 39:2-3,21-23).

divine contact process item. A **process item** involving a person whom God brings to a leader at a crucial moment in a development phase in order to accomplish one or more of the following (or related) functions: affirm leadership potential, encourage leadership potential, give guidance on a special issue, give insights that broaden the leader's capacity, challenge the leader in upward development, and/or open a door to a ministry opportunity.

double confirmation process item. This term refers to the unusual guidance **process item** in which God makes clear His will by reinforcing it through more than one source, each source independent of the others.

early ministry processing. The first **sub-phase** of the **ministry maturity phase**, characterized by processing toward the **entry function**.

emergence patterns. *See* **leadership emergence patterns**.

entry function. The first **development task** described in the **ministry maturing phase**, which has to do with **process items** like **ministry task** and **ministry challenge** and is concerned with initial steps into ministry.

evangelism gift. One of the leadership gifts that is part of the **word gift-cluster** (a secondary word gift); a specific leadership capacity in which one exerts influence over others publicly and/or privately through various means with the message of salvation in Christ and sees them respond by taking initial steps in Christian discipleship.

evolutionary pattern. A three-stage pattern describing the emergence of a **ministry philosophy**: stage 1 — osmosis; stage 2 — implicit to explicit; stage 3 — explicit and integrated.

exhortation gift. One of the leadership gifts that is part of the **word gift-cluster** (a primary word gift). Refers to the capacity to urge people to action in applying scriptural truth, or to encourage people in scriptural truth, or to comfort people through application of scriptural truths to their needs.

faith challenge process item. A **process item** occurring dominantly in the **ministry maturity phase** that God uses to expand a leader's vision and dependence upon Him to accomplish that vision. When the focus of the process item is to test a leader in preparation for expansion, it is termed a faith check or faith test. As a leader matures and establishes habitual patterns of operating in faith, the check aspect drops off and the challenge aspect dominates. *See also* **faith check process item**.

faith check process item. An early form of the **faith challenge process item**, in which God tests a leader's inner conviction as to whether God is going to do something He has revealed to that leader. Expansion usually means a larger capacity to influence toward God's purposes. Synonym: faith test.

faith gift. One of the leadership gifts that is part of the word cluster (a tertiary **word gift**); that unusual capacity to recognize in a given situation what God intends to do and to trust Him for it until He brings it to pass. It is most likely expressed through prayer with God (i.e., the prayer of faith), though it may simply be a belief in what God can and will do in some situation.

faith test. *See* **faith check process item**.

flesh act process item. A guidance **process item** referring to those instances in a leader's life when guidance is presumed and decisions are made either hastily or without proper discernment of God's choice. Such decisions usually involve the working out of guidance by the leader using some human manipulation or other means, bringing ramifications that later affect ministry and life negatively.

focal element. Member of the **giftedness set** (either spiritual gifts, natural abilities, or acquired skills) that lies at the center of a leader's overall ministry efforts and to which the other elements operate supportively.

formal training mode. In leadership training models theory, the term is used to describe deliberate programmatic institutionalized training, leading to credentials or other public recognition of the training.

foundational factors. The generic category label embracing the dominant **process items** in the foundational phase of the **generalized timeline**, including such items as family, contextual, and conversion.

foundational ministry pattern. An observation-statement: "Faithfulness in ministry tasks and ministry assignments along with positive response to the testing element of many of the ministry **process items** leads to expanded ministry and retesting of faithfulness at that new ministry level."

generalized timeline. A **timeline** containing six **development phases** titled **sovereign foundations, inner-life growth, ministry maturing, life maturing, convergence**, and **afterglow**; derived from a synthesis of many unique timelines found in **leadership development studies** of individual leaders.

gift-cluster. A term used in explaining an advanced stage in the **giftedness development pattern**; describes a **gift-mix** in which there is a dominant gift supported by other gifts and used so that the supportive gifts harmonize with the dominant gift to maximize effectiveness.

gift-mix. A term, originating with Dr. C. Peter Wagner, that refers to the set of gifts that a leader evinces in ministry. While all believers have at least one gift, leaders usually repeatedly exercise more than one gift.

gifted power process item. A term describing the **process item** that notes specific instances of the use of a spiritual gift in which it is clear that the Holy Spirit is channeling power in the use of the gift. The stress is on the awareness of this happening and resultant exercise by faith expecting repeated occurrence.

giftedness development pattern. The eight-stage pattern that includes movement from (1) ministry experience, (2) to discovery of gift, (3) to increased use of that gift, (4) to effectiveness in using that gift, (5) to discovery of other gifts, (6) to identification of **gift-mix**, (7) to development of **gift-cluster**, (8) to **convergence**.

giftedness discovery process item. A term describing the **process item** that notes any significant advance along the **giftedness development pattern** and that identifies whatever event, person, or reflection process was instrumental in bringing about the discovery.

giftedness drift. A term that describes the intuitive tendency of a developing potential leader to respond to **ministry challenges** and **ministry assignments** that fit his spiritual gift.

giftedness set. A term describing the set of influence capacity elements of a leader and including the three major elements: spiritual gifts, natural abilities, and acquired skills.

guidance factors. The generic category label embracing the **process items** used by God to give special direction to a leader throughout all **development phases**, often seen during **boundary times**. Includes such items as **divine contacts**, **negative preparation**, **mentoring**, **double confirmation**, **divine affirmation**.

indirect influence. One of the three domains of **sphere of influence** that indicates the totality of people being influenced by miscellaneous influences a leader exerts through others, media, writing, associations, etc. *See also* **direct influence** and **organizational influence**.

influence challenge process item. A **process item** that describes those times when a leader is prompted by God to take steps to expand leadership capacity in terms of **sphere of influence**.

influence-mix. A term describing the combination of **sphere of influence** elements— **direct**, **indirect**, and **organizational**.

informal apprenticeship. A technical term in leadership training models theory, describing an informal training model that involves a master training an apprentice in skills or knowledge either by modeling or by minimal instruction, with the result that the apprentice uses what has been learned.

informal training mode. In leadership training model theory, the training mode that deliberately uses life-activities as the basis for purposeful training.

information mapping. A writing technique for creating self-study materials that uses reference learning techniques to facilitate rapid assimilation of essential data and later referencing of the same.

inner-life growth factors. The generic category label embracing the dominant **process items** in the **inner-life growth phase** of the **generalized timeline**, including such items as **integrity checks**, **obedience checks**, and **word checks**.

inner-life growth phase. A term used to label the second **development phase** of the **generalized timeline**.

integrity check process item. A **process item** found dominantly in the **inner-life growth phase** that refers to the special kind of process test God uses to evaluate intentions and as a springboard to expansion of the leader's capacity.

isolation process item. A **maturity factor** item in which a leader is separated from normal ministry, while in the natural context in which ministry has been occurring, usually for an extended time, and thus experiences God in a new or deeper way.

later ministry processing. The final **sub-phase** of the **ministry maturing phase** characterized by processing toward the **relational function** and **discernment function**.

leader. In the biblical context, a person with a God-given capacity and a God-given responsibility to influence a specific group of God's people toward His purposes for the group.

leadership. In leadership theory, leadership is technically defined as a dynamic process over an extended period of time in which a leader (utilizing leadership resources and by specific leadership behaviors) influences the thoughts and activities of followers, toward accomplishment of aims—usually mutually beneficial for leaders, followers, and the macro context of which they are a part.

leadership backlash process item. A **process item** describing the condition when followers react against a course of action taken by a leader; usually due to unforeseen complications arising after the followers have previously approved of the action.

leadership development. A measure of a leader's changing capacity to influence, in terms of various factors, over time; also used to indicate the actual patterns, processes, and principles that summarize development.

leadership development study. The end product of a research approach that assesses emergence of leadership potential by utilizing a life-history analysis of a leader, integrating internal influences (personal/psychological), external influences (social/contextual), and divine influence (God's providential working) upon the leader's influence capacity.

leadership emergence patterns. A special **leadership development** phrase used to indicate patterns (or underlying processes or principles) that are particularly useful in the early identification of potential leaders; helpful to existing leadership as they select and develop future leaders. The concept is extended to ongoing emergence of further capacities of leaders.

leadership selection. This term describes a major leadership responsibility that involves recognition and facilitation of emerging leaders in the early **entry function** and **training function**.

leadership types. A typology scale used to indicate different kinds of leaders based on **influence-mix**, time involved, support status, and type of ministry (direct or indirect). Types A and B are local leaders not fully supported. Type C is a local leader fully supported doing primarily direct ministry. Types D and E are fully supported doing primarily indirect ministry. Type E would be a leader with international influence.

legitimate authority. A technical term in leadership theory, describing the manifest form of power a leader uses to obtain compliance from a follower by using influence pressure consonant with expectations (jointly held by leader and followers) of the role or position held.

life-crisis item. A specialized form of a **crises process item**, referring to a time of crisis characterized by intense pressure in which the meaning and purpose of life are searched out, and the leader has experienced God in a new way as the Source of life, the Sustainer of life, and the Focus of life.

life-maturing phase. A term used to label the fourth **development phase** of the **generalized timeline**.

like attracts like pattern. An observation describing an early emergence pattern, concerning **giftedness discovery**: "Potential leaders are intuitively attracted to leaders who have like spiritual gifts."

limited apprenticeship. A technical term in leadership training models theory, describing an informal training model that involves a master training an apprentice in skills or knowledge, who agree to minimal training goals; more formal (stated limited goals, agreed upon methods, time, etc.) than an **informal apprenticeship**.

literary process item. A **process item** that refers to the means whereby God is able to teach lessons to leaders for their own lives through others' writing. This ability to learn for one's own life personally from the lessons seen in the lives of others is sometimes called vicarious learning.

love gifts. A term describing the **gift-cluster** used by God to demonstrate His love through His people to believers and unbelievers; includes mercy, giving, helps, and governments.

Luke 16:10 principle. A principle derived from observation of emergent leaders in the **inner-life growth phase** and early **ministry maturing phase**: "Faithfulness in a small responsibility is an indicator of faithfulness in a larger responsibility."

maturity cluster. A cluster of **process items** whose effect is to deepen character; includes **destiny** revelation, **word** items, **literary** items, **contextual** items, **guidance** items, **life crisis**, **isolation**, and **spiritual authority** discovery.

maturity factors. The generic category embracing the dominant **process items** in the maturing phase of the **generalized timeline**; includes **crisis**, **isolation**, **destiny**, inner **conflict**, and **influence-mix**.

mentor. A term in leadership development theory that refers to a leader who, at an opportune moment, facilitates, in any one of a variety of ways, the development of an emergent leader toward realization of potential. A mentor is a special case of a **divine contact**. Mentors may influence by seemingly small actions or important ones, including timely advice, risking a reputation in order to support, bridging, modeling, supplying information, giving financially, co-ministering, etc.

mentoring. A special kind of **divine contact process item** that refers to the process whereby a person with a serving, giving, encouraging attitude (the mentor) sees leadership potential in a still-to-be developed person (the protégé) and is able to promote or otherwise significantly influence the protégé toward the realization of potential.

middle ministry processing. The second **sub-phase** of the **ministry maturing phase** characterized by processing toward the **training function** and **relational function**.

mini-convergence. Two or more **convergence factors**, whether major (**giftedness set**, role, **influence-mix**, upward dependence) or minor (experience, geography, prophecy, **destiny process items**, personality shaping, etc.) or some combination, support each other to increase a leader's influence at a given point in time.

ministry affirmation process item. A special kind of **destiny process item** experience in which God gives approval to a leader in some ministry assignment, resulting in a renewed sense of purpose for the leader.

ministry assignments process item. A **process item** describing a ministry experience that is more permanent than a **ministry task**, yet has the same basic pattern of entry, ministry, closure, and transition, through which God gives new insights to expand influence capacity and responsibility toward future leadership.

ministry challenge process item. A **process item** whereby a leader or potential leader is prompted to accept a new ministry assignment and to sense the guidance of God into service.

ministry conflict process item. A **process item** referring to those instances in ministry in which a leader learns either positive or negative lessons about the nature of conflict, possible ways to resolve conflict, possible ways to avoid conflict, ways to creatively use conflict, and how to see conflict in terms of God's processing of the leader's inner life.

ministry dropout. A term referring to the people who do not continue in ministry roles or functions after having experienced conflict; particularly applied to seminary students who after preparation for full-time ministry stay in the ministry only three to five years.

ministry factors. The generic category label embracing the dominant **process items** in the ministry phase of the **generalized timeline** and including such items as **leadership backlash**, structural testing, relationship testing, giftedness, **gifted power**, **prayer power**, **spiritual warfare**, **power encounter**, entry points, **ministry task**, **ministry conflict**, ministry perception, ministry vision, authority tests, spiritual authority perception, innovative perception, etc.

ministry history. A technical term in leadership development theory referring to the identification and cataloging of ministry tasks or ministry assignments or other closure ministry experiences sequentially so that certain aspects of leader development can be analyzed (patterns, processes, influence capacity, etc.).

ministry maturing phase. A term used to label the third **development phase** of the **generalized timeline**.

ministry philosophy. A technical term in leadership development theory referring to ideas, values, and principles (whether implicit or explicit) that a leader uses as guidelines for decision making, for exercising influence, or for evaluating his ministry.

ministry skills process item. A **process item** referring to the acquisition of one or more identifiable skills (relational, group, organizational, word, etc.) that aid one in a ministry assignment. The prime process item in developing ministerial formation.

ministry task continuum. A horizontal line on which one can plot ministry tasks in terms of their main emphasis in function. Toward the left of the line are plotted ministry tasks that function primarily for developing the person doing the task; toward the right of the line are plotted tasks that function primarily for the accomplishment of the task.

ministry task process item. This term refers to a **process item** that occurs during the transition from the **inner-life growth phase** to the **ministry maturing phase** (dominantly in the latter); refers to an assignment from God that primarily tests a person's faithfulness and obedience, but often also allows use of ministry gifts in the context of a task that has closure, accountability, and evaluation.

negative preparation process item. A sovereign **guidance factor** referring to the special processing that involves God's use of events, people, conflict, persecution, experiences, etc., to focus on the negative in order to free a person to enter the next **sub-phase** or **development phase** with abandonment and revitalized interest.

networking power process item. A **process item** that points out God's unusual use of **mentors**, **divine contacts**, or other related leaders to open doors or accomplish goals for a leader so that the leader senses the importance of relationships with other leaders and knows the touch of God through networks of people.

nonformal training mode. In leadership training models theory, the term is used to describe deliberate non-programmatic, non-institutionalized training leading to functional skills for ministry.

obedience check process item. A **process item** found dominantly in the **inner-life growth phase**; refers to the special category of process item in which God tests personal response to revealed truth and uses as a springboard to expansion of the leader's capacity.

organizational influence. This term is used to describe one of the three domains of **sphere of influence** that indicates the totality of people being influenced by a leader via organizational structures. *See also* **direct influence** and **indirect influence**.

pastoring gift. One of the leadership gifts that is part of the **word gift-cluster** (a secondary word gift); refers to a specific leadership capacity in which one exerts influence over others to care for them, nurture them, edify them, direct them, and answer to God for them.

patience problem. An observation, concerning a tendency toward a guidance pattern, that states, "Leaders tend to move ahead in major decisions before receiving a certainty word of guidance."

pattern. A term used to describe a repetitive cycle in **leadership development**. The cycle may involve periods of time, combinations of **process items**, or combinations of identifiable concepts such as **testing-expansion**.

plateau barrier. A term describing the major hindrance to expansion of capacity by a leader; a comfortable range of ministry skills allows one to "get by."

plateau pattern. The tendency for leaders to appropriate fewer and fewer ministry skills as they move from early and middle ministry processing to latter ministry processing.

power base. The source of credibility, power differential, or resources that enables a leader to have authority for influencing followers.

power cluster. A general phrase describing the cluster of power **process items** (including **gifted power**, **prayer encounter**, **prayer power**, **spiritual warfare**) that focus on accomplishment of the **discernment function** in a leader during the **ministry maturing phase**.

power encounter process item. A **process item** representing a crisis in which there is confrontation between people representing God and people representing other supernatural forces in which the issue is power. God's credibility is at stake and is vindicated in the unusual demonstration of God's power.

power gifts. A term describing the **gift-cluster** that demonstrates the authenticity, credibility, power, and reality of the unseen God, such as **word of wisdom**, **word of knowledge**, **prophecy gift**, kinds of healings, operations of power (miracles), discernings of spirits, kinds of tongues, interpretation of tongues, and faith.

prayer challenge principle. A principle describing the responsibility function exercised by many leaders in the Bible concerning their ministry: "If God calls you to a ministry then He calls you to pray for that ministry."

prayer challenge process item. A **process item** referring to instances in ministry when God in an unusual way impresses a leader with the lesson that he must pray for that ministry, and in which there is positive growth that will affect later ministry.

prayer power process item. A **process item** referring to a specific instance of prayer to meet a situation in such a way that it is clear that God has answered the prayer and demonstrated the authenticity of the leader's **spiritual authority**.

principle. This word is used to describe a generalized truth that is repeatedly observed in various leadership situations and can be taught with varying degrees of authority to other leaders for transfer to their leadership situations. Principles are usually analyzed as suggestions (lowest authority level), guidelines (next highest authority level), and requirements (highest authority level).

process items. A phrase referring to providential events, people, circumstances, special interventions, inner-life lessons, and/or anything else that God uses in the **leadership selection** process of a person to indicate leadership potential (inner integrity and influence capacity), to develop that potential, to confirm appointment to the ministry role or responsibility, or to move the leader toward God's appointed ministry level for realized potential.

prophecy gift. One of the leadership gifts that functions as part of the **word gift-cluster** (a primary word gift) and **power cluster**; refers to the capacity to express truth (of a predictive, explanatory, or corrective nature) from God in order to admonish, edify, or correct the church or individuals.

reflective evaluation pattern. A maturity pattern that observes that repeatedly God breaks into a leader's life in order to prod maturity growth. The pattern usually has five steps: (1) gaining attention via intense processing; (2) serious reflection about ministry, life, and ultimate reality; (3) evaluation and a redirection commitment;

(4) renewed determination to know God more deeply; and
(5) God's blessing on the commitment.

relational function. The third **development task** described in the **ministry maturing phase** that has to do with capacity to relate to superiors, peers, other leaders, and followers so as to effectively influence.

relational insights process item. A **process item** occurring in the middle ministry **sub-phase** that refers to those instances in ministry in which a leader learns either positive or negative lessons with regard to relating to other Christians or non-Christians in the light of ministry decisions or other influence means; such lessons significantly affect future leadership.

seminars. A technical term in leadership training models theory describing a short nonformal training model in which an expert shares knowledge, new insights, or perspectives to groups of people. Because of the numbers of people involved, mass communication methods are used. Seminars are primarily cognitive in focus and motivational rather than skill oriented, as **workshops** are.

sovereign foundations phase. A term used to label the first **development phase** of the **generalized timeline**.

sphere of influence. A term in leadership development theory referring to the totality of people being influenced and for whom a leader will give an account to God. This can be broken down further to personal **direct influence** (face-to-face present ministry), **indirect influence** (not time bound), or **organizational influence** (flowing through organizational structures).

spiritual authority. A term in leadership development theory referring to a source of credibility from God that permits leaders to influence followers. More technically, that characteristic of a God-anointed leader developed upon an experiential **power base** that enables him to influence followers through persuasion, force of modeling, and moral expertise.

spiritual dynamics. A phrase connoting the patterns, processes, and principles underlying the spiritual formation aspects of **leadership development**.

spiritual formation. A term referring to the development of the inner life of a person, so that the person experiences more of Christ as the Source of life, reflects more Christlike characteristics in personality and in everyday relationships, and increasingly knows the power and presence of Christ in ministry.

spiritual gifts. Those special capacities given by the Holy Spirit to every believer and energized by the Holy Spirit in the believer's ministry.

spiritual warfare process item. One of the **power cluster process items** that refers to those instances in ministry where the leader discerns that **ministry conflict** is primarily supernatural in its source and essence, and resorts to various power items to solve the problem in such a way that leadership capacities, notably **spiritual authority**, are expanded.

sub-phases. Identifiable periods of time within a development phase that exhibit the characteristics of a development phase to a lesser degree.

submission cluster. A group of **process items** that cluster around the **relational function** (notably the **authority problem**) and focus on expanding a leader's understanding of authority, structures of authority, and influence means. Process items such as **authority insights**, **relational insights**, **ministry conflict**, and **leadership backlash** form this cluster.

teaching gift. One of the leadership gifts that is part of the **word gift-cluster** (a primary word gift); refers to the capacity to express God's truth in such a way as to clarify it, explain it, and expose it so that its understanding and application to life are very probable.

testing-expansion cycle. A pattern that is the primary basis for **leadership development** in the **inner-life growth phase**. When operating positively for development it usually has three parts: a test, a positive response to the test, and an expansion of leadership capacity. When operating negatively it has three parts: a test, a failure of the test, and remedial action by God for the leader.

timeline. A horizontal line, representing the length of life of a leader, marked off into **development phases** for the purpose of recording information in columns underneath the development phases; used in an integrative analysis of the leader's development. *See also* **generalized timeline**.

training function. This term refers to the second development task described in the **ministry maturing phase**; covers acquisition of skills and development of gifts to increase ministerial formation.

training progress process item. A **process item** that focuses on a closure experience, usually some form of divine affirmation, that stimulates expectation for future leadership after further training in formal, nonformal, or informal modes. The item is characterized by identifiable progress in influence capacity, leader responsibility, or self-confidence.

union life. A phrase indicating the acme of spiritual formation; refers both to the believer's union with the resurrected Christ and the process of that union being lived out.

upward development pattern. A pattern occurring throughout a leader's lifetime that is a repeated cyclic spiraling of growth in being and doing. In each "being" cycle there is an increased depth of experiencing God and knowing God and in each "doing" cycle there is increased depth of effective service to God. The final result of the upward development pattern is a fusion of being and doing.

vicarious learning. *See* **literary process item**.

word check process item. A special kind of **word process item** found dominantly in the **inner-life growth phase** that refers to the special kind of test God uses to evaluate a leader's ability to understand or receive a word from God and to see it worked out in life. Positive response leads to increased sensitivity, to more truth, increased spiritual authority, and increased capacity.

word gifts. A term describing the **gift-cluster** that is specifically used by God to reveal and clarify truth about Himself and His purposes and that will edify the believers and instill hope in them concerning God's present and future activity. The primary word gifts are exhortation, prophecy, and teaching. The secondary word gifts are apostleship, evangelism, and pastoring. The tertiary word gifts are **word of wisdom**, **word of knowledge**, and faith.

word of knowledge. A **spiritual gift** that functions in the **power cluster** of gifts and word cluster (tertiary) and is defined as a special revelation of knowledge from God concerning something the Spirit wants communicated.

word of wisdom. A **spiritual gift** that functions in the **power cluster** of gifts and word cluster (tertiary) and is defined as the capacity to know the mind of the Spirit in a given situation and to communicate clearly the situation, facts, truth, or application of facts and truth to meet the needs of the situation.

word process item. This term refers to an instance in which a leader receives a word from God that affects significantly a leader's guidance, commitment, decision making, personal value system, **spiritual formation**, **spiritual authority**, or **ministry philosophy**. A **word check** is a special kind of word **process item**.

workshops. A technical term in leadership training models theory describing a short nonformal training model in which an expert shares knowledge and skills to a small group of people so that those people will be able to apply that knowledge or those skills at the end of the training. Numbers are kept small enough so that individual attention and practice of the knowledge or skills can be observed and improved upon. Workshops are primarily experiential and motivation is an assumed prerequisite.

BIBLIOGRAPHY

Booth, Carlton. *On the Mountaintop*. Wheaton, IL: Tyndale, 1984.

Carmichael, Amy. *If*. Fort Washington, PA: Christian Literature Crusade, 1992.

Chen, James. *Meet Brother Nee*. Goleta, CA: Christian Books, 1976.

Clinton, Dr. J. Robert. "Apostolic Functions." 2001. (This leadership article is available in *1 and 2 Timothy: Apostolic Leadership, Picking Up the Mantle*.)

————. "Apostolic Functions—Comparison of Titus and Timothy." 2001. (This leadership article is available in *1 and 2 Timothy: Apostolic Leadership, Picking Up the Mantle*.)

————. "Apostolic Giftedness—Multiple Gifted Leaders." 2001. (This leadership article is available in *1 and 2 Timothy: Apostolic Leadership, Picking Up the Mantle*.)

————. "Boundary Processing—Looking at Critical Transition Times in Leaders' Lives." 1992. (A PDF version of this position paper is available in the Resource Store at my website, www.bobbyclinton.com.)

————. *Clinton's Biblical Leadership Commentary: Leadership Insights from Eight Important Bible Books on Leadership*. Altadena, CA: Barnabas Publishers, 1999.

————. *Figures and Idioms*. Altadena, CA: Barnabas Publishers, 1983. (A PDF version is available in the Resource Store at my website, www.bobbyclinton.com.)

————. "Finishing Well—The Challenge of a Lifetime." 1994. (A PDF version of this position paper is available in the Resource Store at my website, www.bobbyclinton.com.)

————. "Five Enhancements." 1999. This leadership article was first published in *Clinton's Biblical Leadership Commentary*. (See appendix D of this book.)

————. *Habakkuk: Hope for a Leader in Troubled Times*. 2002. (Available in PDF in the Resource Store at my website, www.bobbyclinton.com.)

————. "Influence, Power, and Authority." 2003. (This leadership article is available in *1 and 2 Corinthians: Problematic Apostolic Leadership*.)

————. "Interview Notes with Pastor Johnson." Unpublished research notes of interview in August 1987.

————. "Isolation Processing: Learning Deep Lessons from God." 1995, 2011. (This position paper is available in a PDF version in the Resource Store at my website, www.bobbyclinton.com.)

————. *John: Jesus' Incarnational Leadership*. 2007. (Available in PDF in the Resource Store at my website, www.bobbyclinton.com.)

————. *Jonah: Seeing God's Perspective—A Crucial Paradigm Shift*. 2002. (Available in PDF in the Resource Store at my website, www.bobbyclinton.com.)

————. *Leadership Emergence Theory: A Self-Study Manual for Analyzing the Development of a Christian Leader*. Altadena, CA: Barnabas Publishers, 1989. (Hard copy available through Fuller Theological Seminary Bookstore; PDF version available in the Resource Store at my website, www.bobbyclinton.com.)

————. *Leadership Perspectives: How to Study the Bible for Leadership Insights*. 1993. (Hard copy available through Fuller Theological Seminary Bookstore; PDF version available in the Resource Store at my website, www.bobbyclinton.com.)

————. *Leadership Training Model: A Self-Study Manual for Evaluating and Designing Training*. Altadena, CA: Barnabas Publishers, 1986, 2006. (PDF version available in the Resource Store at my website, www.bobbyclinton.com.)

———. "Leading with a Developmental Bias." 1996. This leadership article was published separately in 1996 and included in *Clinton's Biblical Leadership Commentary*, published in 1999.

———. "Listen Up Leaders!" 1989. (A PDF version of this position paper is available in the Resource Store at my website, www.bobbyclinton.com.)

———. "The Mantle of the Mentor: An Exhortation to Finish Well." 1993. (A PDF version of this position paper is available in the Resource Store at my website, www.bobbyclinton.com.)

———. *ML524 Values Reader*. 2010. (PDF version available in the Resource Store at my website, www.bobbyclinton.com.)

———. "Passing On My Heritage." 2000. (A PDF version of this position paper is available in the Resource Store at my website, www.bobbyclinton.com.)

———. "A Personal Ministry Philosophy: One Key to Effective Leadership." 1992. (A PDF version of this position paper is available in the Resource Store at my website, www.bobbyclinton.com.)

———. *Philemon: A Study in Leadership Style*. 2006. (Available in PDF in the Resource Store at my website, www.bobbyclinton.com.)

———. *Philippians: Apostolic Modeling in Tough Times*. 2006. (Available in PDF in the Resource Store at my website, www.bobbyclinton.com.)

———. "Six Characteristics." 1999. This leadership article was first published in *Clinton's Biblical Leadership Commentary*. (See appendix D of this book.)

———. "Six Major Barriers." 1999. This leadership article was first published in *Clinton's Biblical Leadership Commentary*. (See appendix D of this book.)

———. "Sovereign Mindset." 1999. This leadership article was first published in *Clinton's Biblical Leadership Commentary*.

———. "Spiritual Authority: Six Characteristics." 1999. This leadership article was first published in *Clinton's Biblical Leadership Commentary*.

————. *Spiritual Gifts.* Alberta, Canada: Horizon House, 1985.

————. *Strategic Concepts That Clarify a Focused Life: A Self-Study Manual Defining and Applying Focused Life Concepts to Leaders Today.* 1995. (Hard copy available through Fuller Theological Seminary Bookstore; PDF version available in the Resource Store at my website, www.bobbyclinton.com.)

————. *Titus: Apostolic Leadership.* 2001. (Available in PDF in the Resource Store at my website, www.bobbyclinton.com.)

————. "Union Life." 1999. This leadership article was first published in *Clinton's Biblical Leadership Commentary.*

————. "Value Driven Leadership." 2009. (A PDF version of this position paper is available in the Resource Store at my website, www.bobbyclinton.com.)

————. *Various Inputs on Guidance: A Compendium.* 2010. (PDF version available in the Resource Store at my website, www .bobbyclinton.com.)

————. *1 and 2 Corinthians: Problematic, Apostolic Leadership.* 2003. (Available in PDF in the Resource Store at my website, www .bobbyclinton.com.)

————. *1, 2 Samuel: Comparative Study of Leaders in an Emerging Kingdom: The Major Leaders in 1, 2 Samuel: Hannah, Eli, Samuel, Saul, Jonathan, Abner, David, Abigail, Joab, Absalom, Ahithophel, Hushai, Nathan.* 2010. (Available in PDF in the Resource Store at my website, www.bobbyclinton.com.)

————. *1 and 2 Timothy: Apostolic Leadership, Picking Up the Mantle.* 2006. (Available in PDF in the Resource Store at my website, www.bobbyclinton.com.)

Clinton, Dr. J. Robert, and Dr. Daniel Allen. *Nehemiah: Focused Leadership.* 2002. (Available in PDF in the Resource Store at my website, www.bobbyclinton.com.)

Clinton, Dr. J. Robert, and Dr. Richard W. Clinton. *The Mentor Handbook: Detailed Guidelines and Helps for Christian Mentors and Mentorees.* Altadena, CA: Barnabas Publishers, 1991. (Hard copy available through Fuller Theological Seminary Bookstore; PDF version available in the Resource Store on my website, www .bobbyclinton.com.)

———. *Unlocking Your Giftedness: What Leaders Need to Know to Develop Themselves and Others*. Altadena, CA: Barnabas Publishers, 1993. (Hard copy available through Fuller Theological Seminary Bookstore; PDF version available in the Resource Store at my website, www.bobbyclinton.com.) *Note:* This publication replaced my former book on gifts, *Spiritual Gifts*.

Clinton, Dr. J. Robert, and Mike Hannah. *Haggai: Restoring a Work of God—Inspirational, Task-Oriented Leadership*. 2001. (Available in PDF in the Resource Store at my website, www.bobbyclinton.com.)

Clinton, Dr. J. Robert, and Paul D. Stanley. *Connecting: The Mentoring Relationships You Need to Succeed in Life*. Colorado Springs, CO: NavPress, 1992.

Clinton, Dr. J. Robert, and Kenichi Yoshida. *Obadiah: God, the Promise Keeper*. 2003. (Available in PDF in the Resource Store at my website, www.bobbyclinton.com.)

Easton, Burton Scott. *The Pastoral Epistles: Introduction, Translation, Commentary, and Word Studies*. London: SCM Press, 1948.

Fant, David J. *A. W. Tozer: A Twentieth-Century Prophet*. Harrisburg, PA: Christian Publications, 1964.

Goodwin, Bennie. *The Effective Leader: A Basic Guide to Christian Leadership*. Downers Grove, IL: InterVarsity, 1978.

Grubb, Norman. *Once Caught, No Escape*. Fort Washington, PA: Christian Literature Crusade, 1983.

Kinnear, Angus. *Against the Tide: The Story of Watchman Nee*. Wheaton, IL: Tyndale, 1985.

Kraft, Charles H. *Christianity in Culture: A Study in Dynamic Biblical Theologizing in Cross-Cultural Perspective*. New York: Orbis, 1979.

Kuhn, Isobel. *Green Leaf in Drought*. Singapore: Overseas Missionary Fellowship, 1981.

Levinson, Daniel J., et al. *The Seasons of a Man's Life*. New York: Knopf, 1978.

Merriam-Webster's Collegiate Dictionary, Tenth Edition. Springfield, MA: G. & C. Merriam Company Publishers, 1999.

Mintzberg, Henry. *Structure in Fives: Designing Effective Organizations*. Englewood Cliffs, NJ: Prentice-Hall, 1993.

Nee, Watchman. *The Normal Christian Life*. Washington, DC: International Students Press, 1962.

———. *Spiritual Authority*. New York: Christian Fellowship Publishers, 1972.

Raab, Laura, and J. R. Clinton. *Barnabas: The Encouraging Exhorter, A Study in Mentoring*. Altadena, CA: Barnabas Publishers, 1985.

Reid, Patricia, and Norma Van Dalen. "An Abiding Work-Leadership Development Study of Amy Carmichael." Pasadena, CA: School of World Mission, 1985. Unpublished research paper.

Skinner, Betty Lee. *Daws: The Story of Dawson Trotman, Founder of The Navigators*. Grand Rapids, MI: Zondervan, 1974.

Stanford, Miles J. *The Green Letters: Principles of Spiritual Growth*. Grand Rapids, MI: Zondervan, 1975.

Taylor, Dr. Howard, and Mrs. Howard Taylor. *Hudson Taylor's Spiritual Secret*. Chicago: Moody, 1955.

Tozer, A. W. *The Knowledge of the Holy: The Attributes of God and Their Meaning in the Christian Life*. New York: HarperOne, 1992.

———. *The Pursuit of God*. Harrisburg, PA: Christian Publications, 1982.

Trebesch, Shelley. *Isolation: A Place of Transformation in the Life of a Leader*. Altadena, CA: Barnabas Publishers, 1997. (Hard copy available through Fuller Theological Seminary Bookstore.)

Wagner, C. Peter. *Your Spiritual Gifts Can Help Your Church Grow*. Ventura, CA: Regal, 1979.

Weigh, K. H. *Watchman Nee's Testimony: A Unique Public Testimony*. Hong Kong: Church Book Room, 1974.

Wiersbe, Warren. "Principles Are the Bottom Line." *Leadership* 1, no. 1 (Winter 1980): 81–88.

Wrong, Dennis H. *Power: Its Forms, Bases, and Uses*. San Francisco: HarperSanFrancisco, 1979.

ABOUT THE AUTHOR

At the time of first writing *The Making of a Leader*, Dr. J. Robert (Bobby) Clinton was assistant professor of leadership and extension at the School of World Mission of Fuller Theological Seminary. Prior, he was an officer in the Marine Corps, an electrical engineer for Bell Telephone Laboratories, an assistant pastor, and a missionary with World Team.

In addition to a BA and an MA in electrical engineering from Auburn University and New York University, Dr. Clinton received an MA from Columbia Bible College and two doctorates from Fuller Theological Seminary.

His ministry experience at that time included the discipleship of laypeople and assignments as assistant pastor in a local church using Bible study groups for evangelism and training, principal of Jamaica Bible College, director of the Learning Resource Center of World Team, and professor in a missions-oriented faculty.

Dr. Clinton went on to become professor of leadership in the School of Intercultural Studies of Fuller Theological Seminary and retired after thirty years of teaching emerging leaders and leaders from around the world.

The Making of a Leader was based on Dr. Clinton's first eight years of researching God's shaping activities of leaders. He continued his research for another twenty-two years. This revised edition of *The Making of a Leader*, while keeping the basics of the first edition, incorporates findings from this later research.

Dr. Clinton specialized in leadership selection, leadership training, leadership theory, change dynamics in Christian organizations, and

Bible-centered leadership. His last fifteen years focused on Bible-centered leadership. During those fifteen years, he wrote sixteen biblical leadership commentaries. Dr. Clinton has also written numerous manuals and study materials. He and Paul Stanley are co-authors of *Connecting: The Mentoring Relationships You Need to Succeed in Life.*

He and his wife, Marilyn, reside in Altadena, California.

GENERAL INDEX

SCRIPTURE INDEX

THE NAVIGATORS® STORY

T HANK YOU for picking up this NavPress book! I hope it has been a blessing to you.

NavPress is a ministry of The Navigators. The Navigators began in the 1930s, when a young California lumberyard worker named Dawson Trotman was impacted by basic discipleship principles and felt called to teach those principles to others. He saw this mission as an echo of 2 Timothy 2:2: "And the things you have heard me say in the presence of many witnesses entrust to reliable people who will also be qualified to teach others" (NIV).

In 1933, Trotman and his friends began discipling members of the US Navy. By the end of World War II, thousands of men on ships and bases around the world were learning the principles of spiritual multiplication by the intentional, person-to-person teaching of God's Word.

After World War II, The Navigators expanded its relational ministry to include college campuses; local churches; the Glen Eyrie Conference Center and Eagle Lake Camps in Colorado Springs, Colorado; and neighborhood and citywide initiatives across the country and around the world.

Today, with more than 2,600 US staff members—and local ministries in more than 100 countries—The Navigators continues the transformational process of making disciples who make more disciples, advancing the Kingdom of God in a world that desperately needs the hope and salvation of Jesus Christ and the encouragement to grow deeper in relationship with Him.

NAVPRESS was created in 1975 to advance the calling of The Navigators by bringing biblically rooted and culturally relevant products to people who want to know and love Christ more deeply. In January 2014, NavPress entered an alliance with Tyndale House Publishers to strengthen and better position our rich content for the future. Through *THE MESSAGE* Bible and other resources, NavPress seeks to bring positive spiritual movement to people's lives.

If you're interested in learning more or becoming involved with The Navigators, go to www.navigators.org. For more discipleship content from The Navigators and NavPress authors, visit www.thedisciplemaker.org. May God bless you in your walk with Him!